GREEN ARROW AND BLACK CANARY

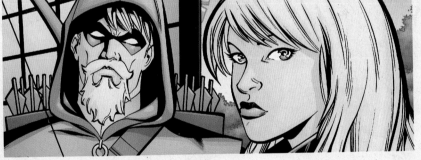

A LEAGUE OF THEIR OWN

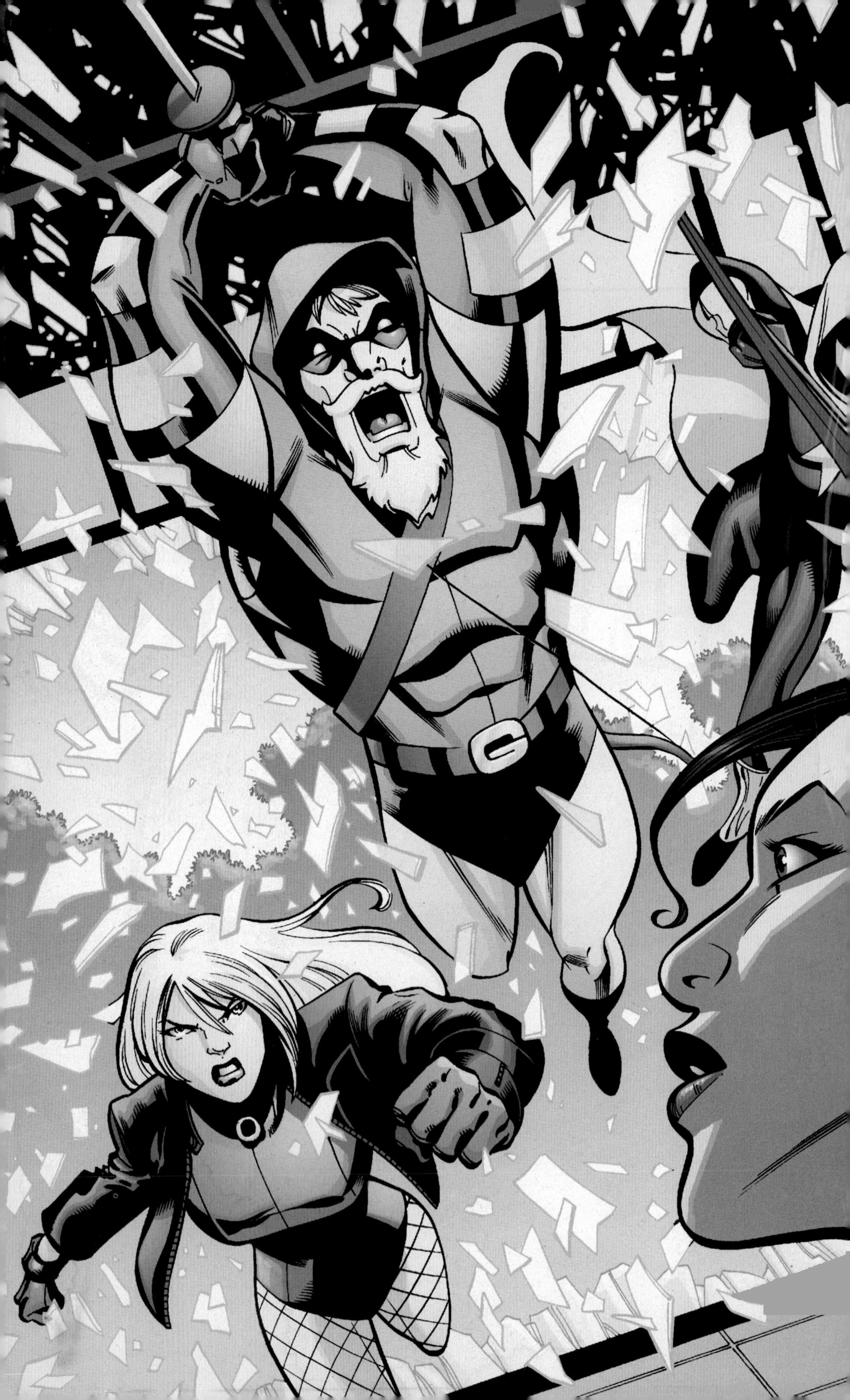

GREEN AND BLACK ARROW CANARY

A LEAGUE OF THEIR OWN

Judd Winick Writer **Mike Norton** Penciller
Wayne Faucher Inker **David Baron** Colorist
Steve Wands / Sal Cipriano Letterers

Original series covers by **Cliff Chiang**

THE PARTING SHOT

Judd Winick Writer **Diego Barreto** Penciller
Robin Riggs Inker **Tom McCraw** Colorist
John Costanza Letterer

Original series cover by **Matt Wagner**

Dan DiDio Senior VP-Executive Editor
Mike Carlin / Ivan Cohen / Bob Schreck Editors-original series
Elisabeth V. Gehrlein Assistant Editor-original series
Bob Joy Editor-collected edition
Robbin Brosterman Senior Art Director
Paul Levitz President & Publisher
Georg Brewer VP-Design & DC Direct Creative
Richard Bruning Senior VP-Creative Director
Patrick Caldon Executive VP-Finance & Operations
Chris Caramalis VP-Finance
John Cunningham VP-Marketing
Terri Cunningham VP-Managing Editor
Amy Genkins Senior VP-Business & Legal Affairs
Alison Gill VP-Manufacturing
David Hyde VP-Publicity
Hank Kanalz VP-General Manager, WildStorm
Jim Lee Editorial Director-WildStorm
Gregory Noveck Senior VP-Creative Affairs
Sue Pohja VP-Book Trade Sales
Steve Rotterdam Senior VP-Sales & Marketing
Cheryl Rubin Senior VP-Brand Management
Alysse Soll VP-Advertising & Custom Publishing
Jeff Trojan VP-Business Development, DC Direct
Bob Wayne VP-Sales

Cover art by Cliff Chiang

GREEN ARROW AND BLACK CANARY: A LEAGUE OF THEIR OWN

DC Comics, 1700 Broadway, New York, NY 10019
A Warner Bros. Entertainment Company
Printed in Canada. First Printing.

ISBN: 978-1-4012-2250-5

SUSTAINABLE FORESTRY INITIATIVE Certified Fiber Sourcing
www.sfiprogram.org

PREVIOUSLY...

During a daring rescue of his father, Green Arrow, an unknown assailant viciously struck down Connor Hawke. Utilizing the greatest scientific technology available, Hawke's life was saved — but he was left in a comatose state.

Shortly afterward, the heartbroken Green Arrow and Black Canary were married in a small private ceremony, only to discover that Connor had been kidnapped in their absence. The newlyweds embarked on a desperate quest around the world — seeking to solve the mystery behind Connor's disappearance.

Along with their sidekick Speedy, self-proclaimed thief Dodger and fellow Justice Leaguers Plastic Man and Batman, the Emerald Archer and Black Canary track down the mysterious eco-terrorist Ra's al Ghul and his deadly League of Assassins. Following the battle, Batman stunned his enemies and allies by announcing that *this* Ra's al Ghul was an impostor, leaving Green Arrow to ponder... Who are the Assassins really working for and what did they do with Connor?

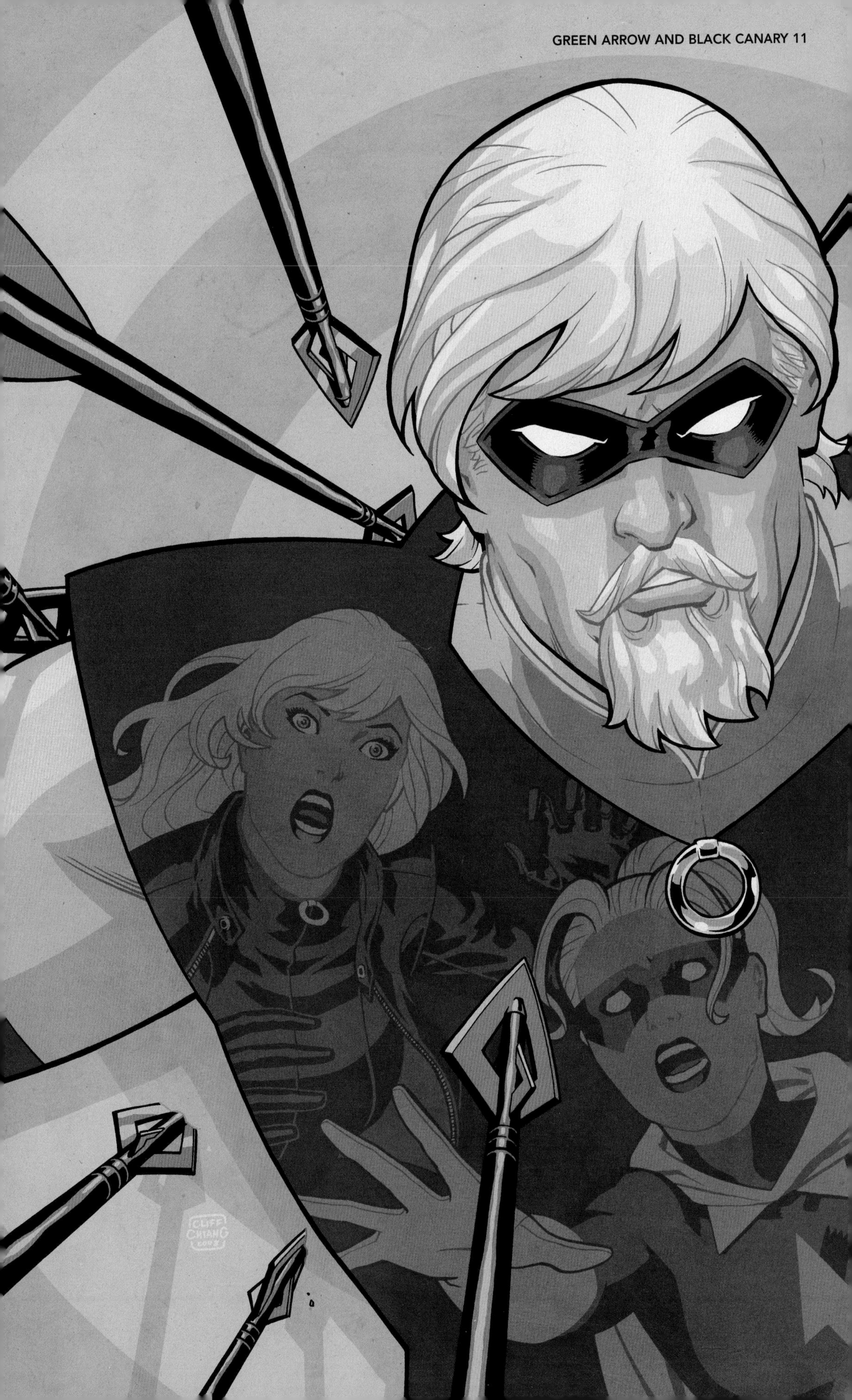
CLIFF CHIANG

A LEAGUE OF THEIR OWN:

THE MAN BEHIND THE CURTAIN

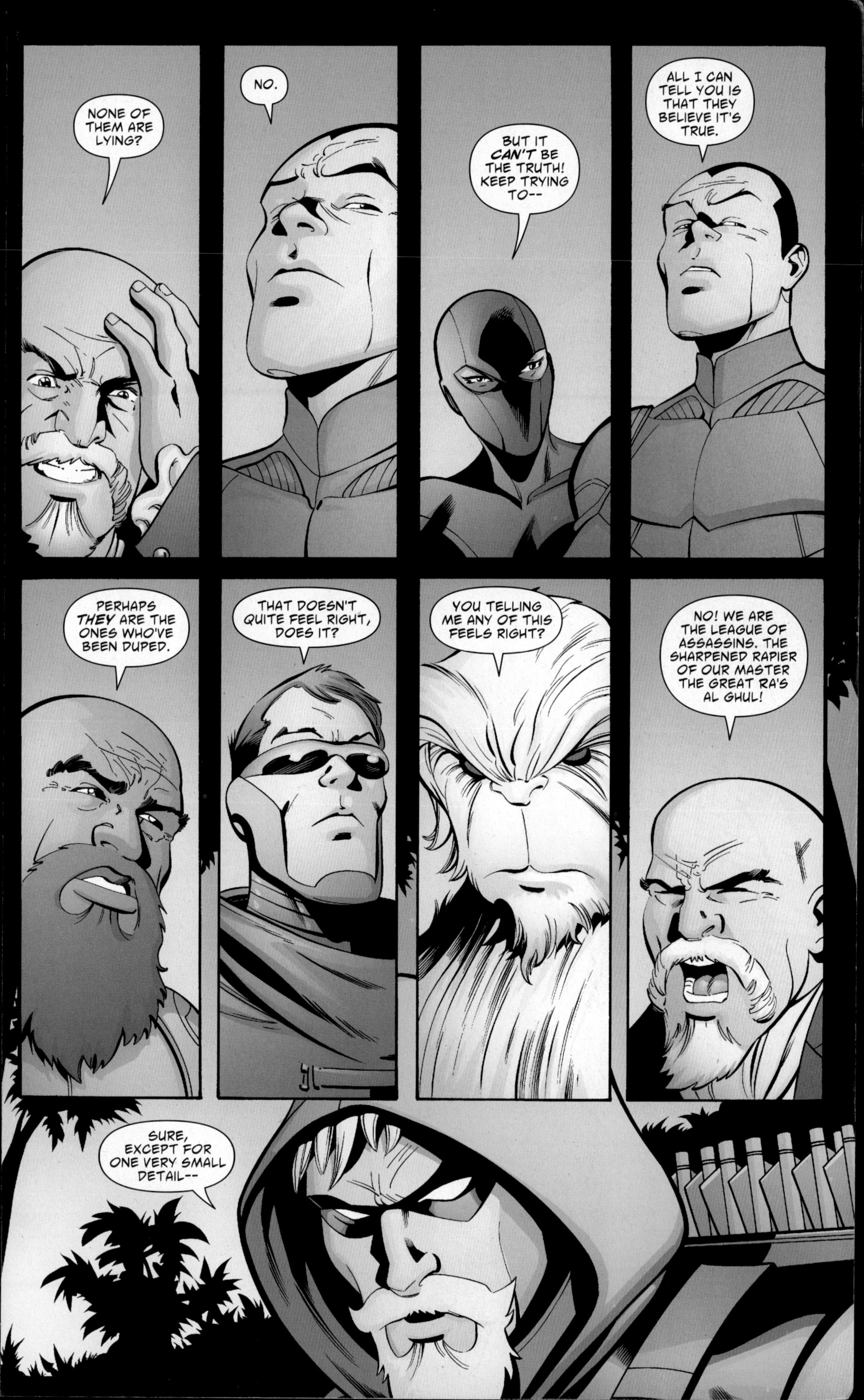
NONE OF THEM ARE LYING?
NO.
BUT IT CAN'T BE THE TRUTH! KEEP TRYING TO--
ALL I CAN TELL YOU IS THAT THEY BELIEVE IT'S TRUE.
PERHAPS THEY ARE THE ONES WHO'VE BEEN DUPED.
THAT DOESN'T QUITE FEEL RIGHT, DOES IT?
YOU TELLING ME ANY OF THIS FEELS RIGHT?
NO! WE ARE THE LEAGUE OF ASSASSINS. THE SHARPENED RAPIER OF OUR MASTER THE GREAT RA'S AL GHUL!
SURE, EXCEPT FOR ONE VERY SMALL DETAIL--

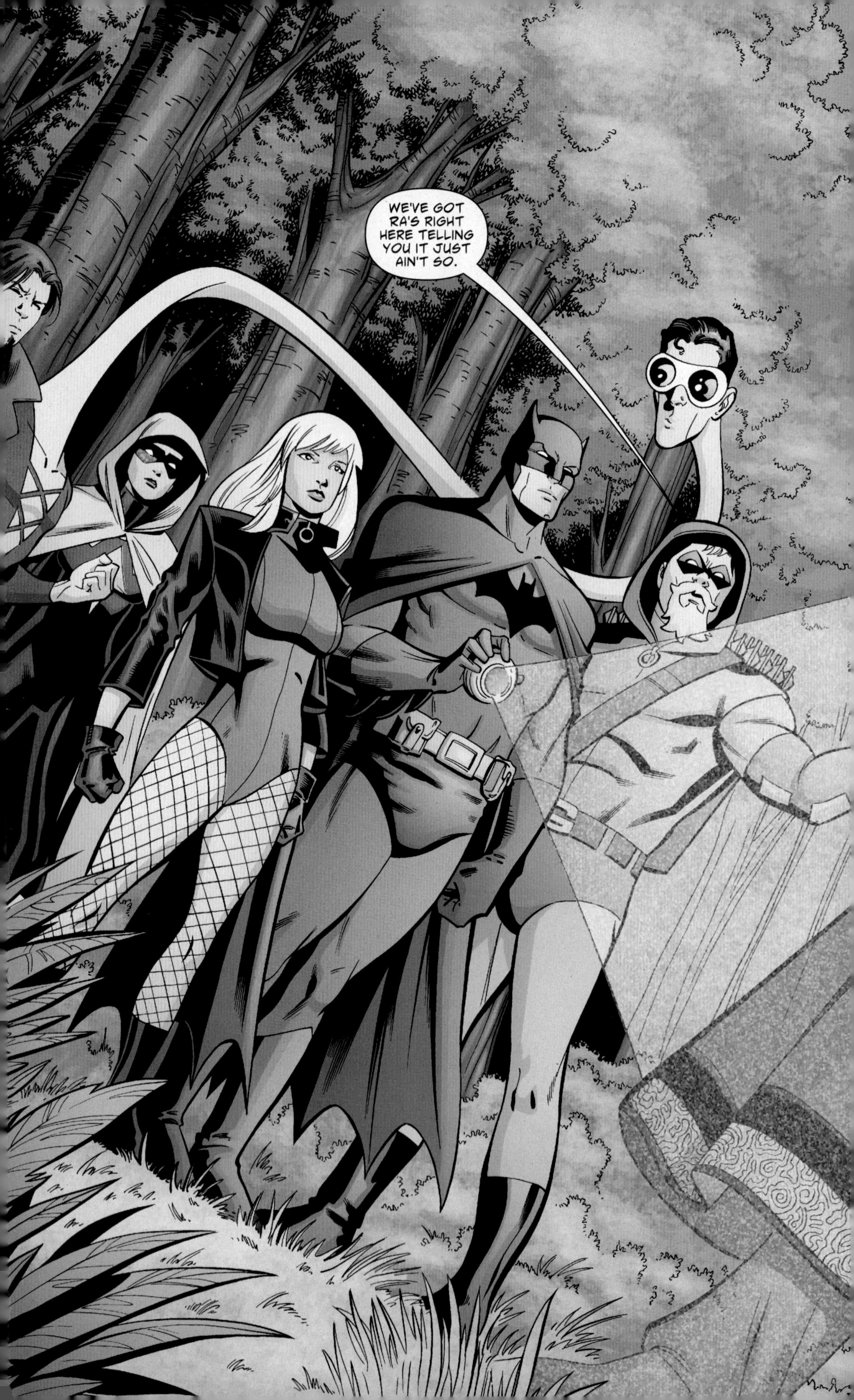
WE'VE GOT RA'S RIGHT HERE TELLING YOU IT JUST AIN'T SO.

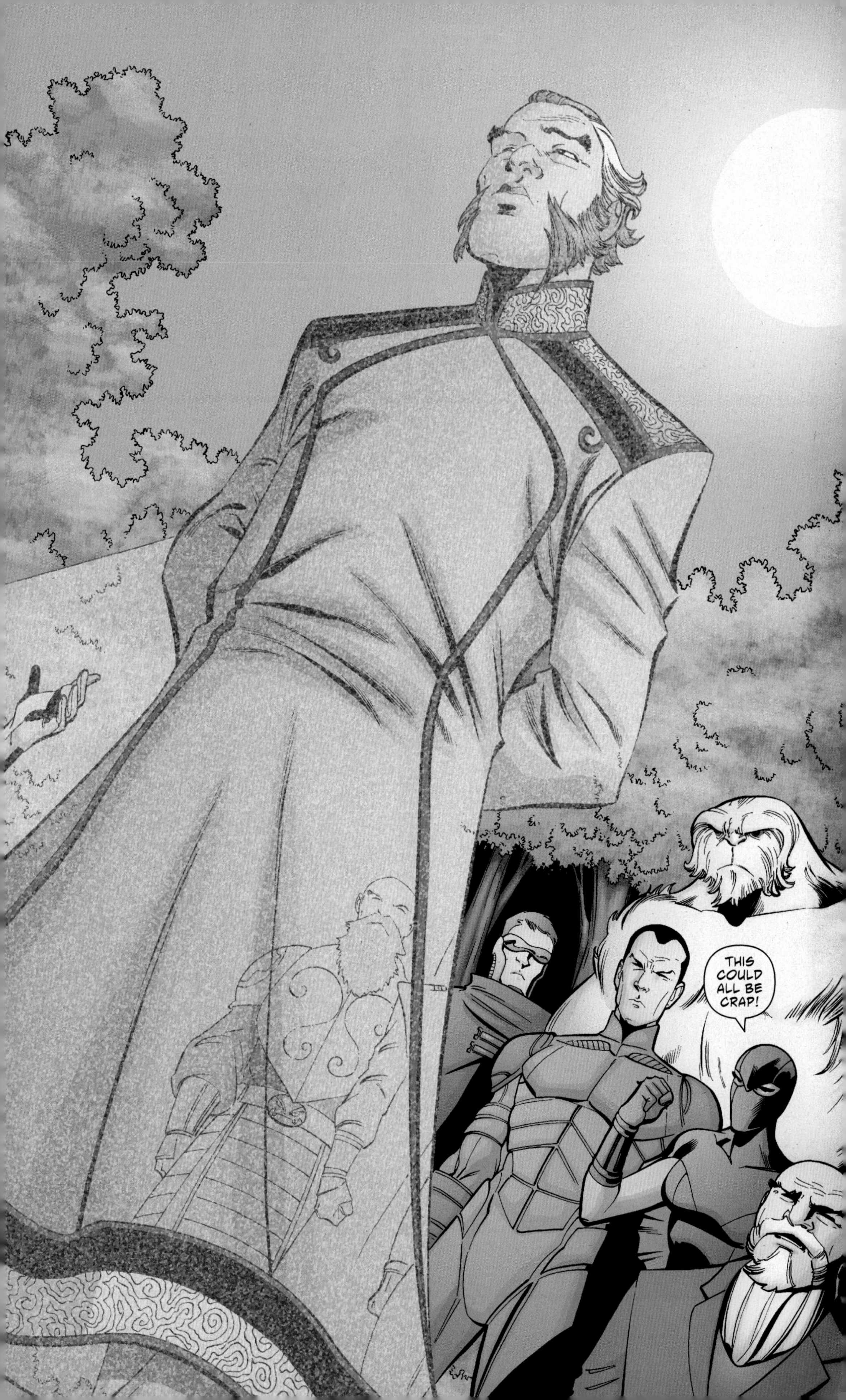
THIS COULD ALL BE CRAP!

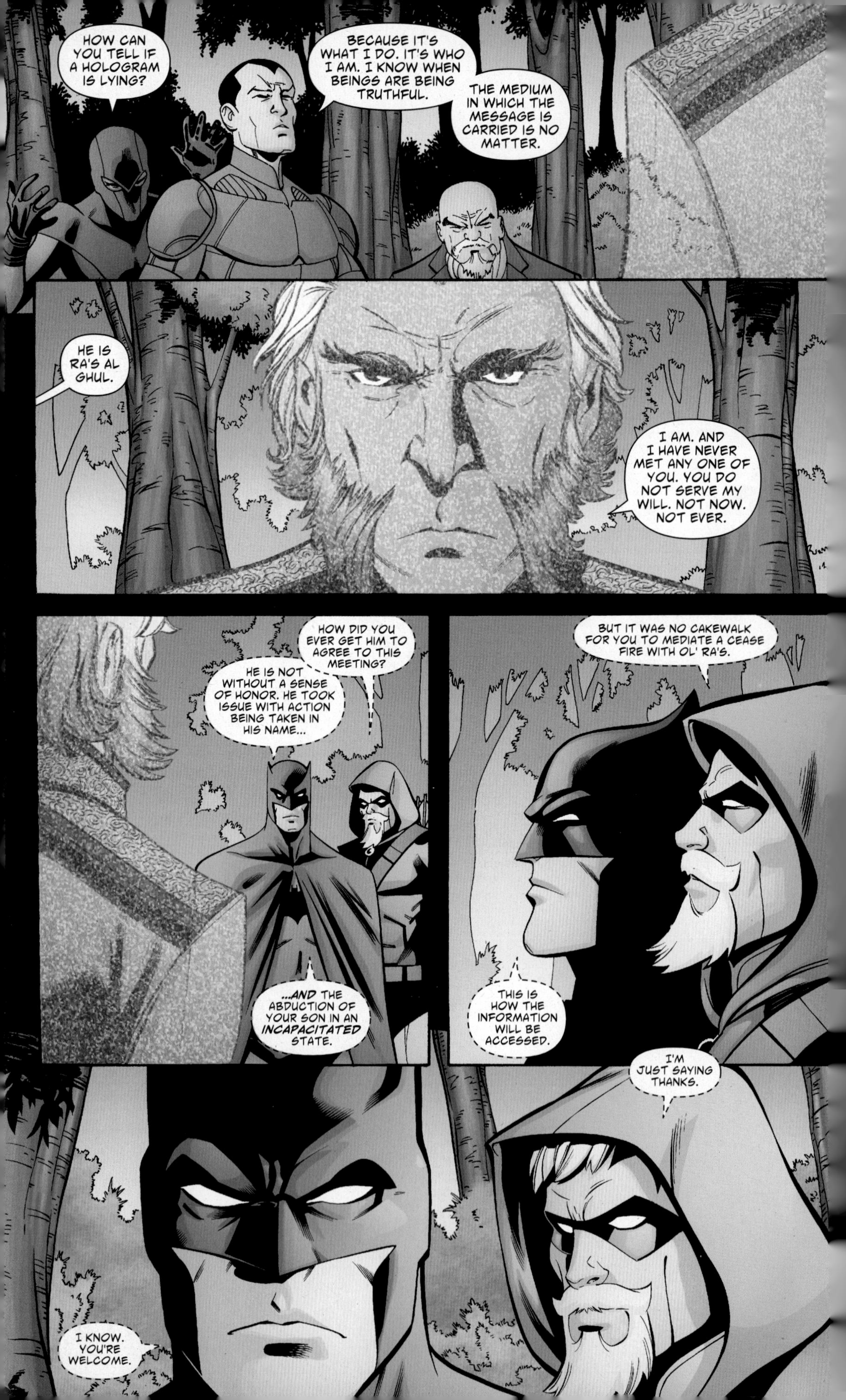
HOW CAN YOU TELL IF A HOLOGRAM IS LYING?
BECAUSE IT'S WHAT I DO. IT'S WHO I AM. I KNOW WHEN BEINGS ARE BEING TRUTHFUL.
THE MEDIUM IN WHICH THE MESSAGE IS CARRIED IS NO MATTER.
HE IS RA'S AL GHUL.
I AM. AND I HAVE NEVER MET ANY ONE OF YOU. YOU DO NOT SERVE MY WILL. NOT NOW. NOT EVER.
HOW DID YOU EVER GET HIM TO AGREE TO THIS MEETING?
HE IS NOT WITHOUT A SENSE OF HONOR. HE TOOK ISSUE WITH ACTION BEING TAKEN IN HIS NAME...
...AND THE ABDUCTION OF YOUR SON IN AN INCAPACITATED STATE.
BUT IT WAS NO CAKEWALK FOR YOU TO MEDIATE A CEASE FIRE WITH OL' RA'S.
THIS IS HOW THE INFORMATION WILL BE ACCESSED.
I'M JUST SAYING THANKS.
I KNOW. YOU'RE WELCOME.

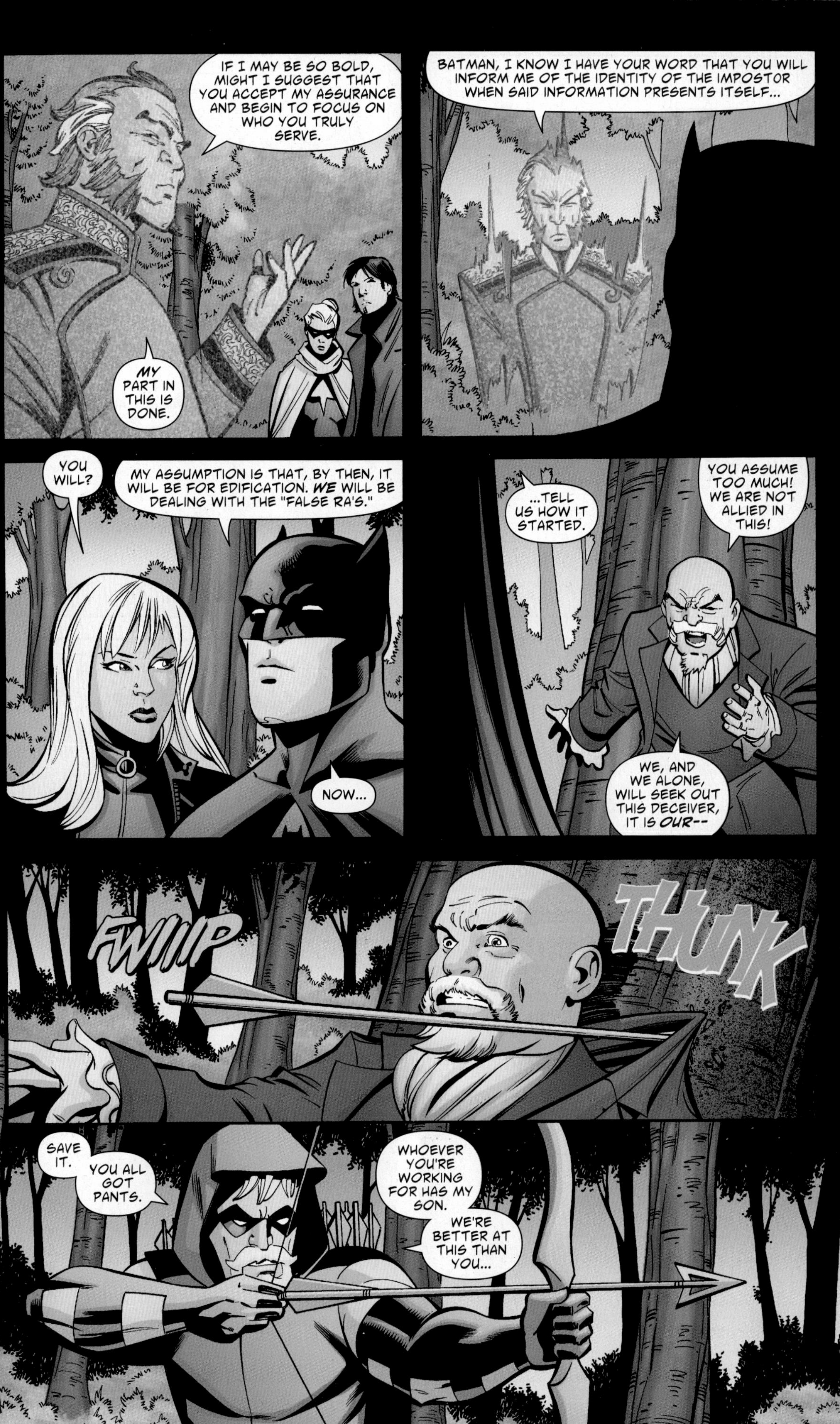
IF I MAY BE SO BOLD, MIGHT I SUGGEST THAT YOU ACCEPT MY ASSURANCE AND BEGIN TO FOCUS ON WHO YOU TRULY SERVE.
MY PART IN THIS IS DONE.
BATMAN, I KNOW I HAVE YOUR WORD THAT YOU WILL INFORM ME OF THE IDENTITY OF THE IMPOSTOR WHEN SAID INFORMATION PRESENTS ITSELF...
YOU WILL?
MY ASSUMPTION IS THAT, BY THEN, IT WILL BE FOR EDIFICATION. WE WILL BE DEALING WITH THE "FALSE RA'S."
NOW...
...TELL US HOW IT STARTED.
YOU ASSUME TOO MUCH! WE ARE NOT ALLIED IN THIS!
WE, AND WE ALONE, WILL SEEK OUT THIS DECEIVER, IT IS OUR--
FWIIIP
THUNK
SAVE IT.
YOU ALL GOT PANTS.
WHOEVER YOU'RE WORKING FOR HAS MY SON.
WE'RE BETTER AT THIS THAN YOU...

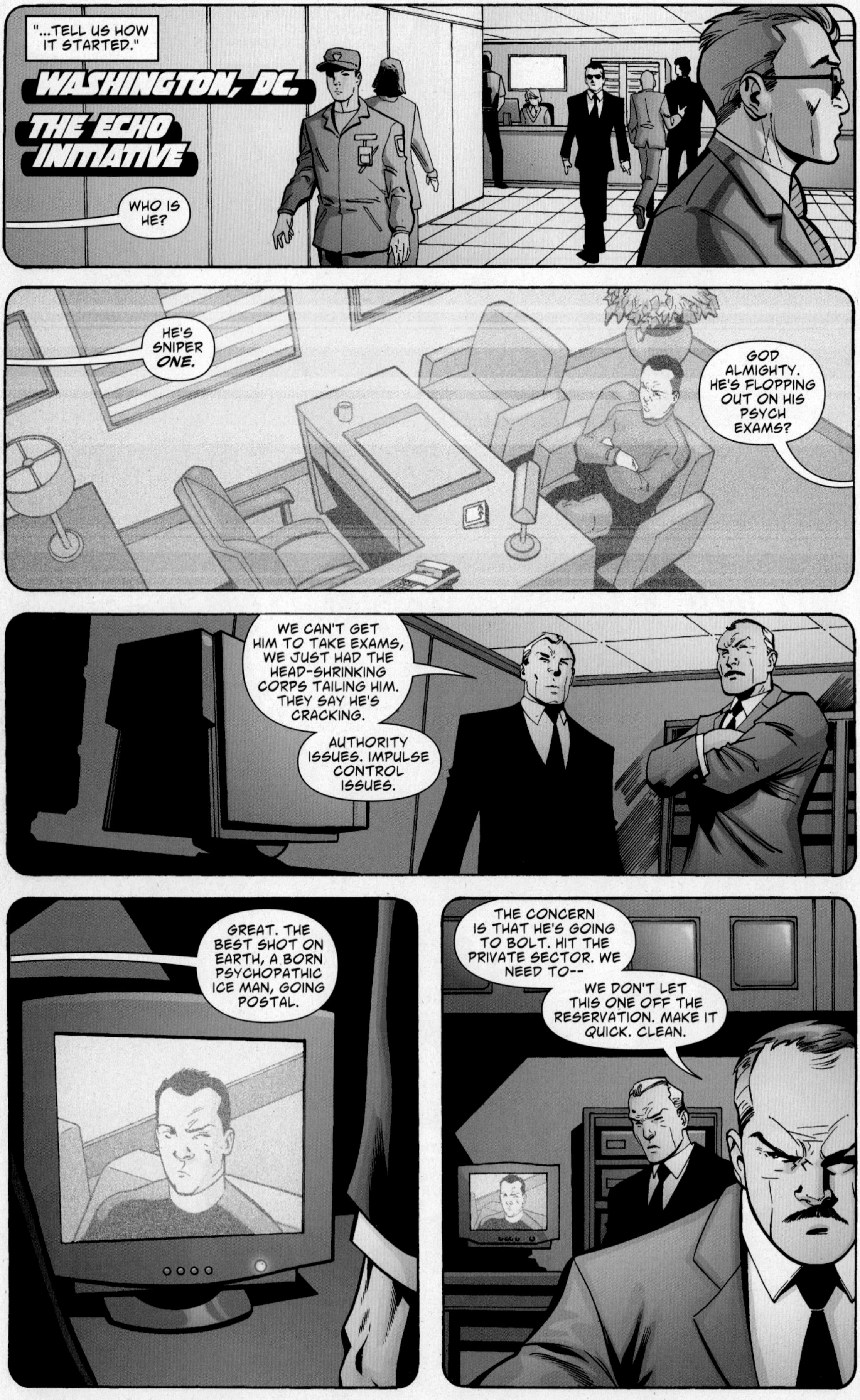
"...TELL US HOW IT STARTED."
WASHINGTON, DC.
THE ECHO INITIATIVE
WHO IS HE?
HE'S SNIPER ONE.
GOD ALMIGHTY. HE'S FLOPPING OUT ON HIS PSYCH EXAMS?
WE CAN'T GET HIM TO TAKE EXAMS, WE JUST HAD THE HEAD-SHRINKING CORPS TAILING HIM. THEY SAY HE'S CRACKING.
AUTHORITY ISSUES. IMPULSE CONTROL ISSUES.
GREAT. THE BEST SHOT ON EARTH, A BORN PSYCHOPATHIC ICE MAN, GOING POSTAL.
THE CONCERN IS THAT HE'S GOING TO BOLT. HIT THE PRIVATE SECTOR. WE NEED TO--
WE DON'T LET THIS ONE OFF THE RESERVATION. MAKE IT QUICK. CLEAN.

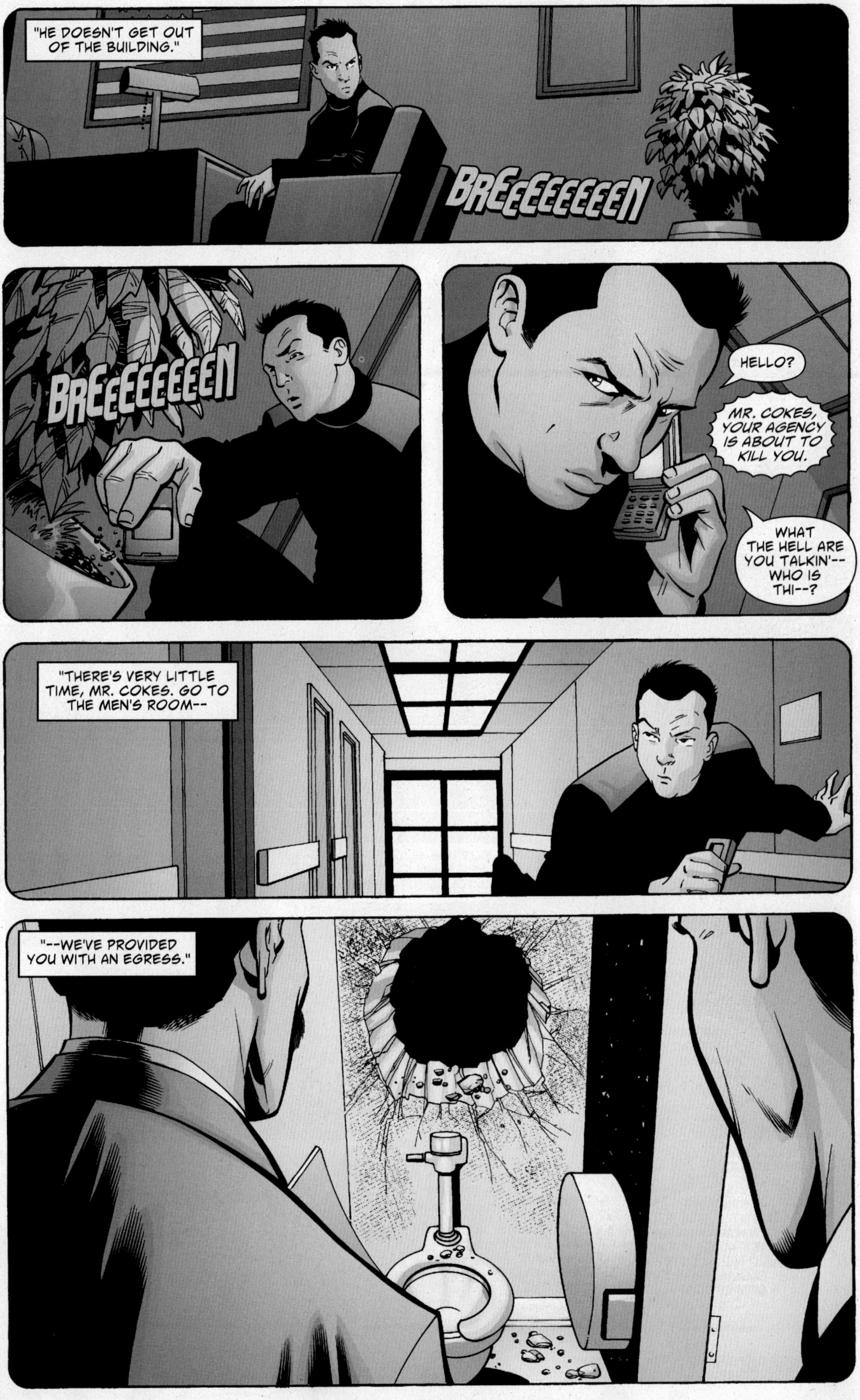
"HE DOESN'T GET OUT OF THE BUILDING."
BREEEEEEEEN
BREEEEEEEEN
HELLO?
MR. COKES, YOUR AGENCY IS ABOUT TO KILL YOU.
WHAT THE HELL ARE YOU TALKIN'-- WHO IS THI--?
"THERE'S VERY LITTLE TIME, MR. COKES. GO TO THE MEN'S ROOM--
"--WE'VE PROVIDED YOU WITH AN EGRESS."

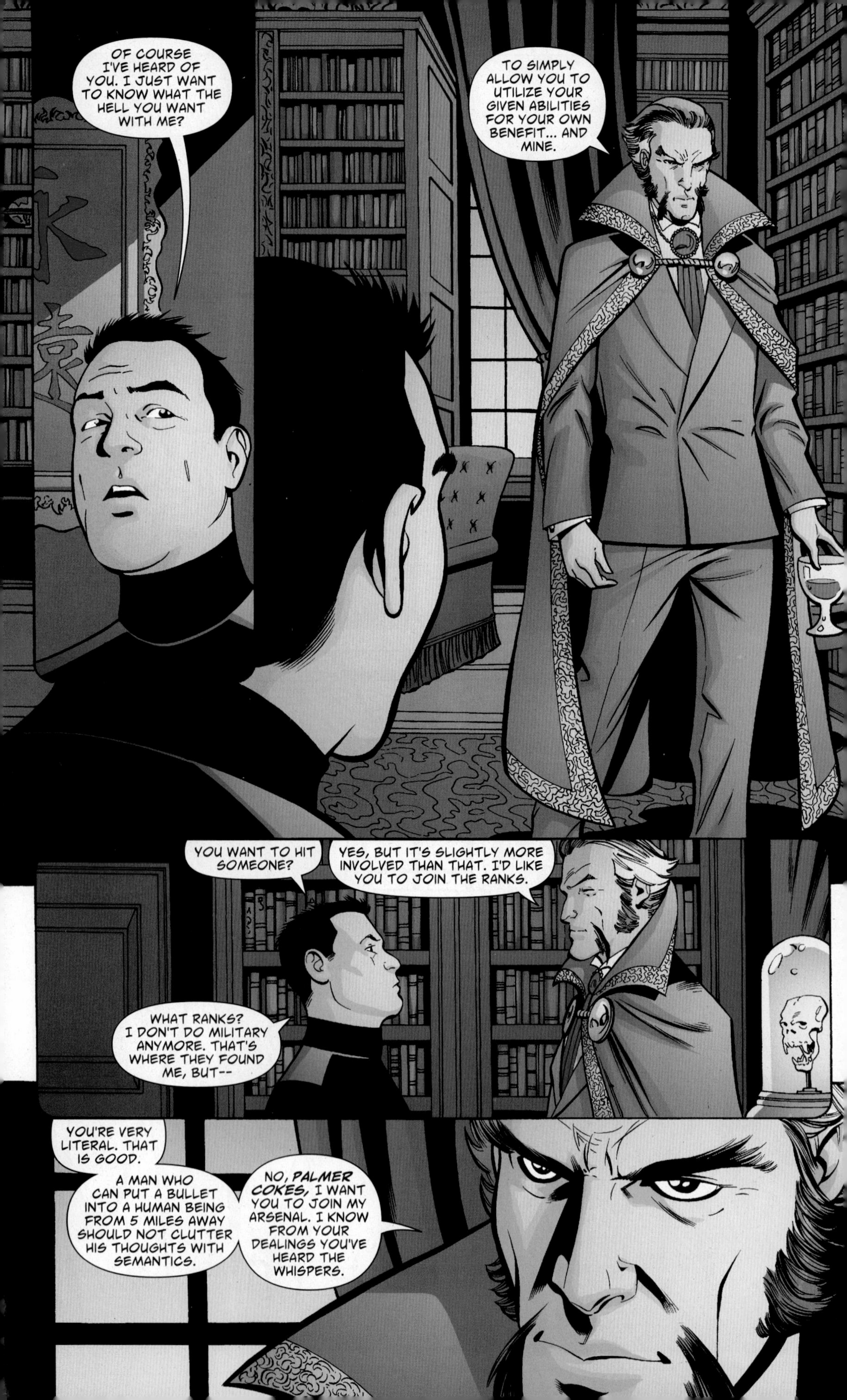
OF COURSE I'VE HEARD OF YOU. I JUST WANT TO KNOW WHAT THE HELL YOU WANT WITH ME?
TO SIMPLY ALLOW YOU TO UTILIZE YOUR GIVEN ABILITIES FOR YOUR OWN BENEFIT... AND MINE.
YOU WANT TO HIT SOMEONE?
YES, BUT IT'S SLIGHTLY MORE INVOLVED THAN THAT. I'D LIKE YOU TO JOIN THE RANKS.
WHAT RANKS? I DON'T DO MILITARY ANYMORE. THAT'S WHERE THEY FOUND ME, BUT--
YOU'RE VERY LITERAL. THAT IS GOOD.
A MAN WHO CAN PUT A BULLET INTO A HUMAN BEING FROM 5 MILES AWAY SHOULD NOT CLUTTER HIS THOUGHTS WITH SEMANTICS.
NO, PALMER COKES, I WANT YOU TO JOIN MY ARSENAL. I KNOW FROM YOUR DEALINGS YOU'VE HEARD THE WHISPERS.

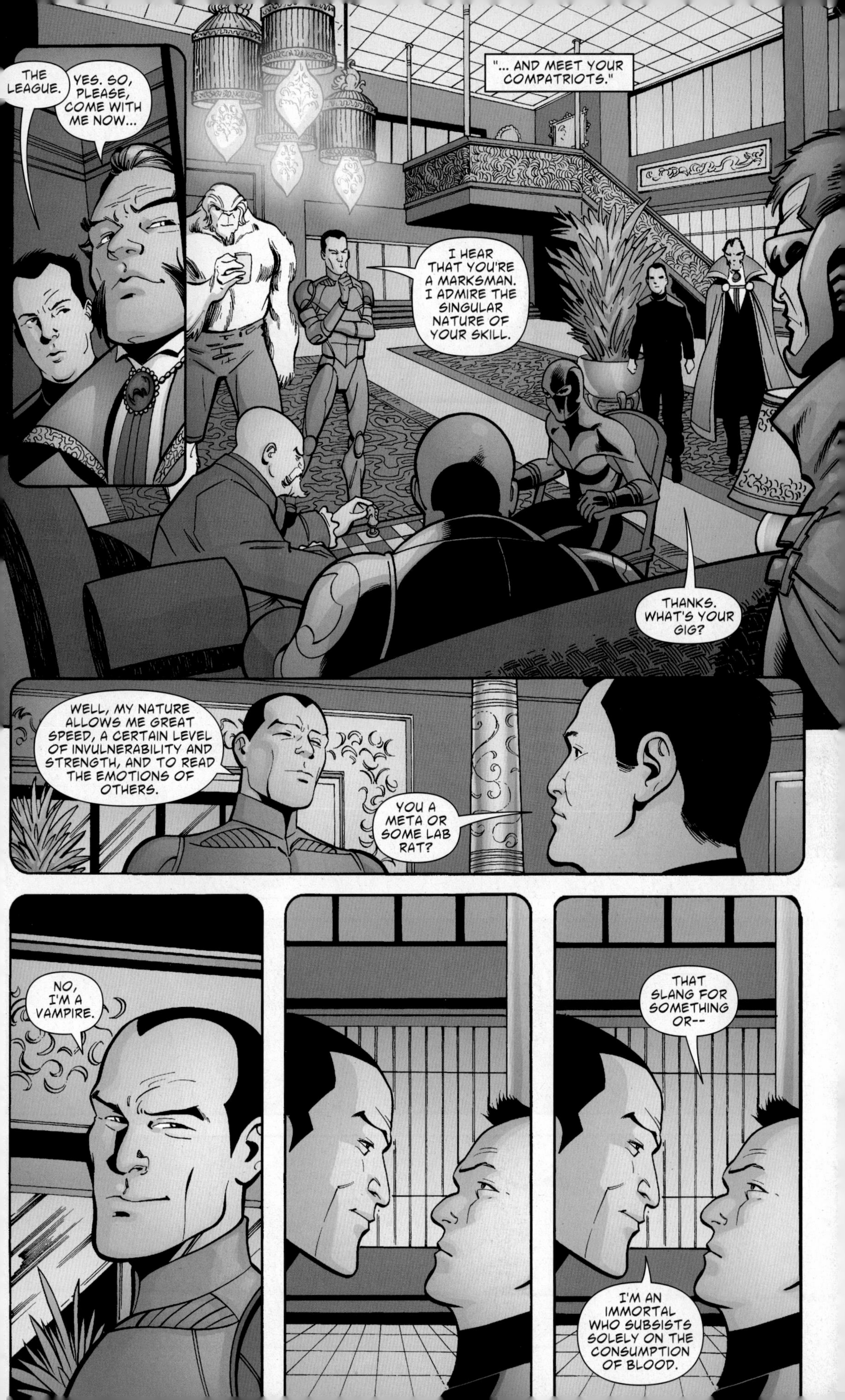
THE LEAGUE.
YES. SO, PLEASE, COME WITH ME NOW...
"... AND MEET YOUR COMPATRIOTS."
I HEAR THAT YOU'RE A MARKSMAN. I ADMIRE THE SINGULAR NATURE OF YOUR SKILL.
THANKS. WHAT'S YOUR GIG?
WELL, MY NATURE ALLOWS ME GREAT SPEED, A CERTAIN LEVEL OF INVULNERABILITY AND STRENGTH, AND TO READ THE EMOTIONS OF OTHERS.
YOU A META OR SOME LAB RAT?
NO, I'M A VAMPIRE.
THAT SLANG FOR SOMETHING OR--
I'M AN IMMORTAL WHO SUBSISTS SOLELY ON THE CONSUMPTION OF BLOOD.

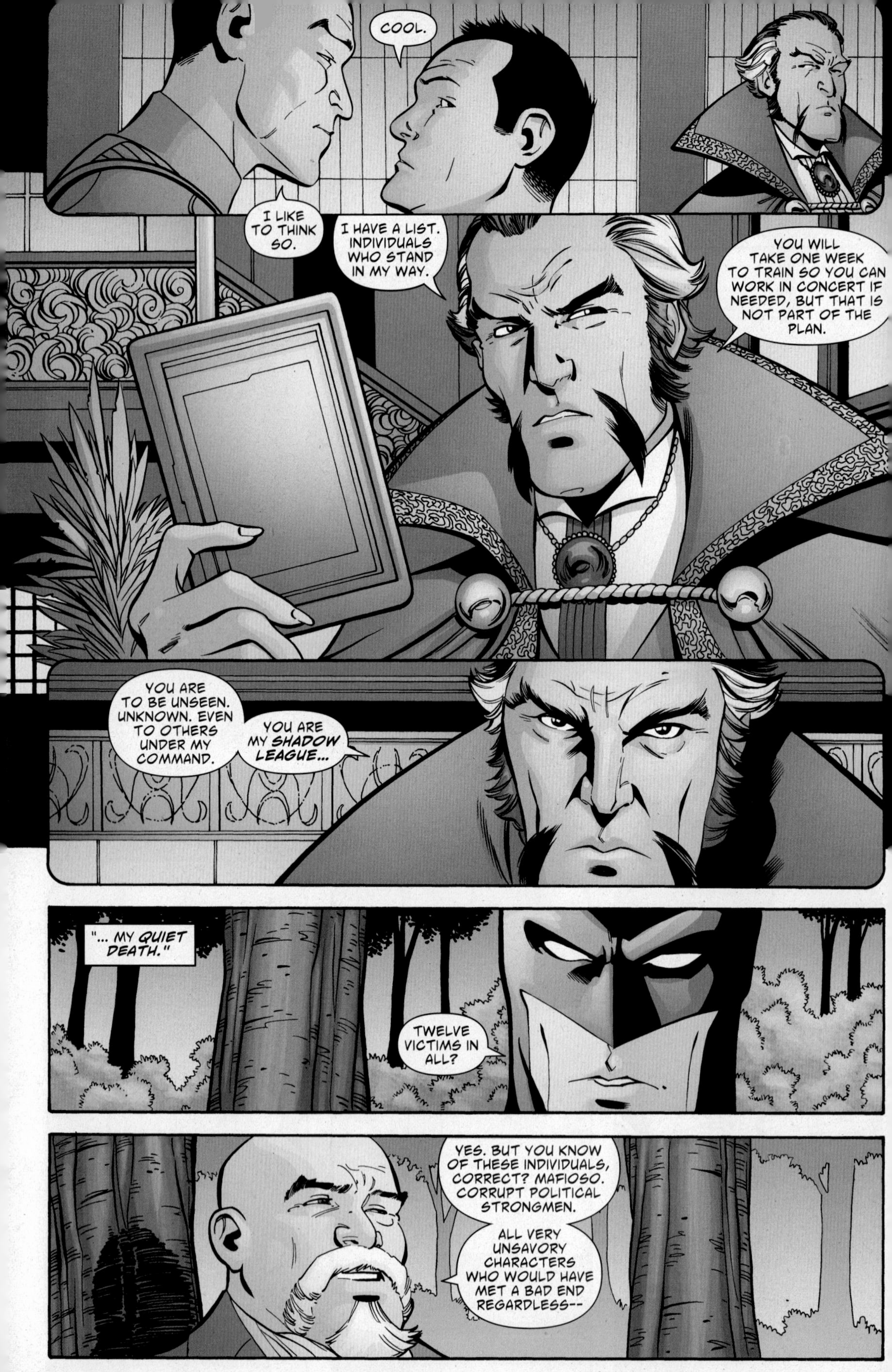
COOL.
I LIKE TO THINK SO.
I HAVE A LIST. INDIVIDUALS WHO STAND IN MY WAY.
YOU WILL TAKE ONE WEEK TO TRAIN SO YOU CAN WORK IN CONCERT IF NEEDED, BUT THAT IS NOT PART OF THE PLAN.
YOU ARE TO BE UNSEEN. UNKNOWN. EVEN TO OTHERS UNDER MY COMMAND.
YOU ARE MY *SHADOW LEAGUE...*
"... MY *QUIET DEATH.*"
TWELVE VICTIMS IN ALL?
YES. BUT YOU KNOW OF THESE INDIVIDUALS, CORRECT? MAFIOSO. CORRUPT POLITICAL STRONGMEN.
ALL VERY UNSAVORY CHARACTERS WHO WOULD HAVE MET A BAD END REGARDLESS--

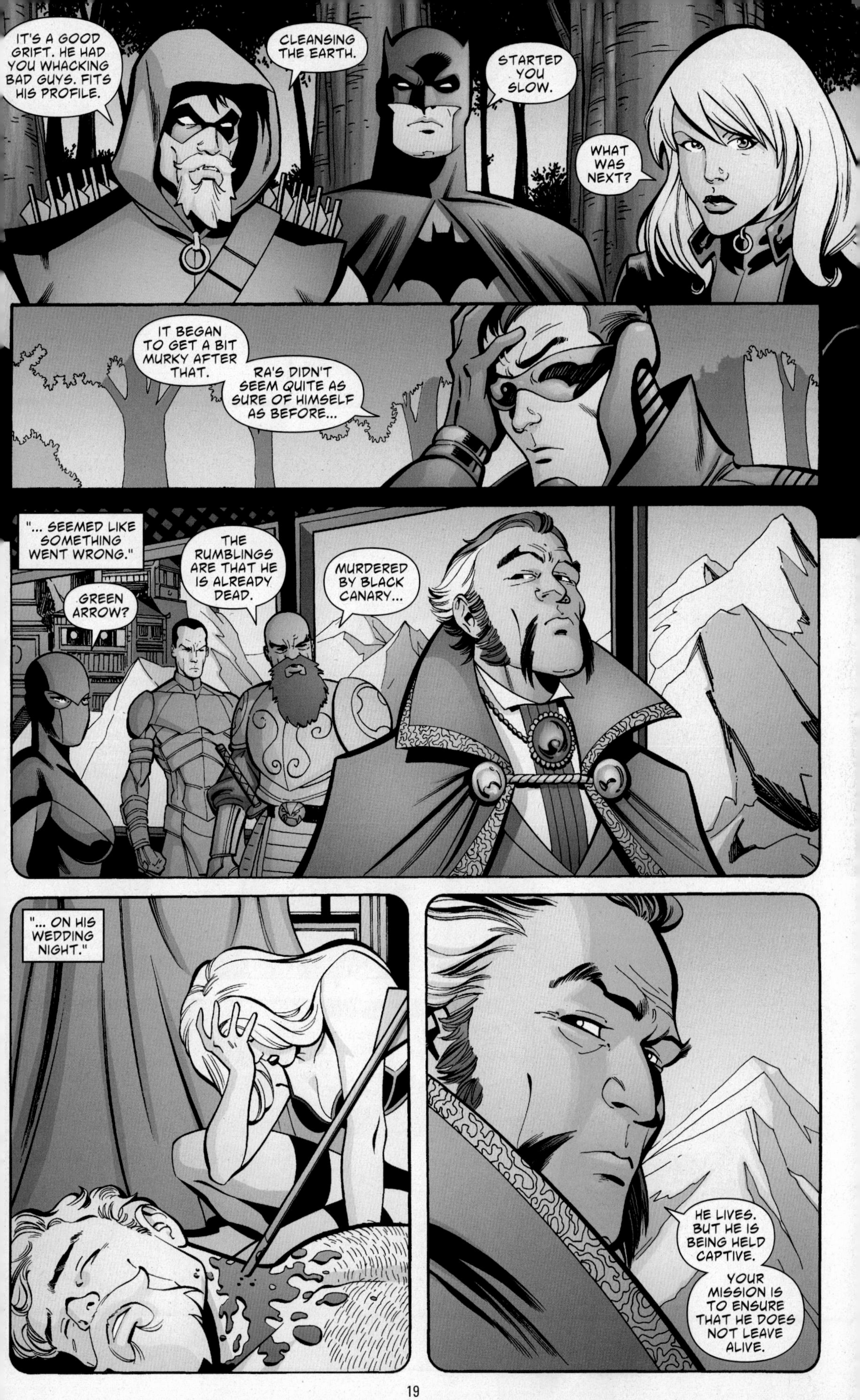
IT'S A GOOD GRIFT. HE HAD YOU WHACKING BAD GUYS. FITS HIS PROFILE.
CLEANSING THE EARTH.
STARTED YOU SLOW.
WHAT WAS NEXT?
IT BEGAN TO GET A BIT MURKY AFTER THAT.
RA'S DIDN'T SEEM QUITE AS SURE OF HIMSELF AS BEFORE...
"... SEEMED LIKE SOMETHING WENT WRONG."
GREEN ARROW?
THE RUMBLINGS ARE THAT HE IS ALREADY DEAD.
MURDERED BY BLACK CANARY...
"... ON HIS WEDDING NIGHT."
HE LIVES. BUT HE IS BEING HELD CAPTIVE.
YOUR MISSION IS TO ENSURE THAT HE DOES NOT LEAVE ALIVE.

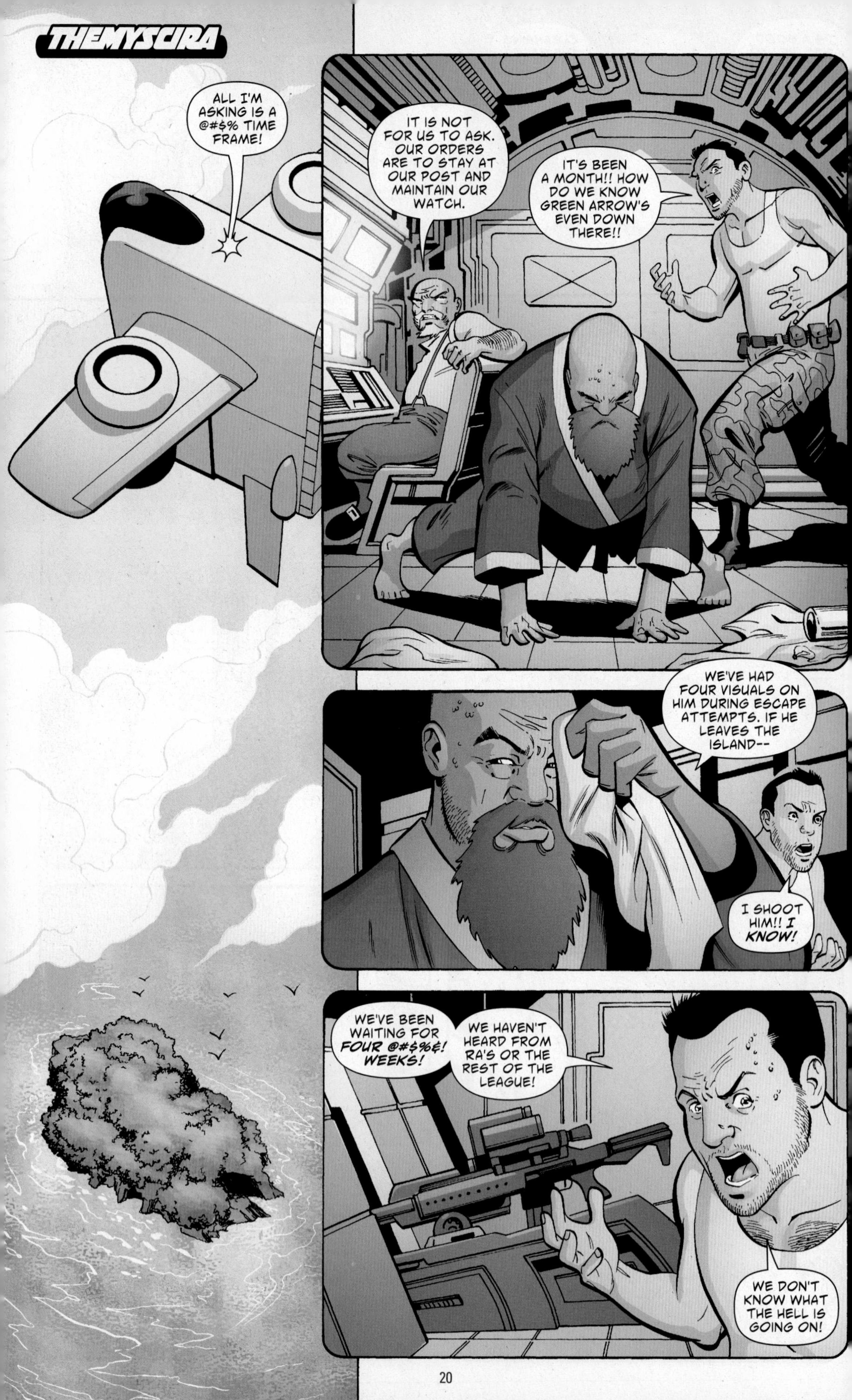
THEMYSCIRA
ALL I'M ASKING IS A @#$% TIME FRAME!
IT IS NOT FOR US TO ASK. OUR ORDERS ARE TO STAY AT OUR POST AND MAINTAIN OUR WATCH.
IT'S BEEN A MONTH!! HOW DO WE KNOW GREEN ARROW'S EVEN DOWN THERE!!
WE'VE HAD FOUR VISUALS ON HIM DURING ESCAPE ATTEMPTS. IF HE LEAVES THE ISLAND--
I SHOOT HIM!! I KNOW!
WE'VE BEEN WAITING FOR FOUR @#$%&! WEEKS!
WE HAVEN'T HEARD FROM RA'S OR THE REST OF THE LEAGUE!
WE DON'T KNOW WHAT THE HELL IS GOING ON!

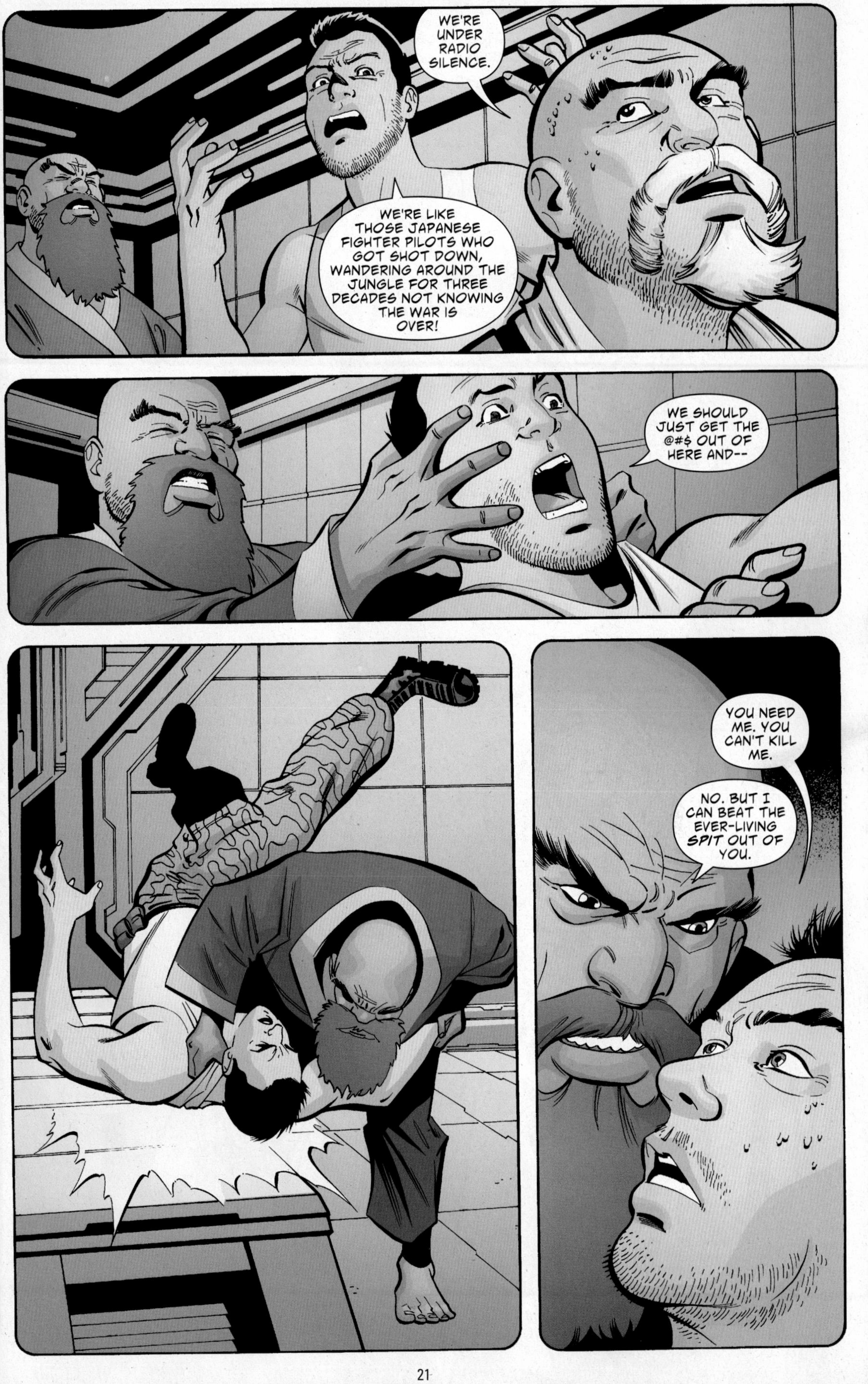
WE'RE UNDER RADIO SILENCE.
WE'RE LIKE THOSE JAPANESE FIGHTER PILOTS WHO GOT SHOT DOWN, WANDERING AROUND THE JUNGLE FOR THREE DECADES NOT KNOWING THE WAR IS OVER!
WE SHOULD JUST GET THE @#$ OUT OF HERE AND--
YOU NEED ME. YOU CAN'T KILL ME.
NO. BUT I CAN BEAT THE EVER-LIVING *SPIT* OUT OF YOU.

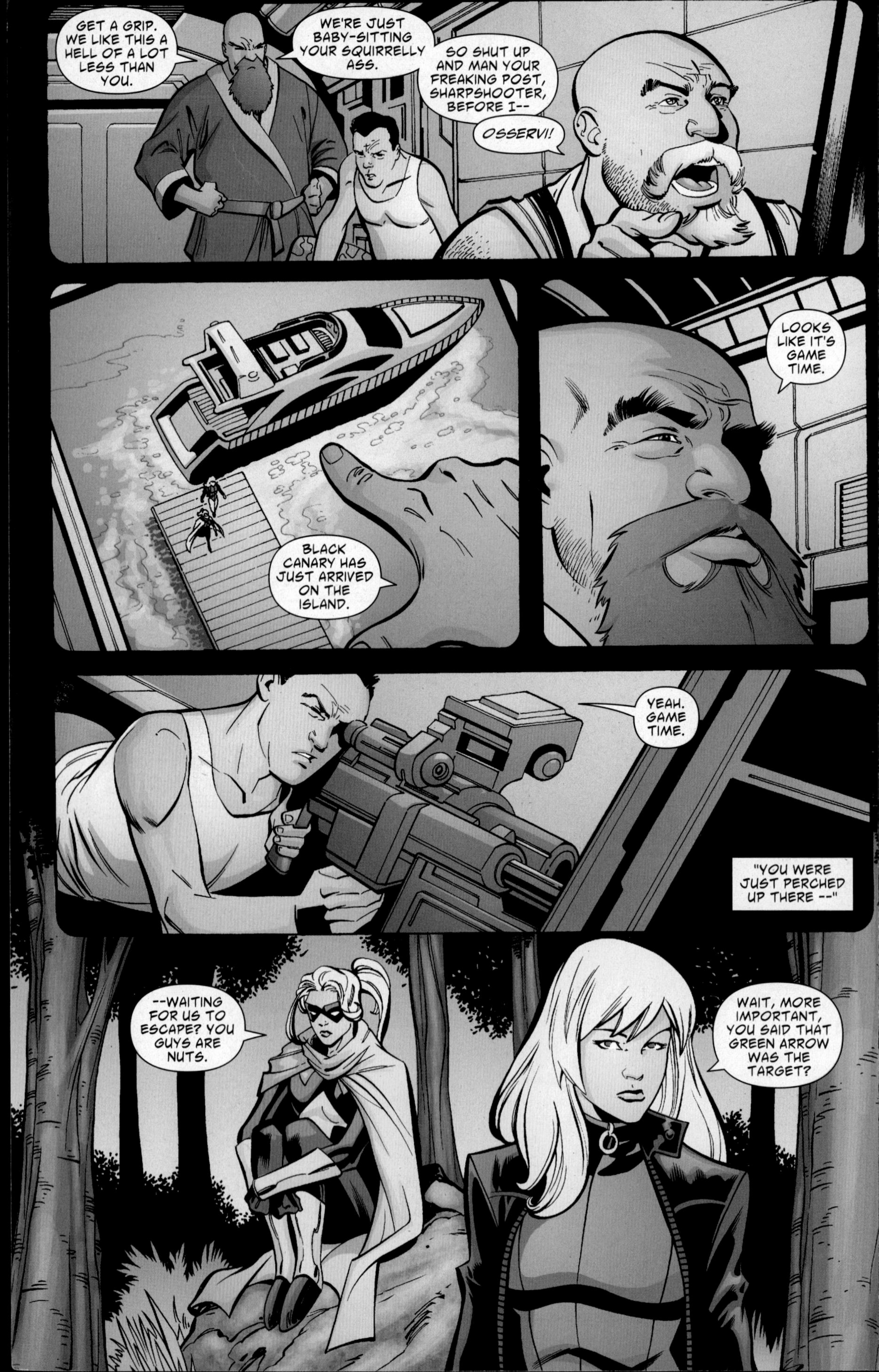
GET A GRIP. WE LIKE THIS A HELL OF A LOT LESS THAN YOU.
WE'RE JUST BABY-SITTING YOUR SQUIRRELLY ASS.
SO SHUT UP AND MAN YOUR FREAKING POST, SHARPSHOOTER, BEFORE I--
OSSERVI!
BLACK CANARY HAS JUST ARRIVED ON THE ISLAND.
LOOKS LIKE IT'S GAME TIME.
YEAH. GAME TIME.
"YOU WERE JUST PERCHED UP THERE --"
--WAITING FOR US TO ESCAPE? YOU GUYS ARE NUTS.
WAIT, MORE IMPORTANT, YOU SAID THAT GREEN ARROW WAS THE TARGET?

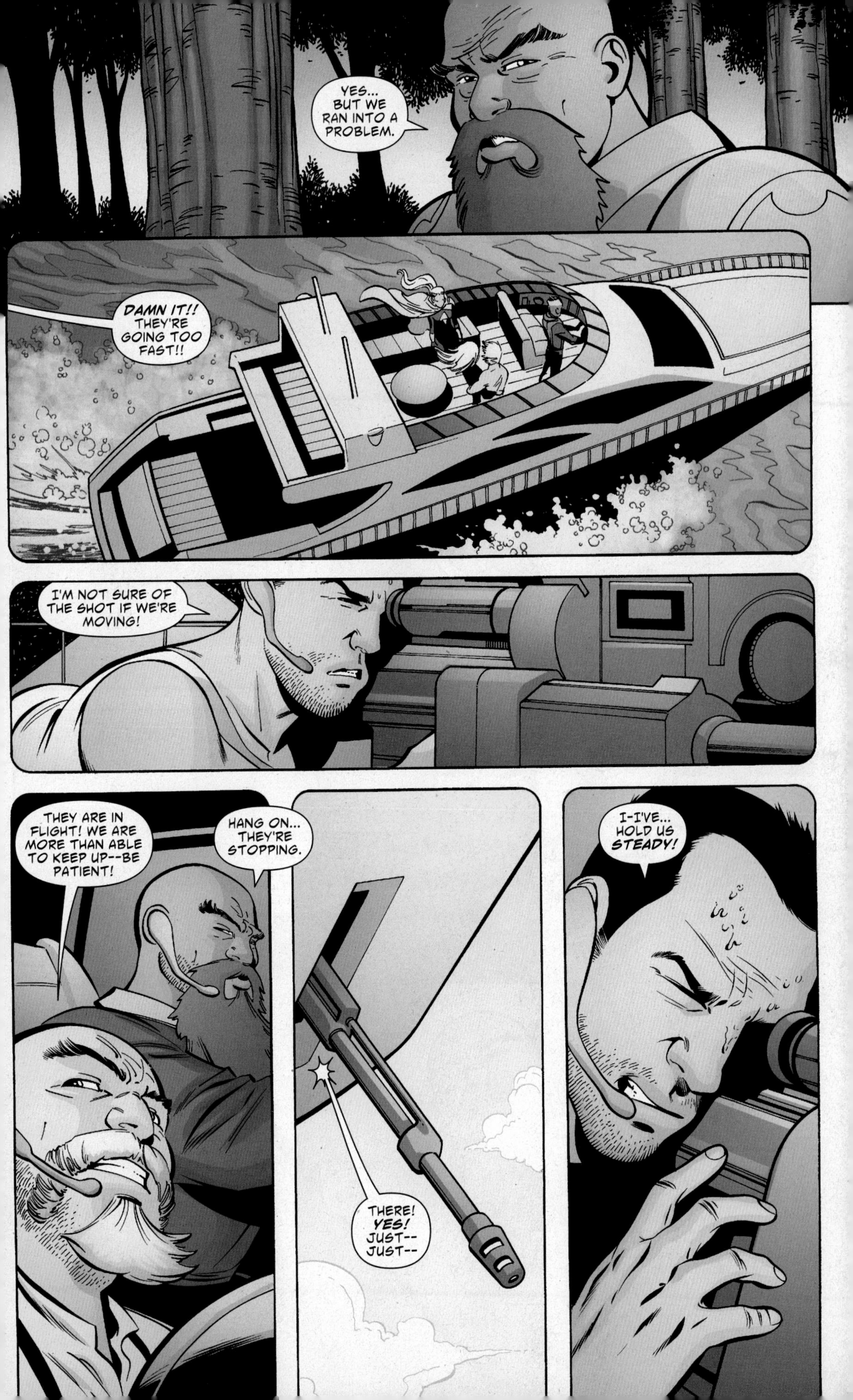
YES... BUT WE RAN INTO A PROBLEM.
DAMN IT!! THEY'RE GOING TOO FAST!!
I'M NOT SURE OF THE SHOT IF WE'RE MOVING!
THEY ARE IN FLIGHT! WE ARE MORE THAN ABLE TO KEEP UP--BE PATIENT!
HANG ON... THEY'RE STOPPING.
THERE! YES! JUST-- JUST--
I-I'VE... HOLD US STEADY!

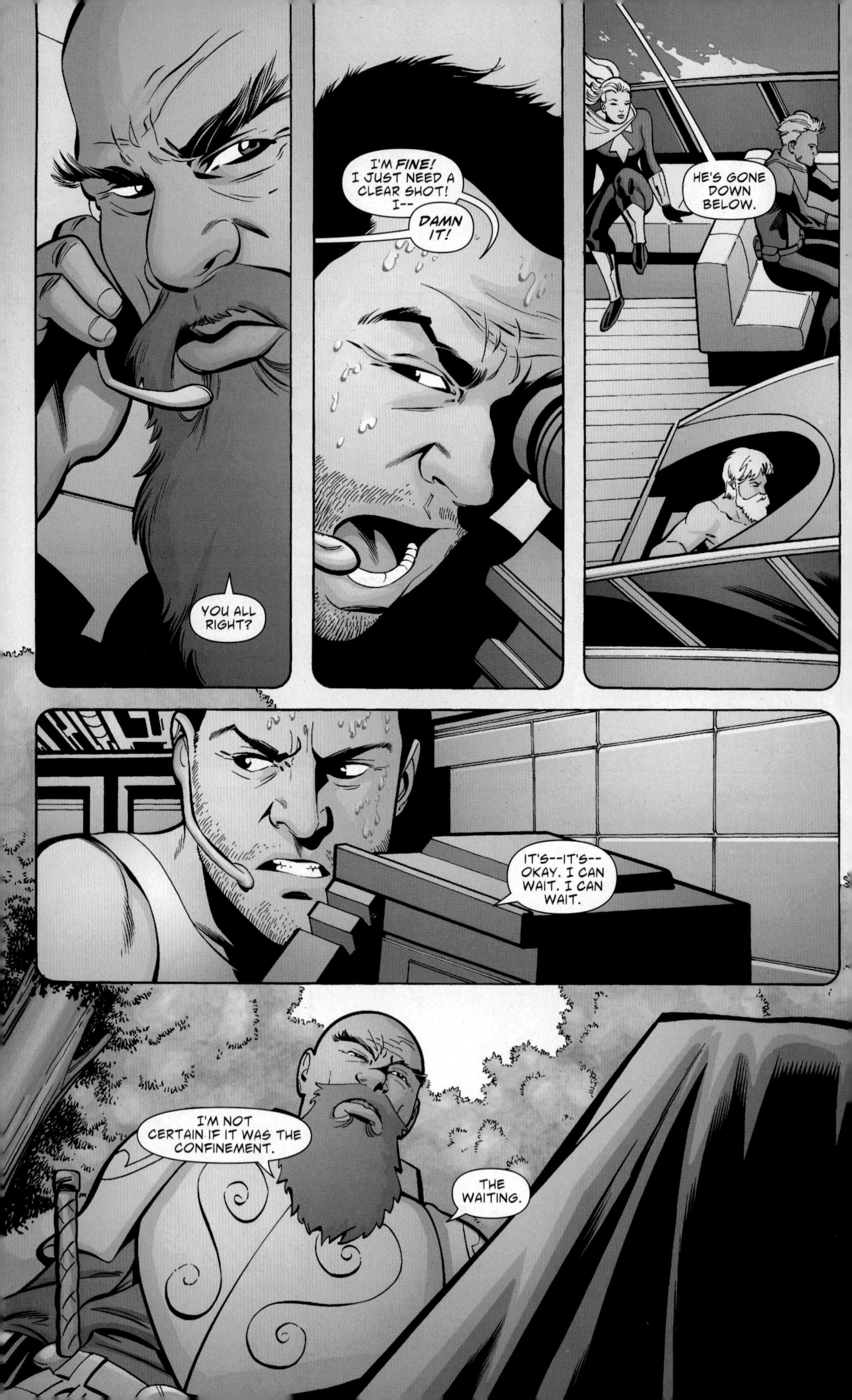
YOU ALL RIGHT?
I'M FINE! I JUST NEED A CLEAR SHOT! I--
DAMN IT!
HE'S GONE DOWN BELOW.
IT'S--IT'S--OKAY. I CAN WAIT. I CAN WAIT.
I'M NOT CERTAIN IF IT WAS THE CONFINEMENT.
THE WAITING.

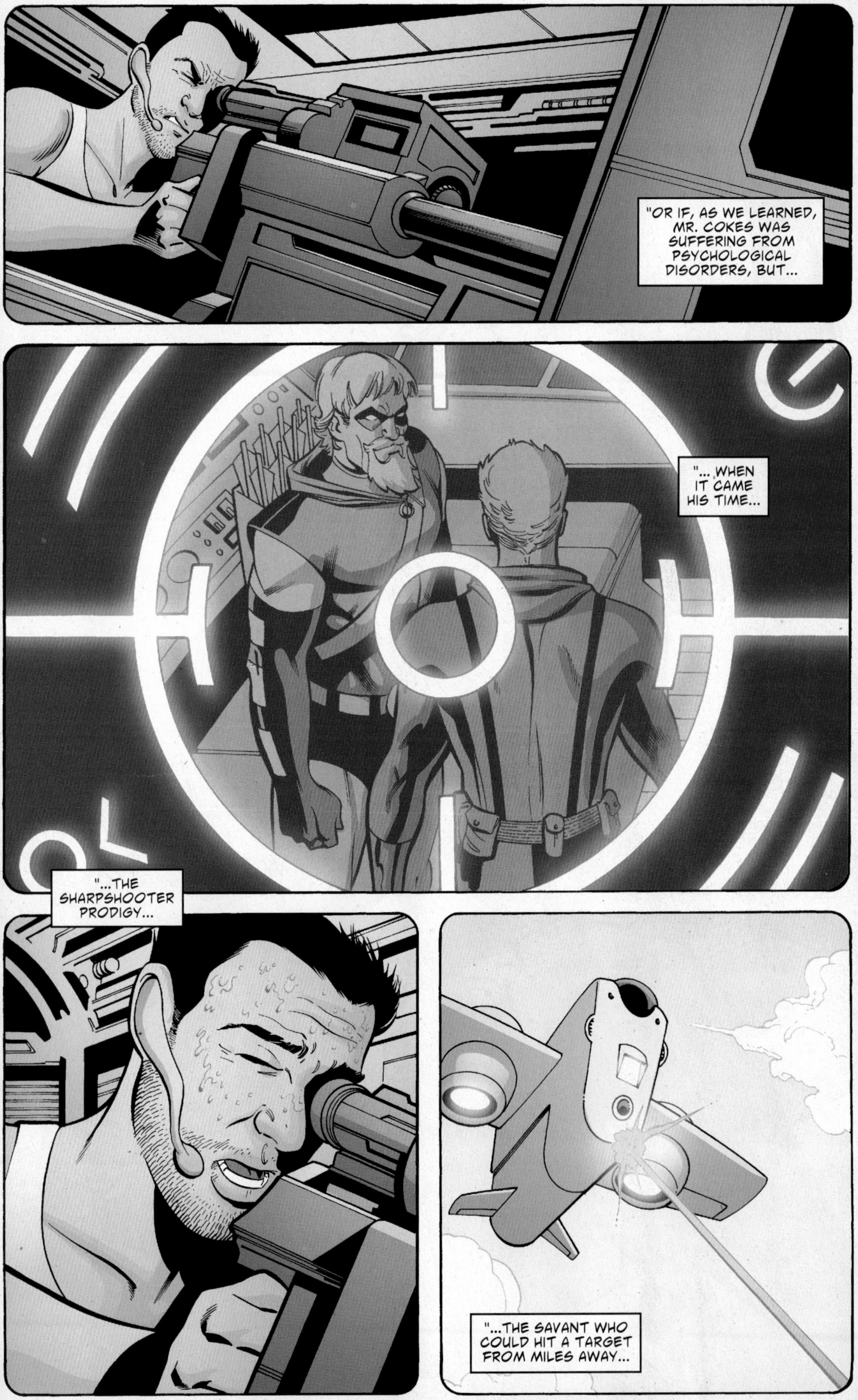
"OR IF, AS WE LEARNED, MR. COKES WAS SUFFERING FROM PSYCHOLOGICAL DISORDERS, BUT...
"... WHEN IT CAME HIS TIME...
"...THE SHARPSHOOTER PRODIGY...
"...THE SAVANT WHO COULD HIT A TARGET FROM MILES AWAY...

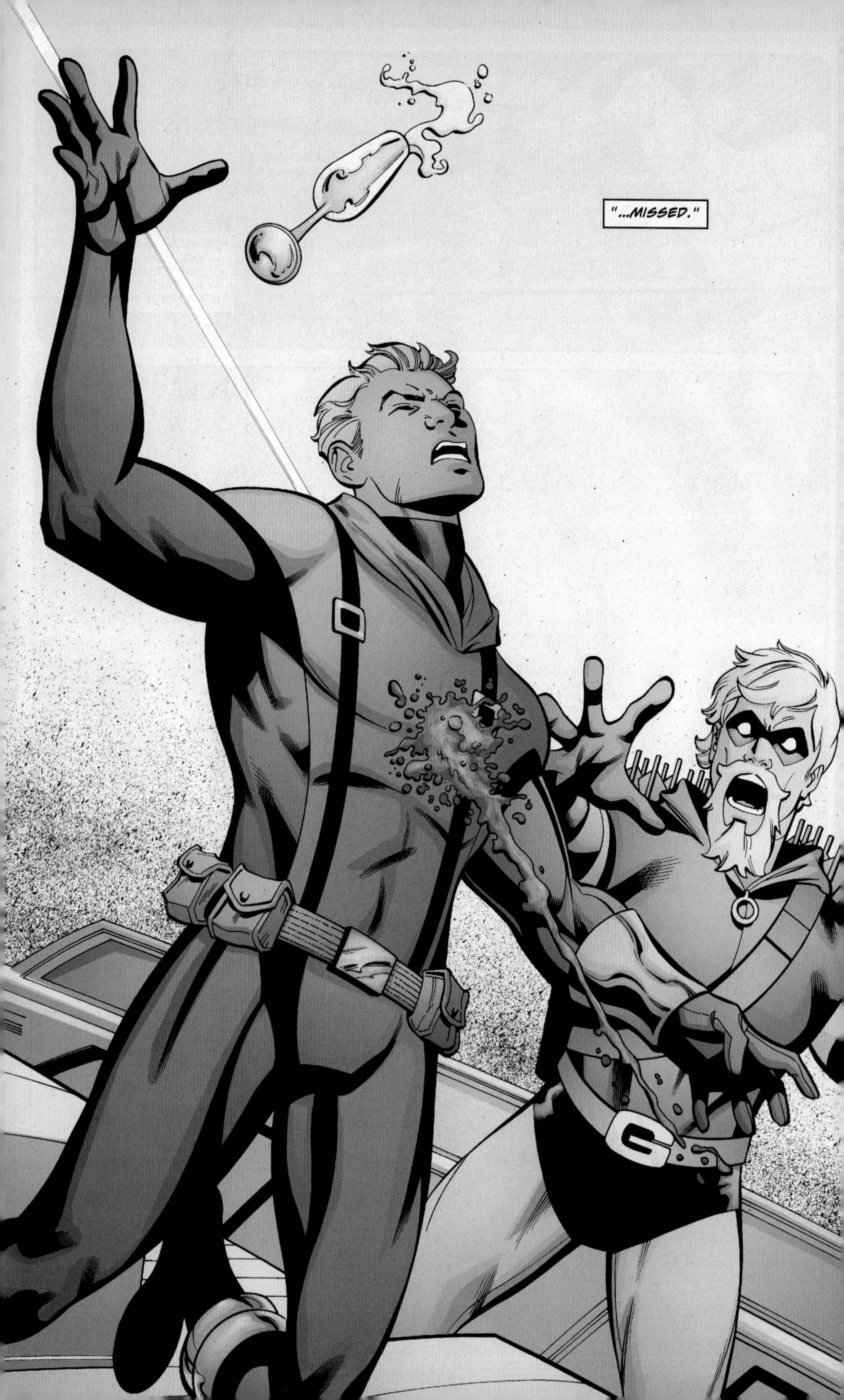
"...MISSED."

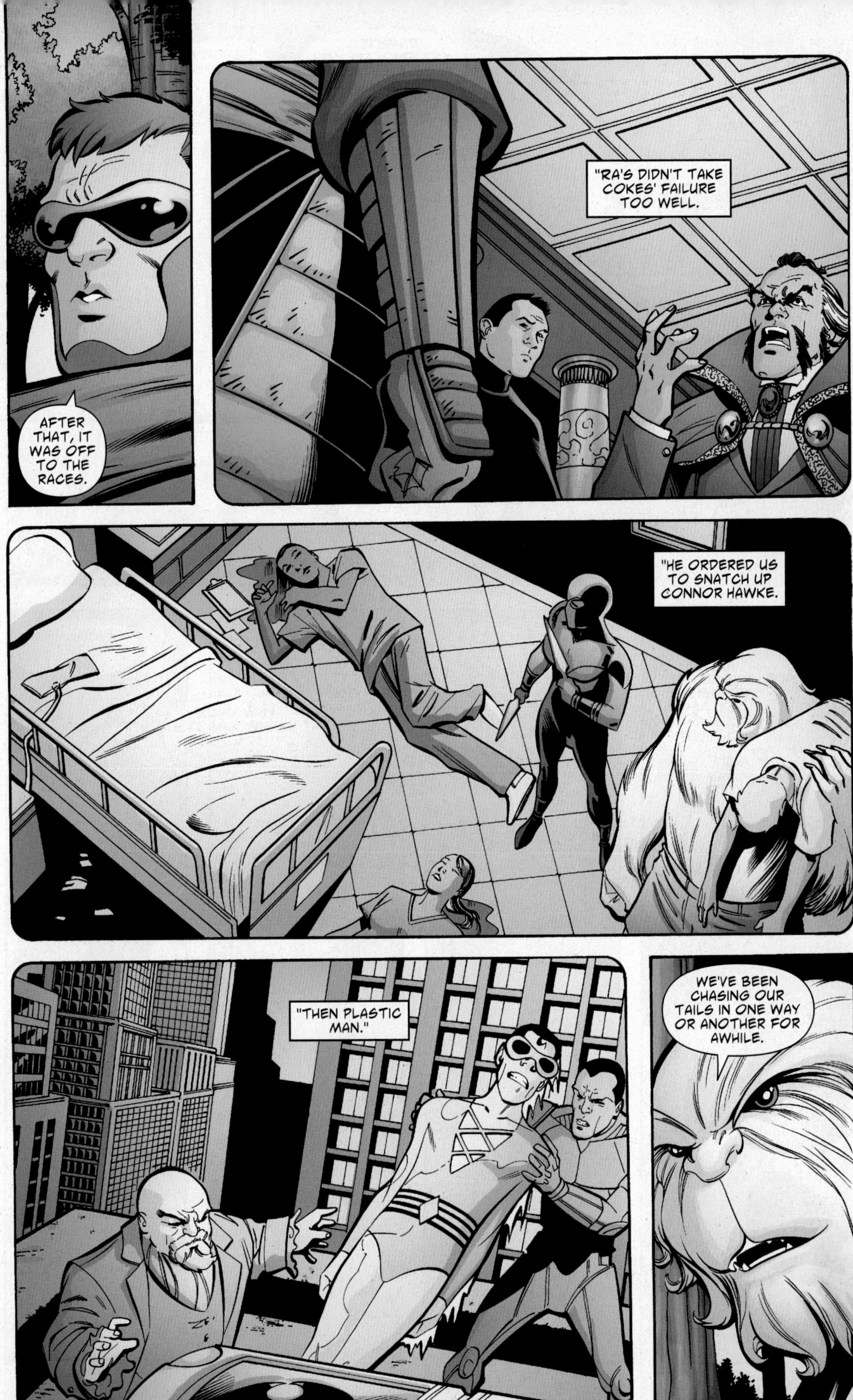
AFTER THAT, IT WAS OFF TO THE RACES.
"RA'S DIDN'T TAKE COKES' FAILURE TOO WELL.
"HE ORDERED US TO SNATCH UP CONNOR HAWKE.
"THEN PLASTIC MAN."
WE'VE BEEN CHASING OUR TAILS IN ONE WAY OR ANOTHER FOR AWHILE.

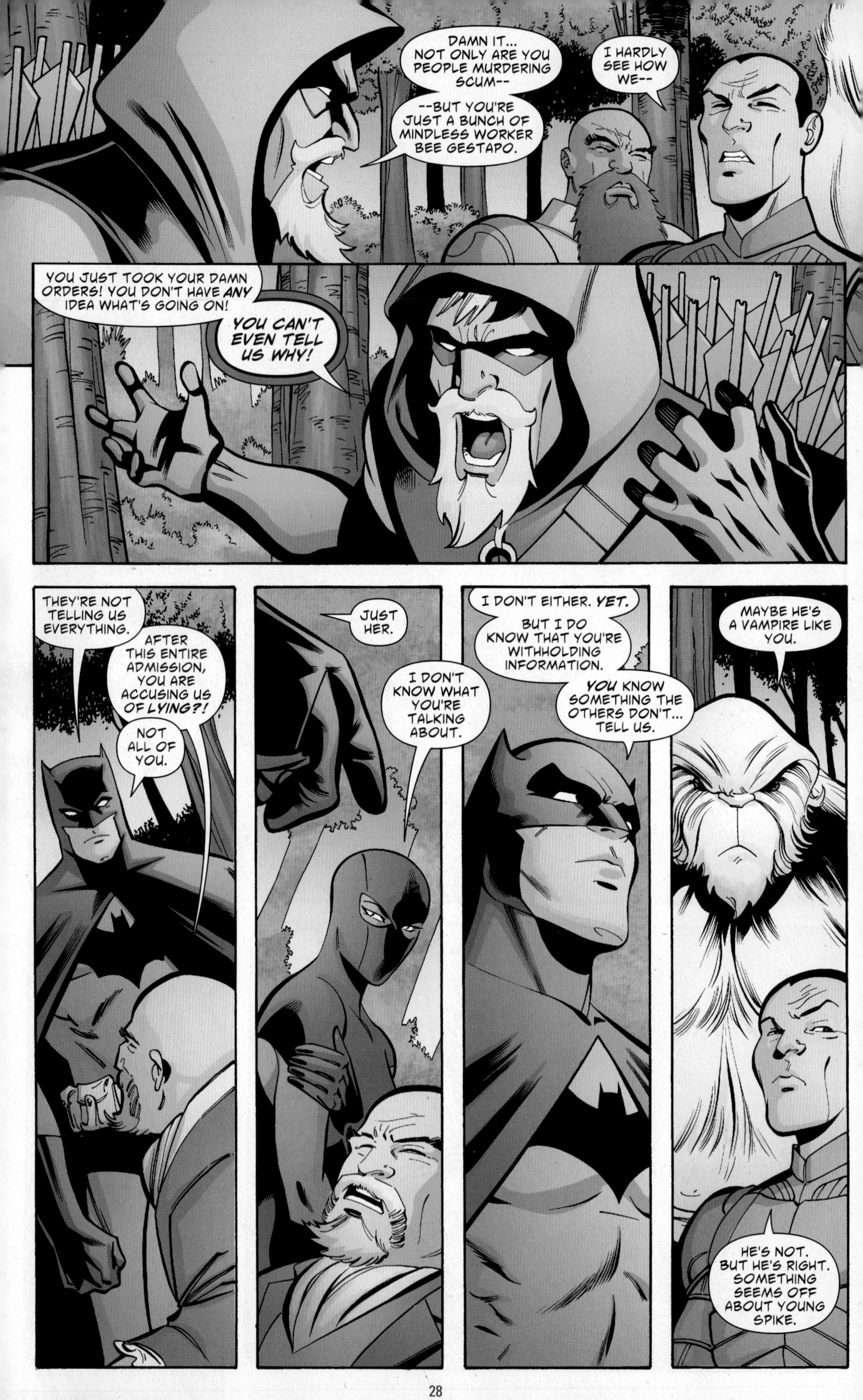
DAMN IT... NOT ONLY ARE YOU PEOPLE MURDERING SCUM--
--BUT YOU'RE JUST A BUNCH OF MINDLESS WORKER BEE GESTAPO.
I HARDLY SEE HOW WE--
YOU JUST TOOK YOUR DAMN ORDERS! YOU DON'T HAVE ANY IDEA WHAT'S GOING ON!
YOU CAN'T EVEN TELL US WHY!
THEY'RE NOT TELLING US EVERYTHING.
AFTER THIS ENTIRE ADMISSION, YOU ARE ACCUSING US OF LYING?!
NOT ALL OF YOU.
JUST HER.
I DON'T KNOW WHAT YOU'RE TALKING ABOUT.
I DON'T EITHER. YET.
BUT I DO KNOW THAT YOU'RE WITHHOLDING INFORMATION.
YOU KNOW SOMETHING THE OTHERS DON'T... TELL US.
MAYBE HE'S A VAMPIRE LIKE YOU.
HE'S NOT. BUT HE'S RIGHT. SOMETHING SEEMS OFF ABOUT YOUNG SPIKE.

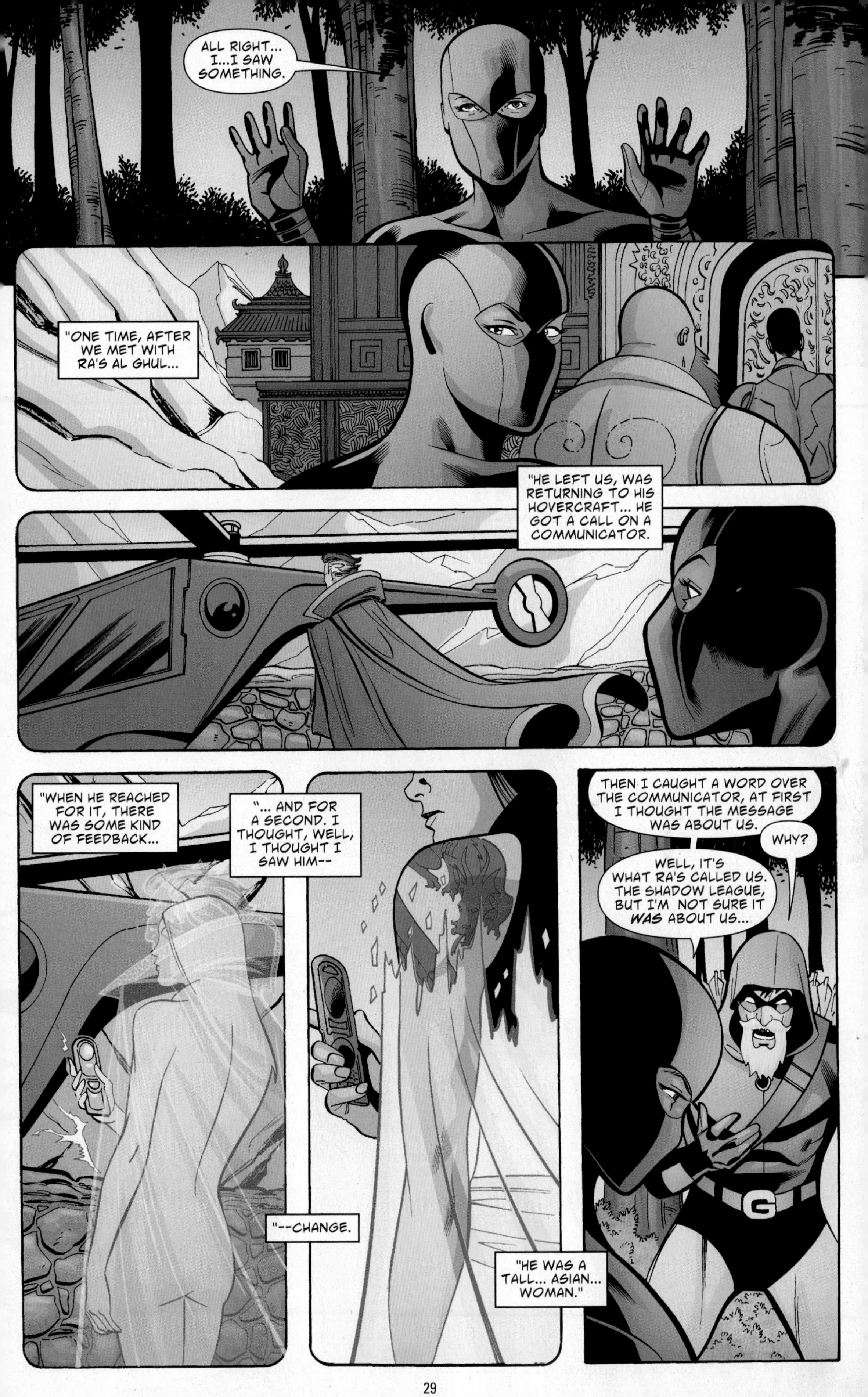
ALL RIGHT... I...I SAW SOMETHING.
"ONE TIME, AFTER WE MET WITH RA'S AL GHUL...
"HE LEFT US, WAS RETURNING TO HIS HOVERCRAFT... HE GOT A CALL ON A COMMUNICATOR.
"WHEN HE REACHED FOR IT, THERE WAS SOME KIND OF FEEDBACK...
"... AND FOR A SECOND. I THOUGHT, WELL, I THOUGHT I SAW HIM--
"--CHANGE.
"HE WAS A TALL... ASIAN... WOMAN."
THEN I CAUGHT A WORD OVER THE COMMUNICATOR, AT FIRST I THOUGHT THE MESSAGE WAS ABOUT US.
WHY?
WELL, IT'S WHAT RA'S CALLED US. THE SHADOW LEAGUE, BUT I'M NOT SURE IT *WAS* ABOUT US...

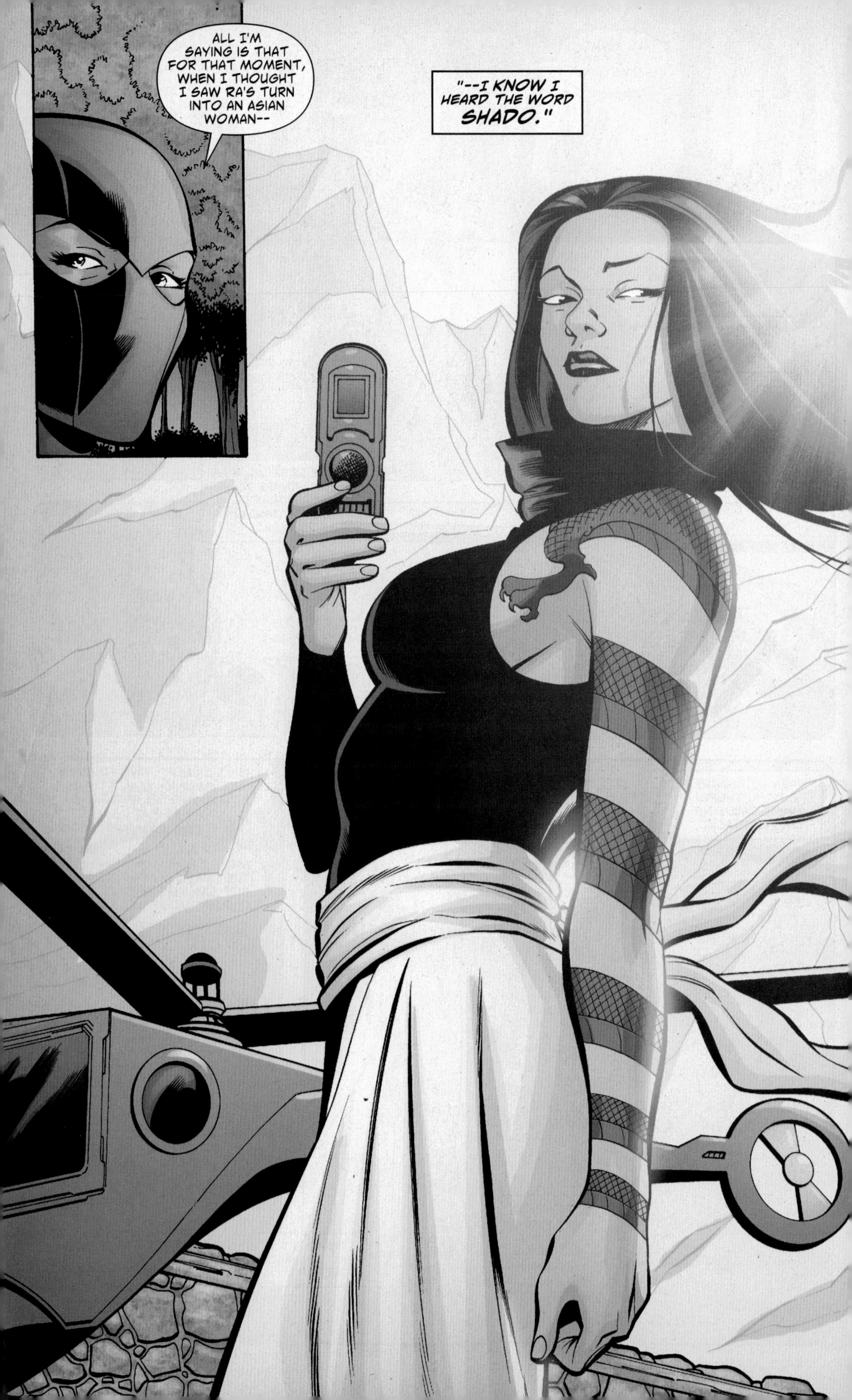
ALL I'M SAYING IS THAT FOR THAT MOMENT, WHEN I THOUGHT I SAW RA'S TURN INTO AN ASIAN WOMAN--
"--I KNOW I HEARD THE WORD SHADO."

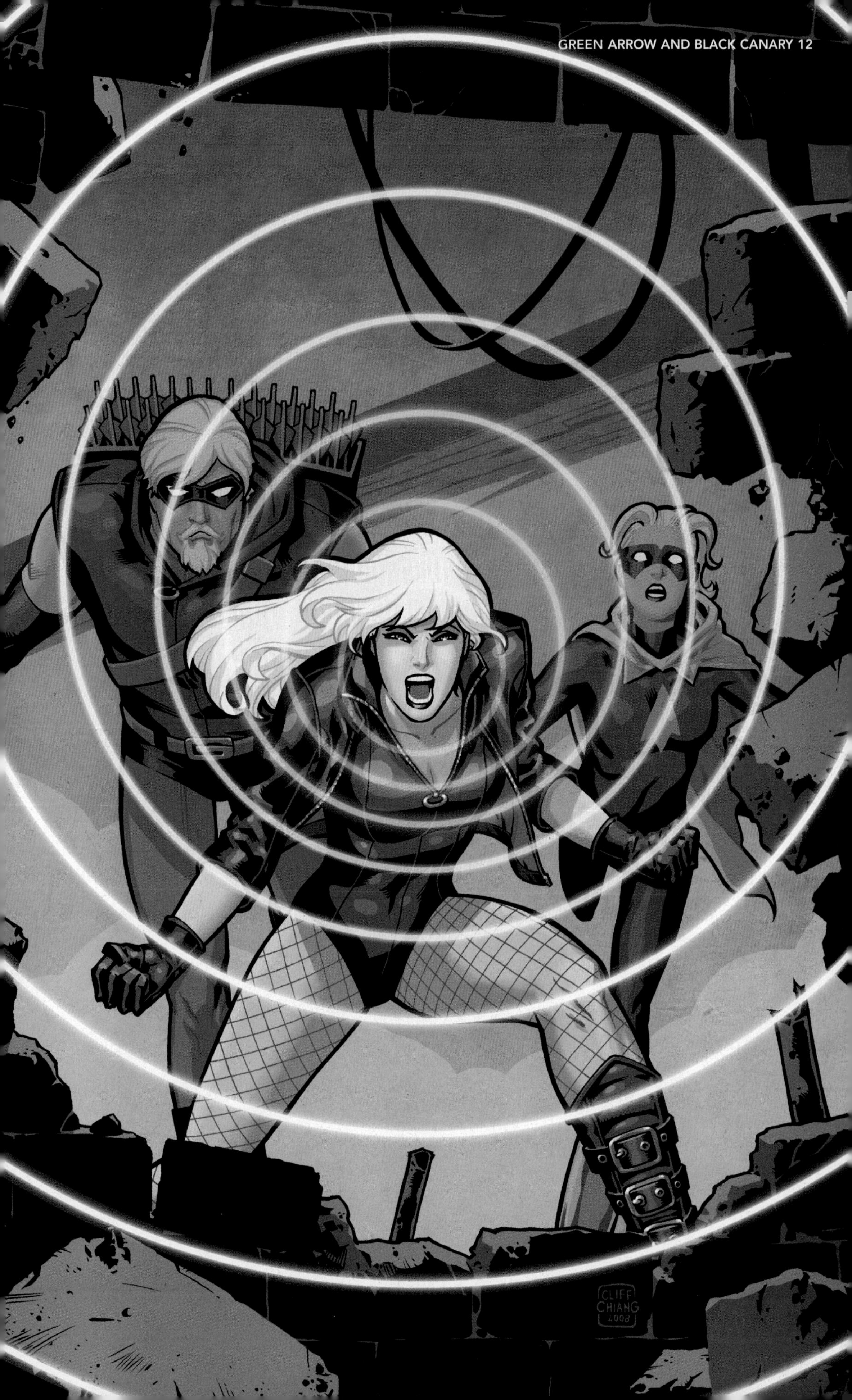
CLIFF CHIANG 2009

A LEAGUE OF THEIR OWN:

**THE SON OF THE FATHER
THE FATHER OF THE SON**

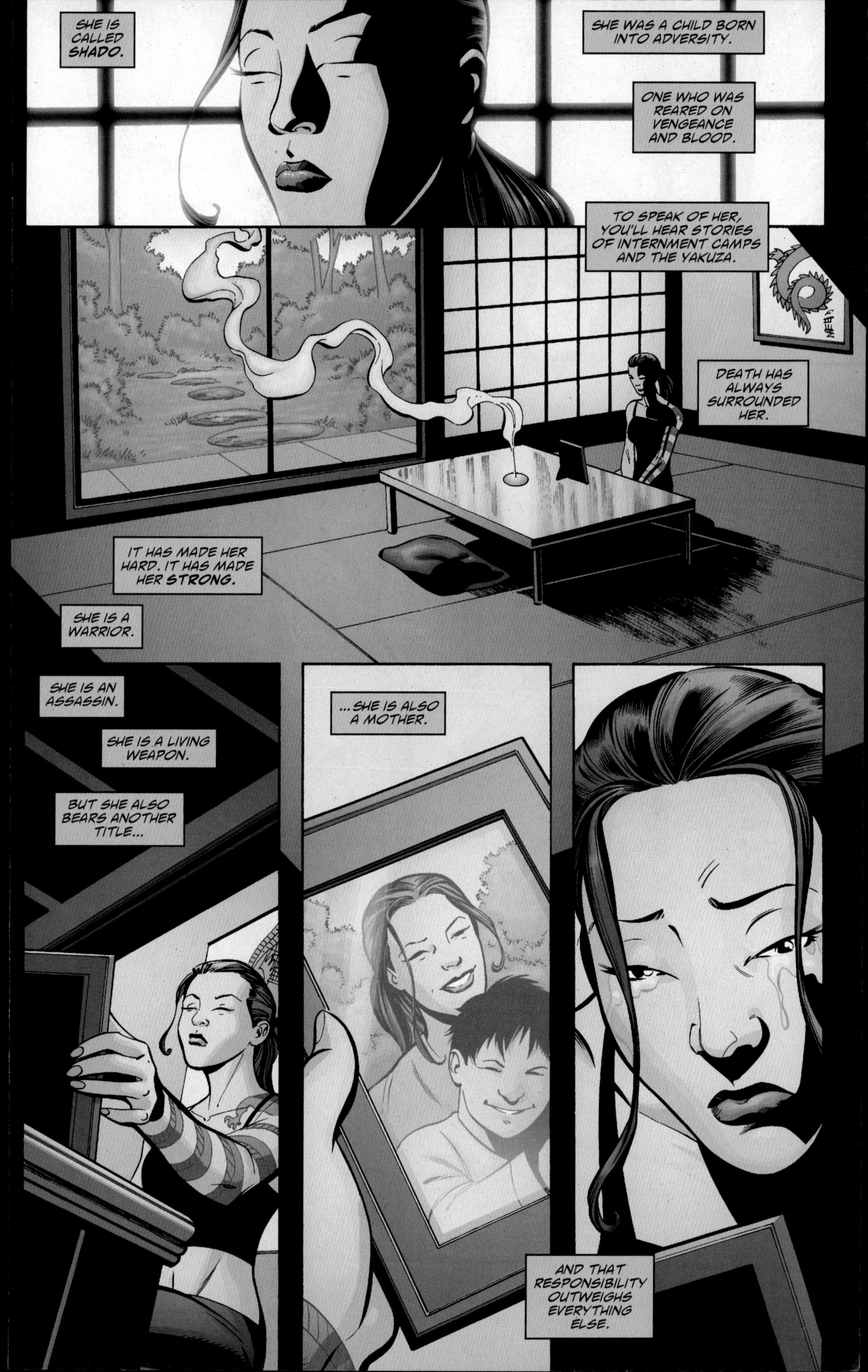
SHE IS CALLED SHADO.
SHE WAS A CHILD BORN INTO ADVERSITY.
ONE WHO WAS REARED ON VENGEANCE AND BLOOD.
TO SPEAK OF HER, YOU'LL HEAR STORIES OF INTERNMENT CAMPS AND THE YAKUZA.
DEATH HAS ALWAYS SURROUNDED HER.
IT HAS MADE HER HARD. IT HAS MADE HER STRONG.
SHE IS A WARRIOR.
SHE IS AN ASSASSIN.
SHE IS A LIVING WEAPON.
BUT SHE ALSO BEARS ANOTHER TITLE...
...SHE IS ALSO A MOTHER.
AND THAT RESPONSIBILITY OUTWEIGHS EVERYTHING ELSE.

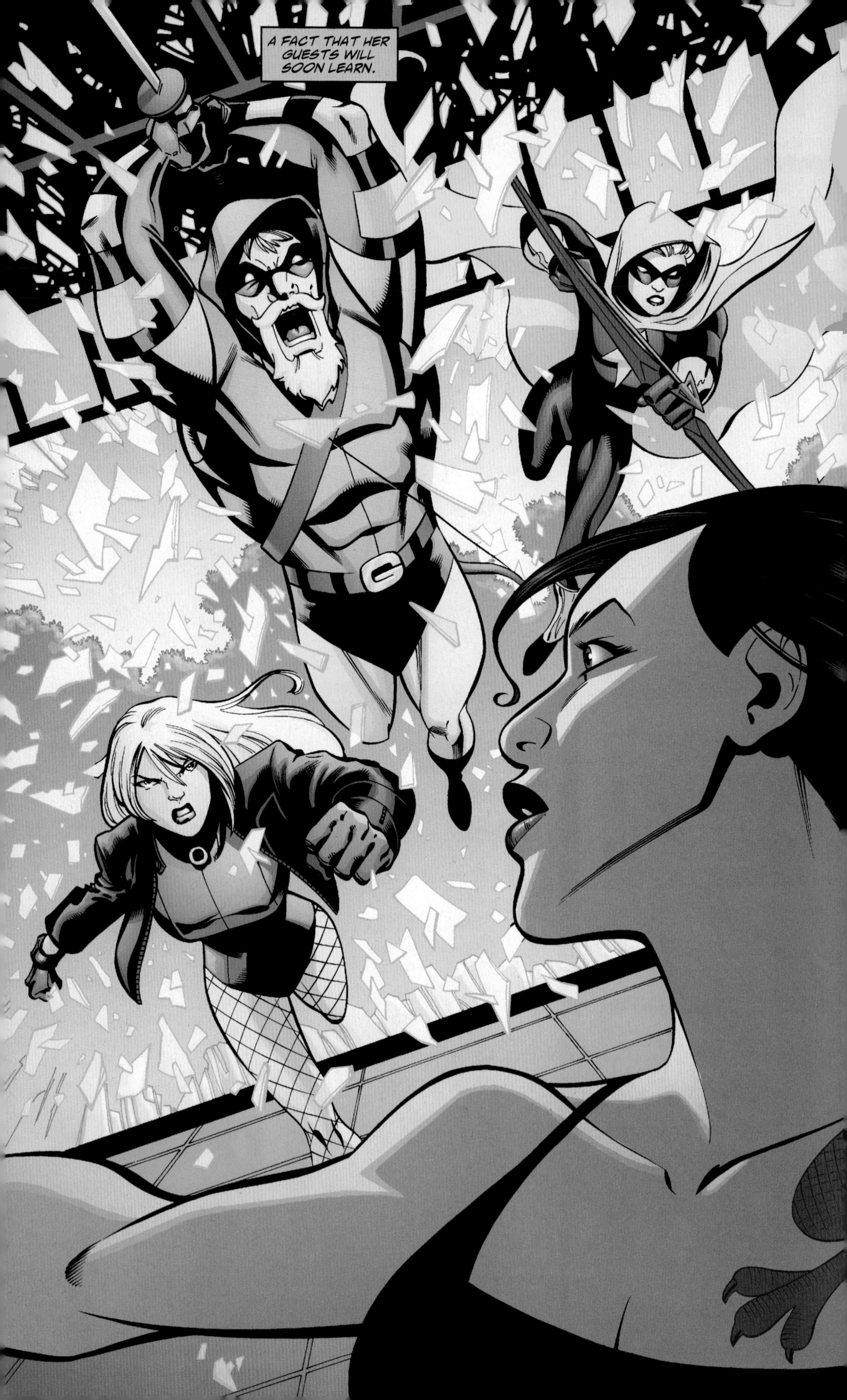
A FACT THAT HER GUESTS WILL SOON LEARN.

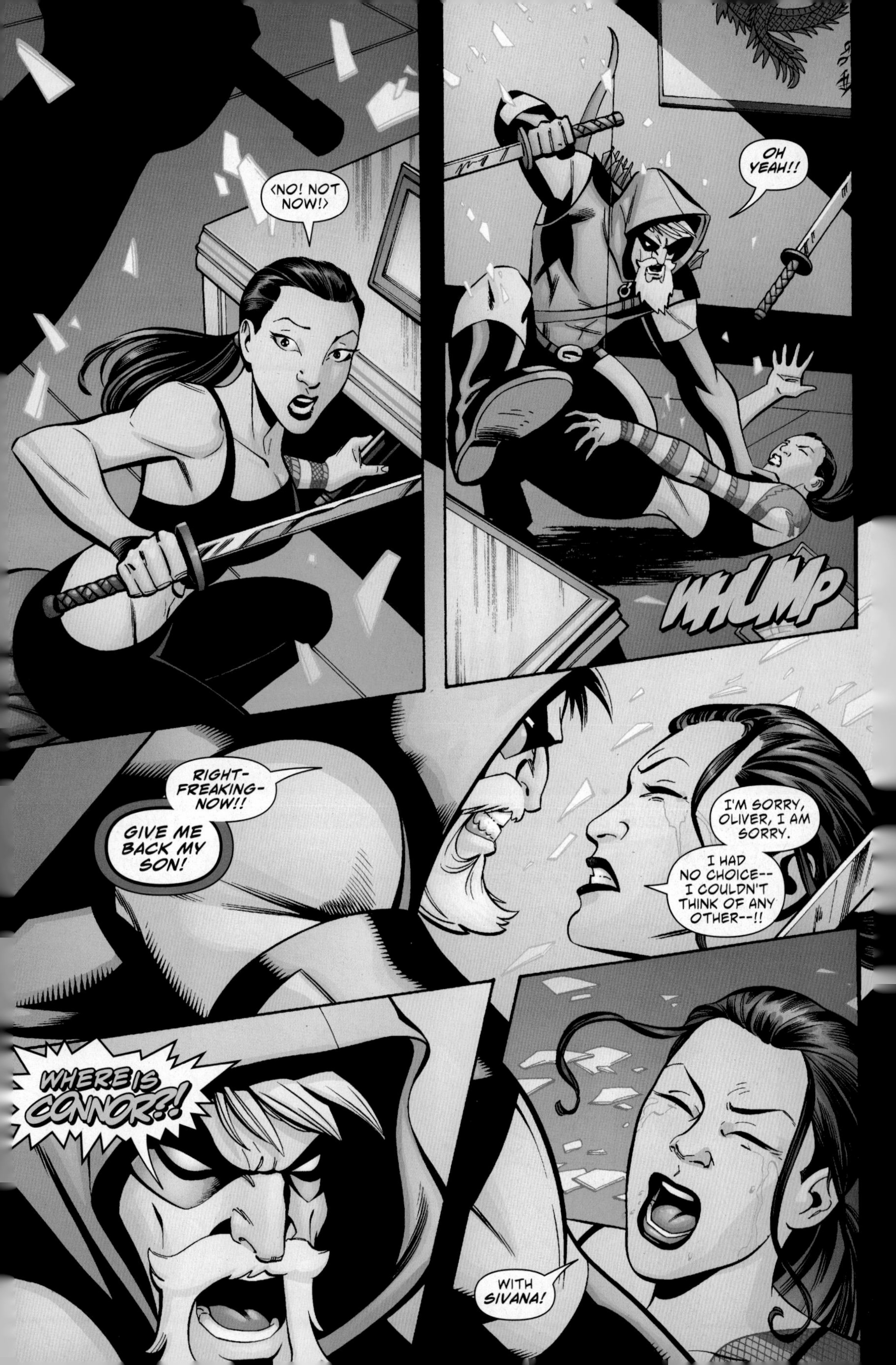
<NO! NOT NOW!>
OH YEAH!!
WHUMP
RIGHT-FREAKING-NOW!!
GIVE ME BACK MY SON!
I'M SORRY, OLIVER, I AM SORRY.
I HAD NO CHOICE-- I COULDN'T THINK OF ANY OTHER--!!
WHERE IS CONNOR?!
WITH SIVANA!

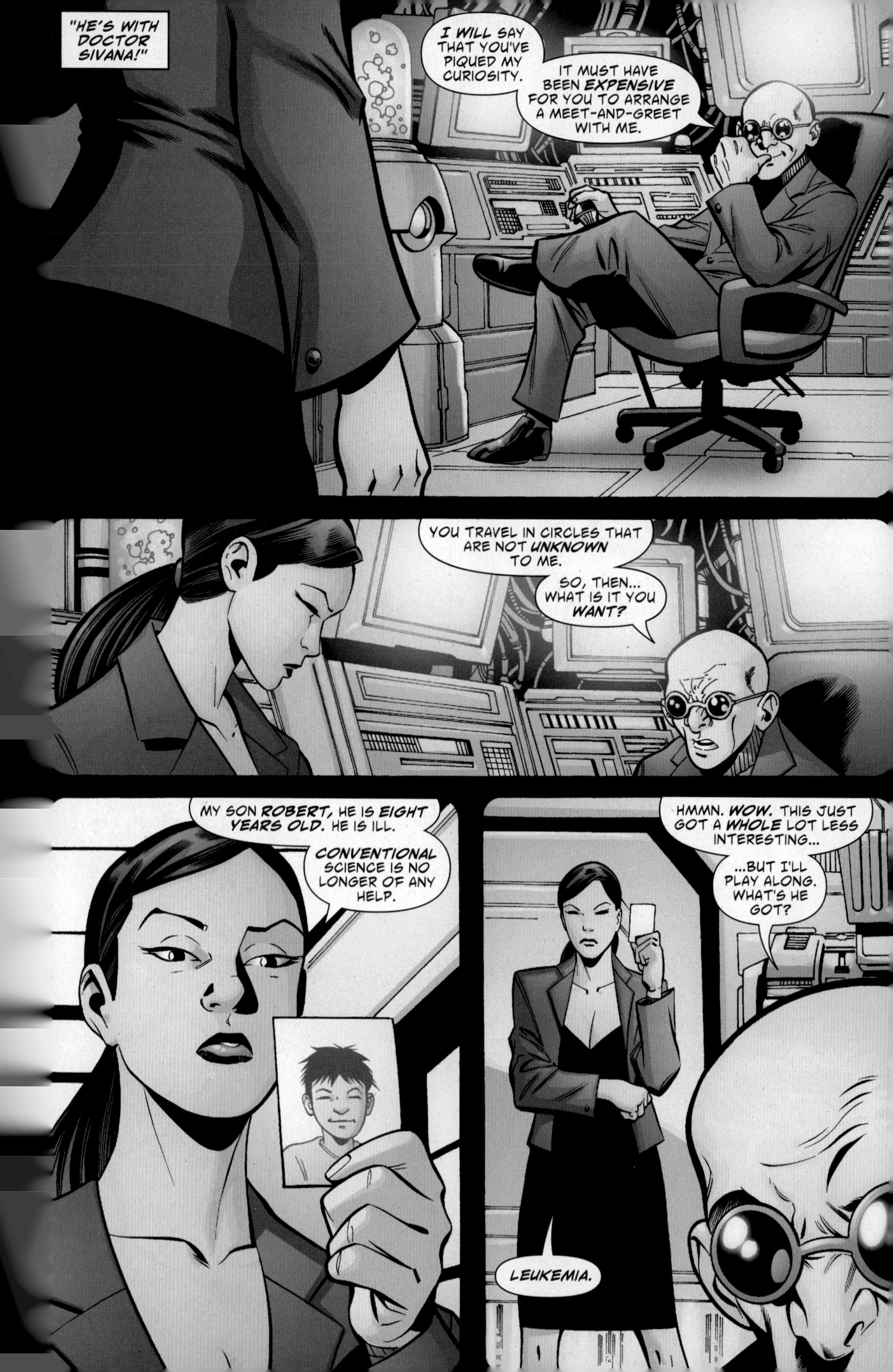
"HE'S WITH DOCTOR SIVANA!"
I WILL SAY THAT YOU'VE PIQUED MY CURIOSITY.
IT MUST HAVE BEEN EXPENSIVE FOR YOU TO ARRANGE A MEET-AND-GREET WITH ME.
YOU TRAVEL IN CIRCLES THAT ARE NOT UNKNOWN TO ME.
SO, THEN... WHAT IS IT YOU WANT?
MY SON ROBERT, HE IS EIGHT YEARS OLD. HE IS ILL.
CONVENTIONAL SCIENCE IS NO LONGER OF ANY HELP.
HMMN. WOW. THIS JUST GOT A WHOLE LOT LESS INTERESTING...
...BUT I'LL PLAY ALONG. WHAT'S HE GOT?
LEUKEMIA.

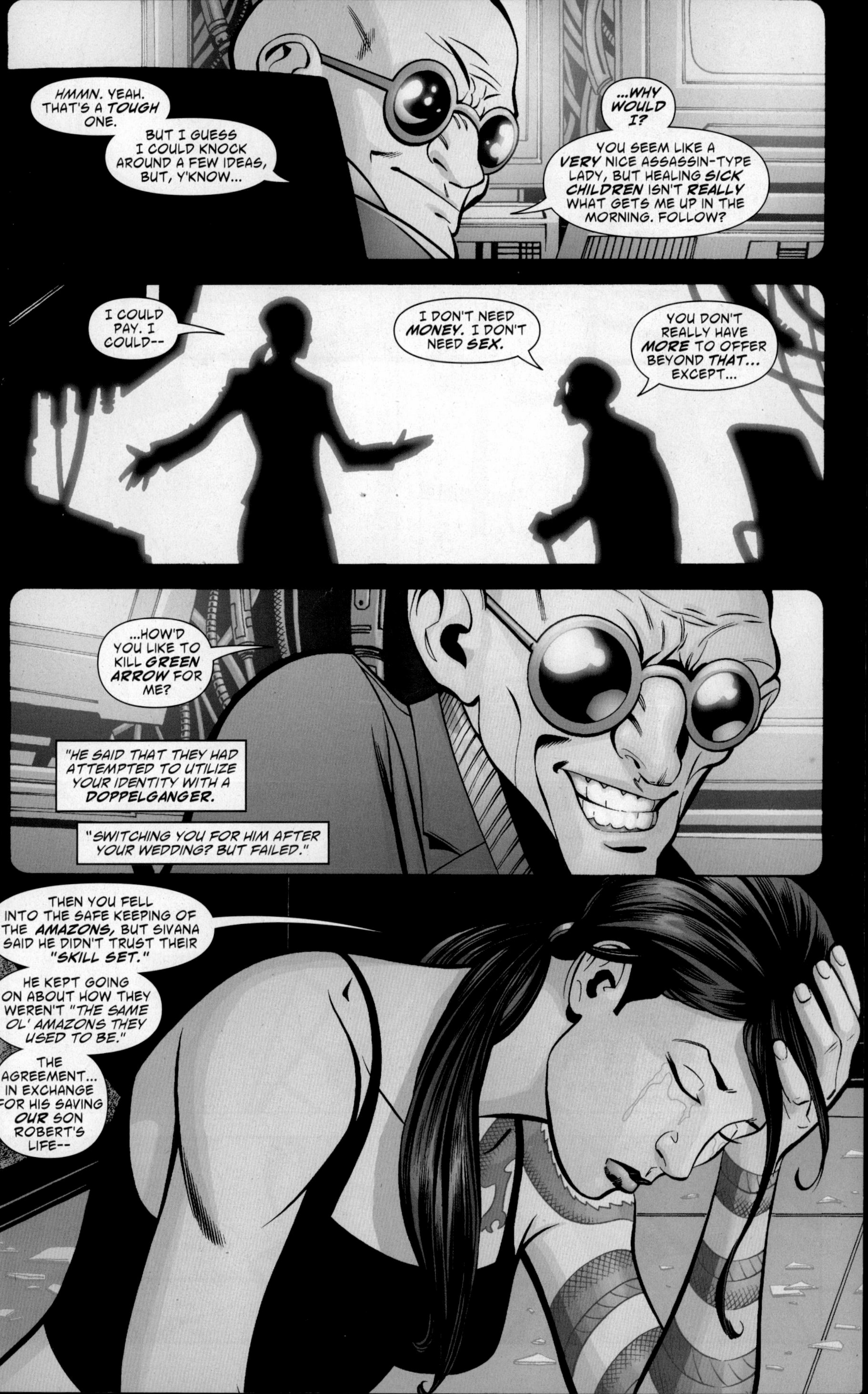
HMMN. YEAH. THAT'S A TOUGH ONE.
BUT I GUESS I COULD KNOCK AROUND A FEW IDEAS, BUT, Y'KNOW...
...WHY WOULD I?
YOU SEEM LIKE A VERY NICE ASSASSIN-TYPE LADY, BUT HEALING SICK CHILDREN ISN'T REALLY WHAT GETS ME UP IN THE MORNING. FOLLOW?
I COULD PAY. I COULD--
I DON'T NEED MONEY. I DON'T NEED SEX.
YOU DON'T REALLY HAVE MORE TO OFFER BEYOND THAT... EXCEPT...
...HOW'D YOU LIKE TO KILL GREEN ARROW FOR ME?
"HE SAID THAT THEY HAD ATTEMPTED TO UTILIZE YOUR IDENTITY WITH A DOPPELGANGER.
"SWITCHING YOU FOR HIM AFTER YOUR WEDDING? BUT FAILED."
THEN YOU FELL INTO THE SAFE KEEPING OF THE AMAZONS, BUT SIVANA SAID HE DIDN'T TRUST THEIR "SKILL SET."
HE KEPT GOING ON ABOUT HOW THEY WEREN'T "THE SAME OL' AMAZONS THEY USED TO BE."
THE AGREEMENT... IN EXCHANGE FOR HIS SAVING OUR SON ROBERT'S LIFE--

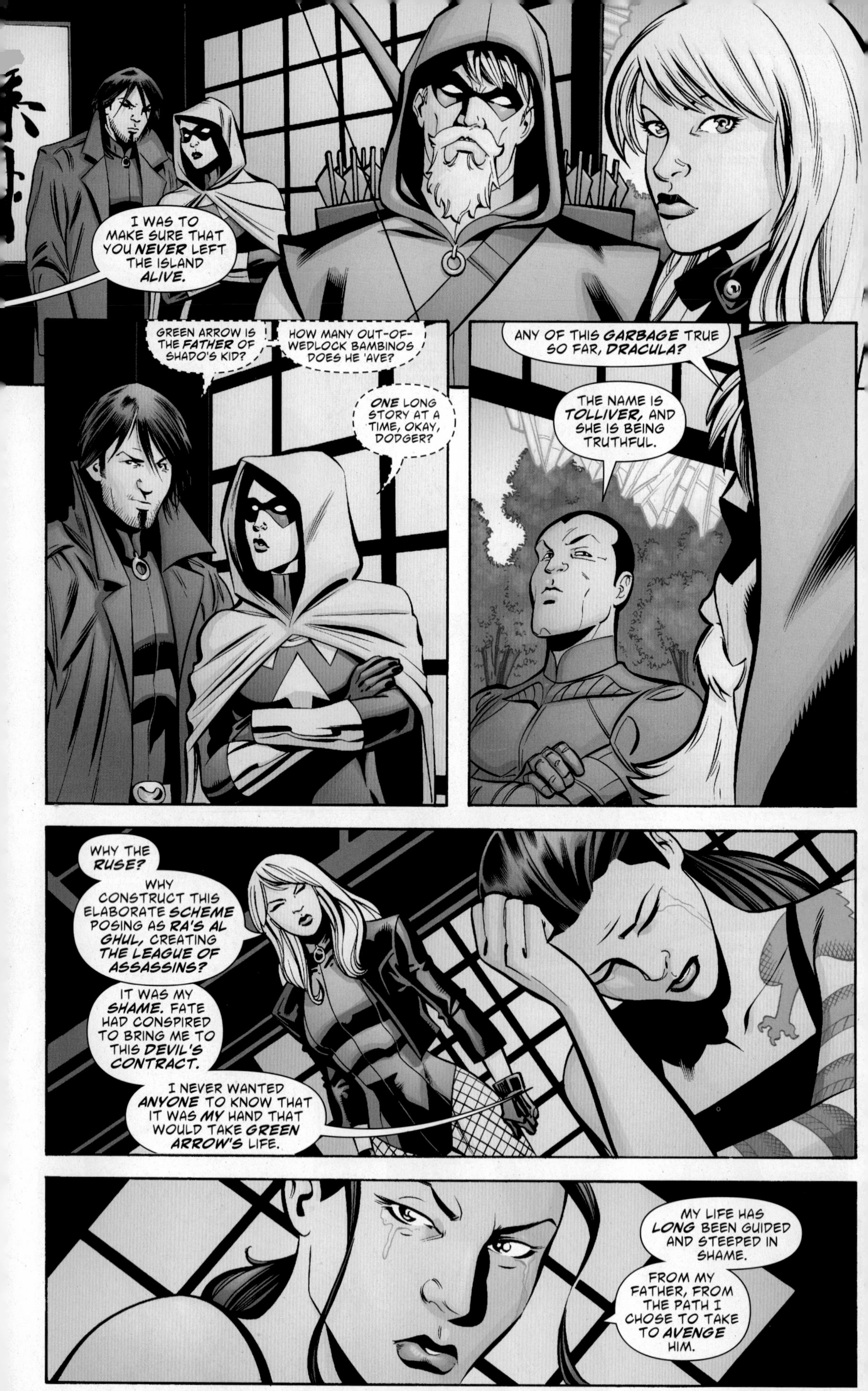

I WAS TO MAKE SURE THAT YOU NEVER LEFT THE ISLAND ALIVE.
GREEN ARROW IS THE FATHER OF SHADO'S KID?
HOW MANY OUT-OF-WEDLOCK BAMBINOS DOES HE 'AVE?
ONE LONG STORY AT A TIME, OKAY, DODGER?
ANY OF THIS GARBAGE TRUE SO FAR, DRACULA?
THE NAME IS TOLLIVER, AND SHE IS BEING TRUTHFUL.
WHY THE RUSE?
WHY CONSTRUCT THIS ELABORATE SCHEME POSING AS RA'S AL GHUL, CREATING THE LEAGUE OF ASSASSINS?
IT WAS MY SHAME. FATE HAD CONSPIRED TO BRING ME TO THIS DEVIL'S CONTRACT.
I NEVER WANTED ANYONE TO KNOW THAT IT WAS MY HAND THAT WOULD TAKE GREEN ARROW'S LIFE.
MY LIFE HAS LONG BEEN GUIDED AND STEEPED IN SHAME.
FROM MY FATHER, FROM THE PATH I CHOSE TO TAKE TO AVENGE HIM.

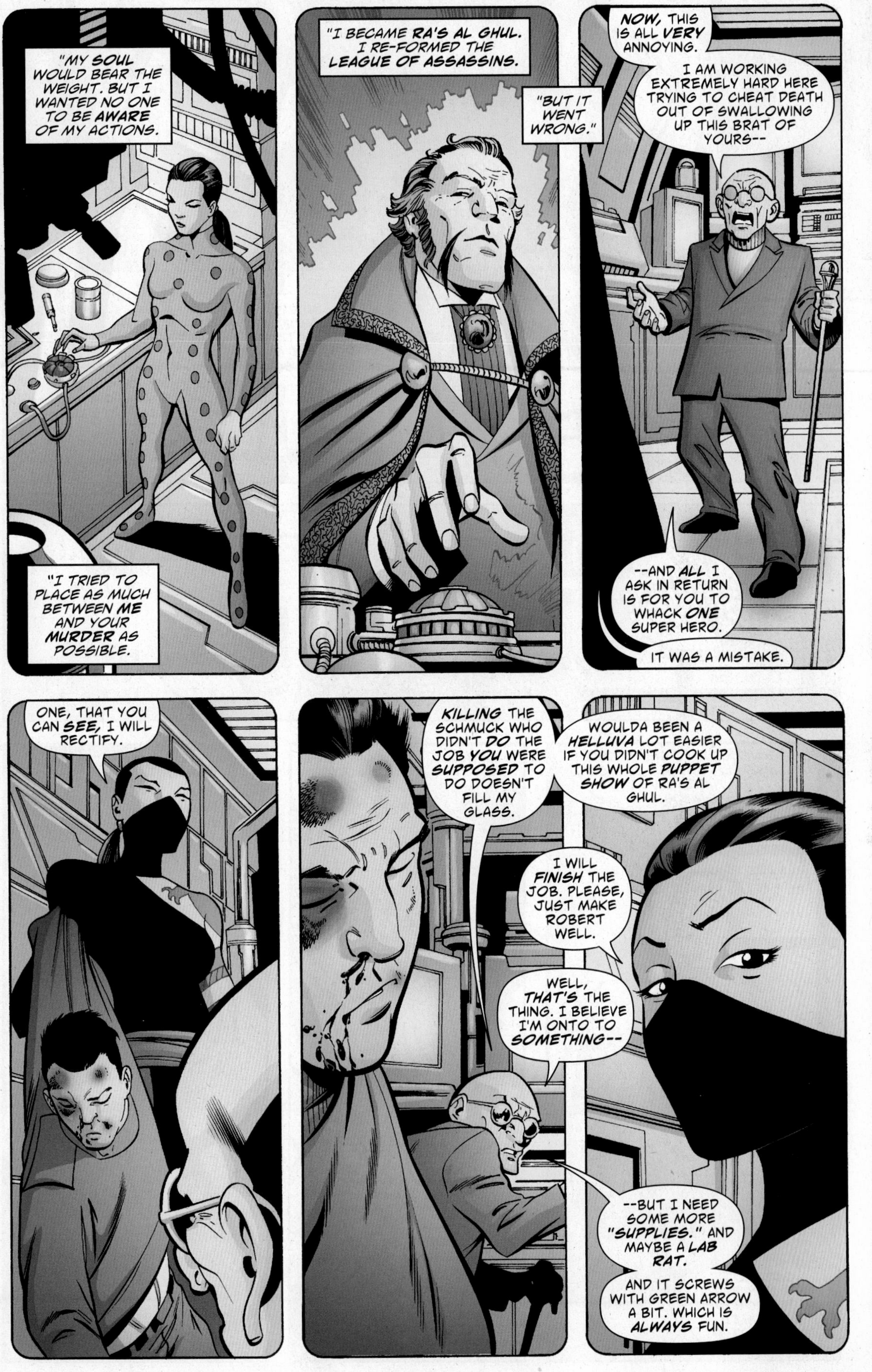
"MY SOUL WOULD BEAR THE WEIGHT. BUT I WANTED NO ONE TO BE AWARE OF MY ACTIONS.
"I TRIED TO PLACE AS MUCH BETWEEN ME AND YOUR MURDER AS POSSIBLE.
"I BECAME RA'S AL GHUL. I RE-FORMED THE LEAGUE OF ASSASSINS.
"BUT IT WENT WRONG."
NOW, THIS IS ALL VERY ANNOYING.
I AM WORKING EXTREMELY HARD HERE TRYING TO CHEAT DEATH OUT OF SWALLOWING UP THIS BRAT OF YOURS--
--AND ALL I ASK IN RETURN IS FOR YOU TO WHACK ONE SUPER HERO.
IT WAS A MISTAKE.
ONE, THAT YOU CAN SEE, I WILL RECTIFY.
KILLING THE SCHMUCK WHO DIDN'T DO THE JOB YOU WERE SUPPOSED TO DO DOESN'T FILL MY GLASS.
WOULDA BEEN A HELLUVA LOT EASIER IF YOU DIDN'T COOK UP THIS WHOLE PUPPET SHOW OF RA'S AL GHUL.
I WILL FINISH THE JOB. PLEASE, JUST MAKE ROBERT WELL.
WELL, THAT'S THE THING. I BELIEVE I'M ONTO TO SOMETHING--
--BUT I NEED SOME MORE "SUPPLIES." AND MAYBE A LAB RAT.
AND IT SCREWS WITH GREEN ARROW A BIT. WHICH IS ALWAYS FUN.

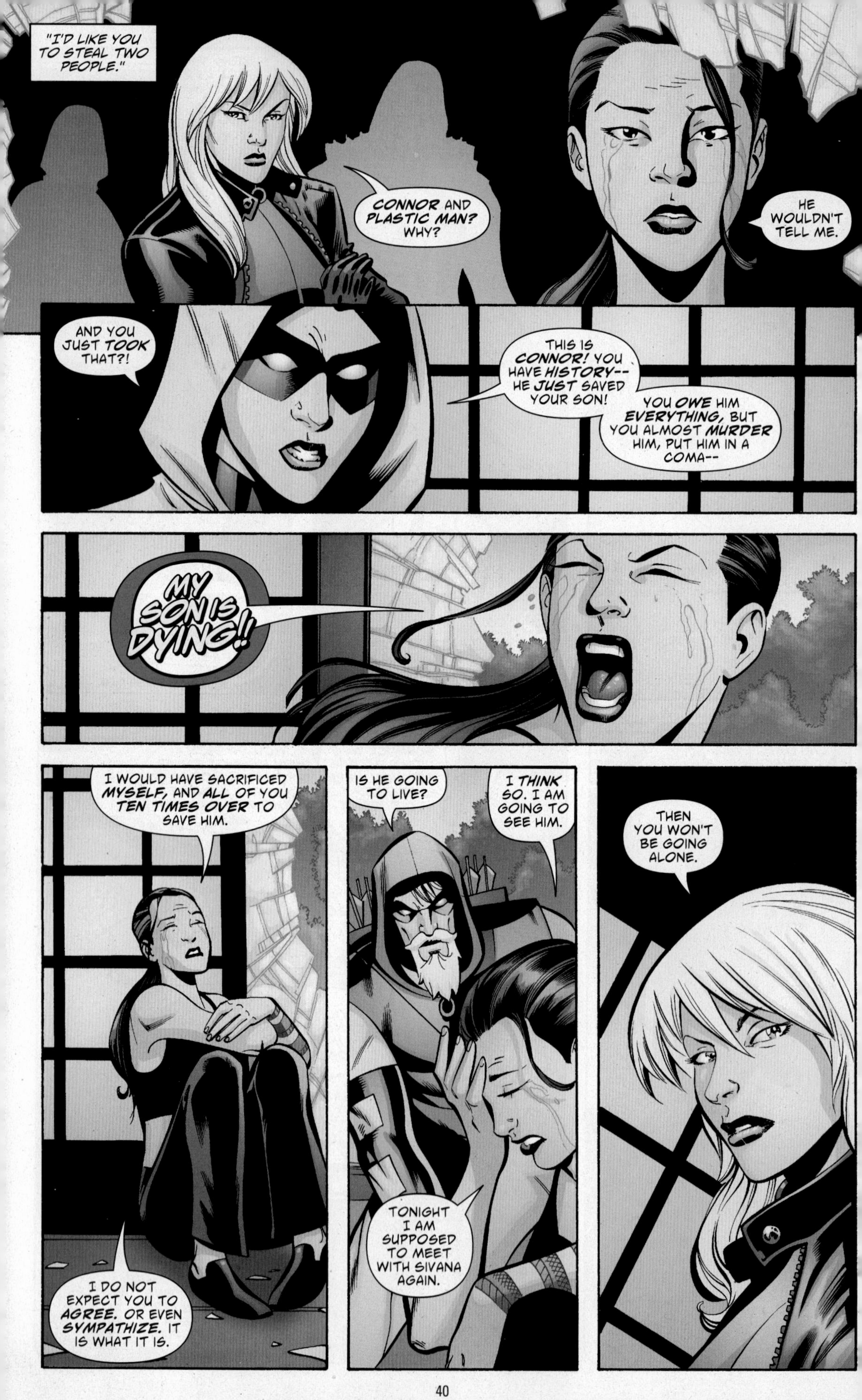
"I'D LIKE YOU TO STEAL TWO PEOPLE."
CONNOR AND PLASTIC MAN? WHY?
HE WOULDN'T TELL ME.
AND YOU JUST TOOK THAT?!
THIS IS CONNOR! YOU HAVE HISTORY-- HE JUST SAVED YOUR SON!
YOU OWE HIM EVERYTHING, BUT YOU ALMOST MURDER HIM, PUT HIM IN A COMA--
MY SON IS DYING!!
I WOULD HAVE SACRIFICED MYSELF, AND ALL OF YOU TEN TIMES OVER TO SAVE HIM.
I DO NOT EXPECT YOU TO AGREE. OR EVEN SYMPATHIZE. IT IS WHAT IT IS.
IS HE GOING TO LIVE?
I THINK SO. I AM GOING TO SEE HIM.
TONIGHT I AM SUPPOSED TO MEET WITH SIVANA AGAIN.
THEN YOU WON'T BE GOING ALONE.

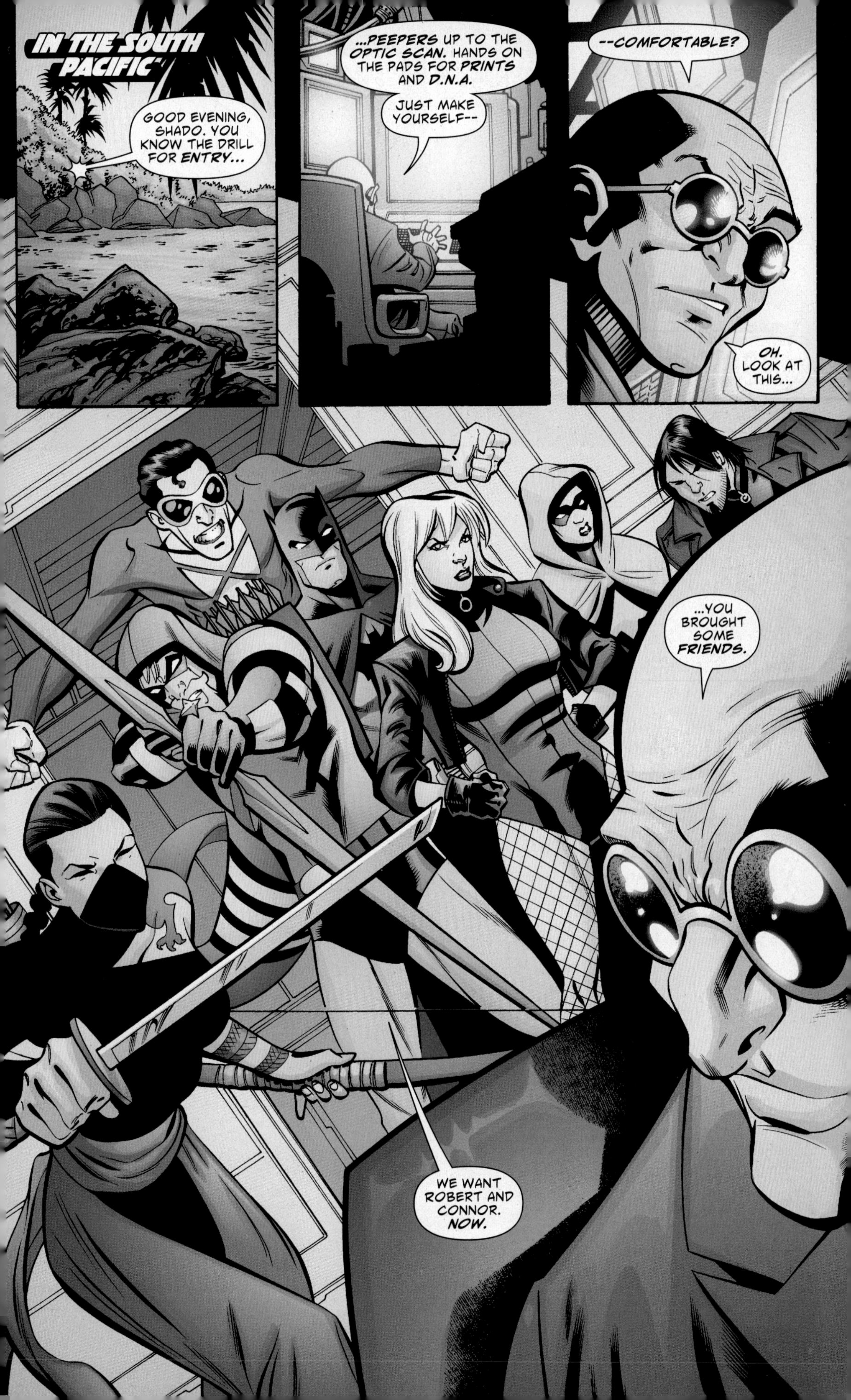
IN THE SOUTH PACIFIC
GOOD EVENING, SHADO. YOU KNOW THE DRILL FOR ENTRY...
...PEEPERS UP TO THE OPTIC SCAN. HANDS ON THE PADS FOR PRINTS AND D.N.A.
JUST MAKE YOURSELF--
--COMFORTABLE?
OH. LOOK AT THIS...
...YOU BROUGHT SOME FRIENDS.
WE WANT ROBERT AND CONNOR. NOW.

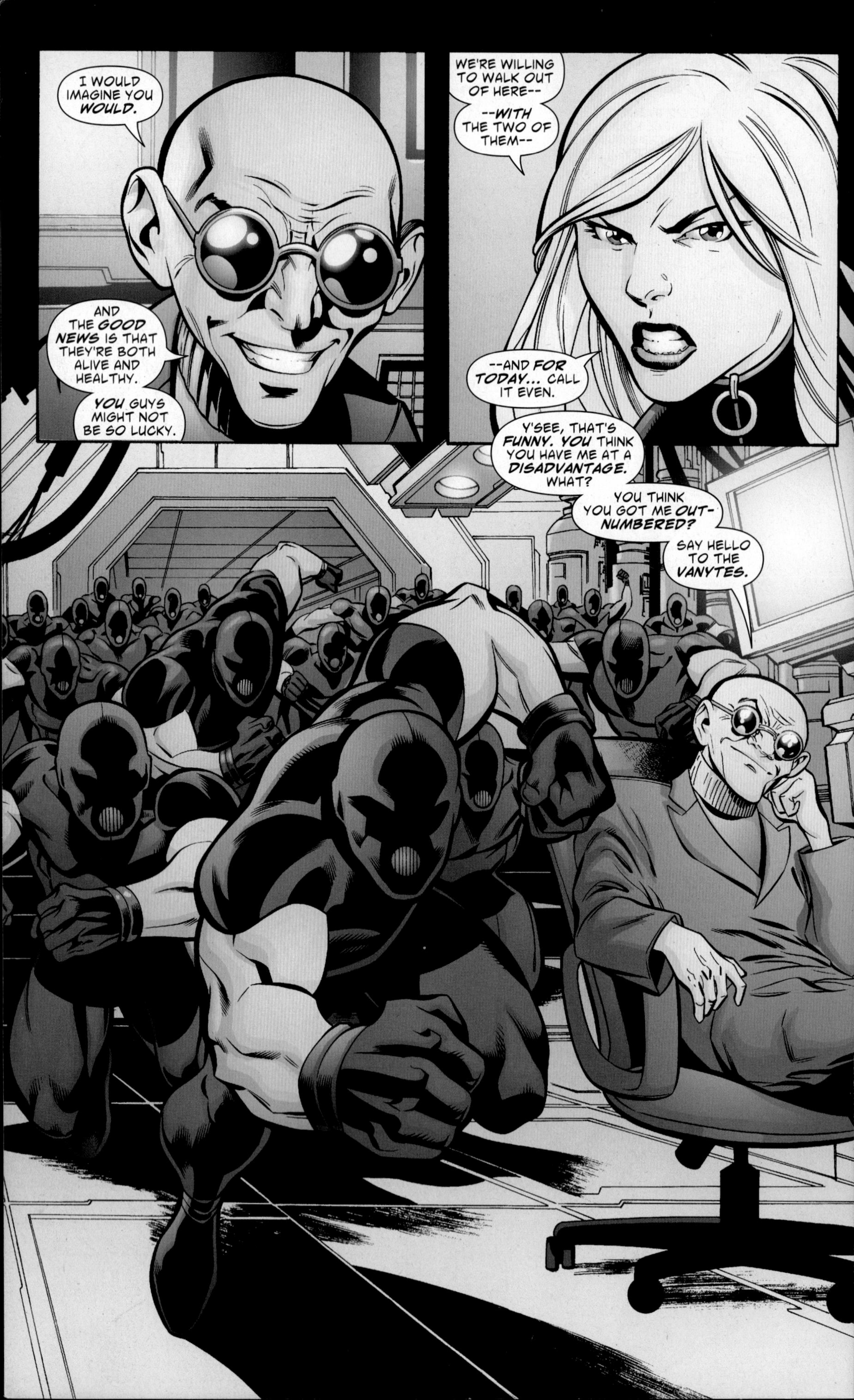
I WOULD IMAGINE YOU **WOULD.**
AND THE **GOOD NEWS** IS THAT THEY'RE BOTH ALIVE AND HEALTHY.
YOU GUYS MIGHT NOT BE SO LUCKY.
WE'RE WILLING TO WALK OUT OF HERE--
--**WITH** THE TWO OF THEM--
--AND **FOR TODAY...** CALL IT EVEN.
Y'SEE, THAT'S **FUNNY. YOU** THINK YOU HAVE ME AT A **DISADVANTAGE.** WHAT?
YOU THINK YOU GOT ME **OUT-NUMBERED?**
SAY HELLO TO THE **VANYTES.**

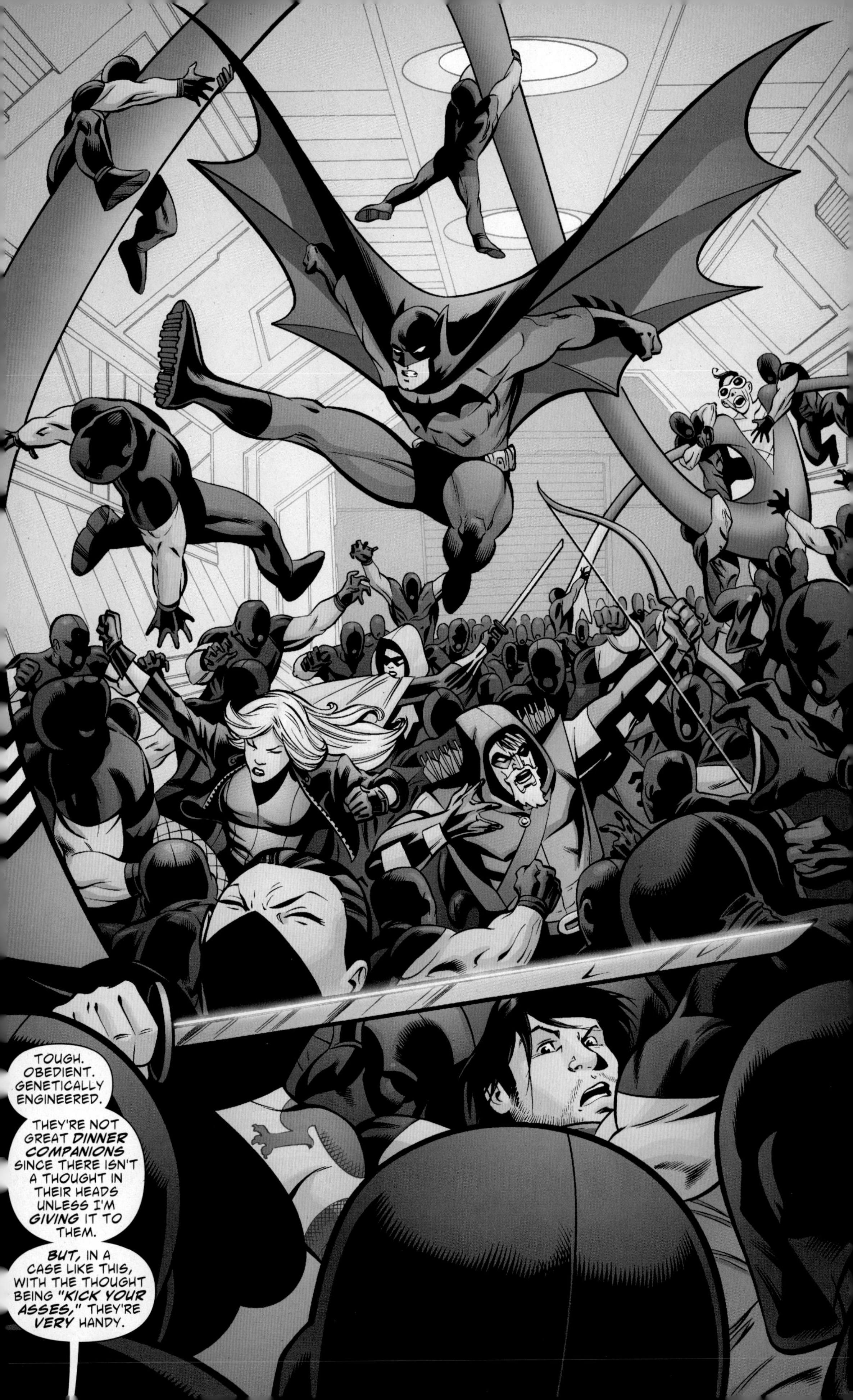
TOUGH. OBEDIENT. GENETICALLY ENGINEERED.
THEY'RE NOT GREAT DINNER COMPANIONS SINCE THERE ISN'T A THOUGHT IN THEIR HEADS UNLESS I'M GIVING IT TO THEM.
BUT, IN A CASE LIKE THIS, WITH THE THOUGHT BEING "KICK YOUR ASSES," THEY'RE VERY HANDY.

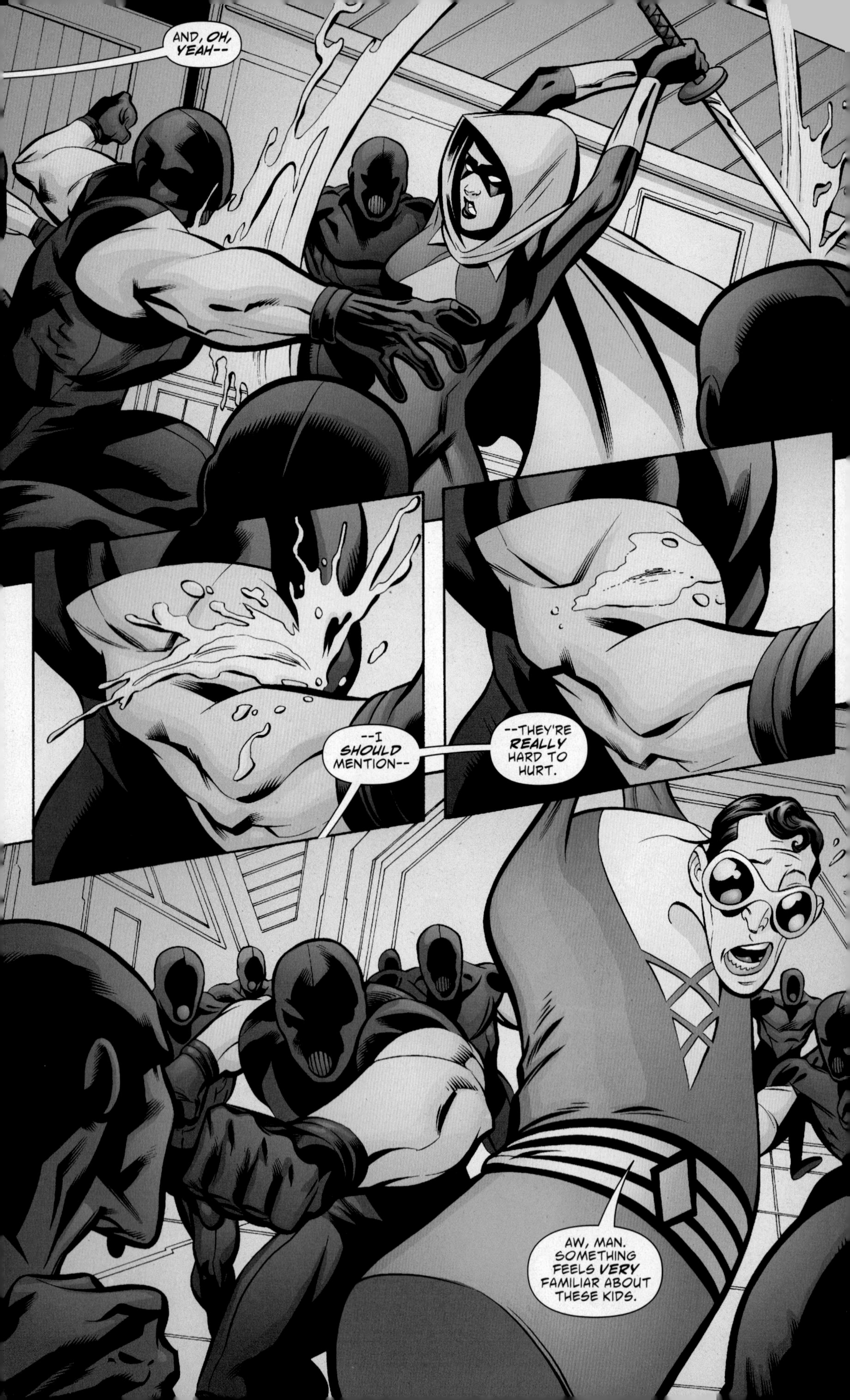
AND, OH, YEAH--
--I SHOULD MENTION--
--THEY'RE REALLY HARD TO HURT.
AW, MAN. SOMETHING FEELS VERY FAMILIAR ABOUT THESE KIDS.

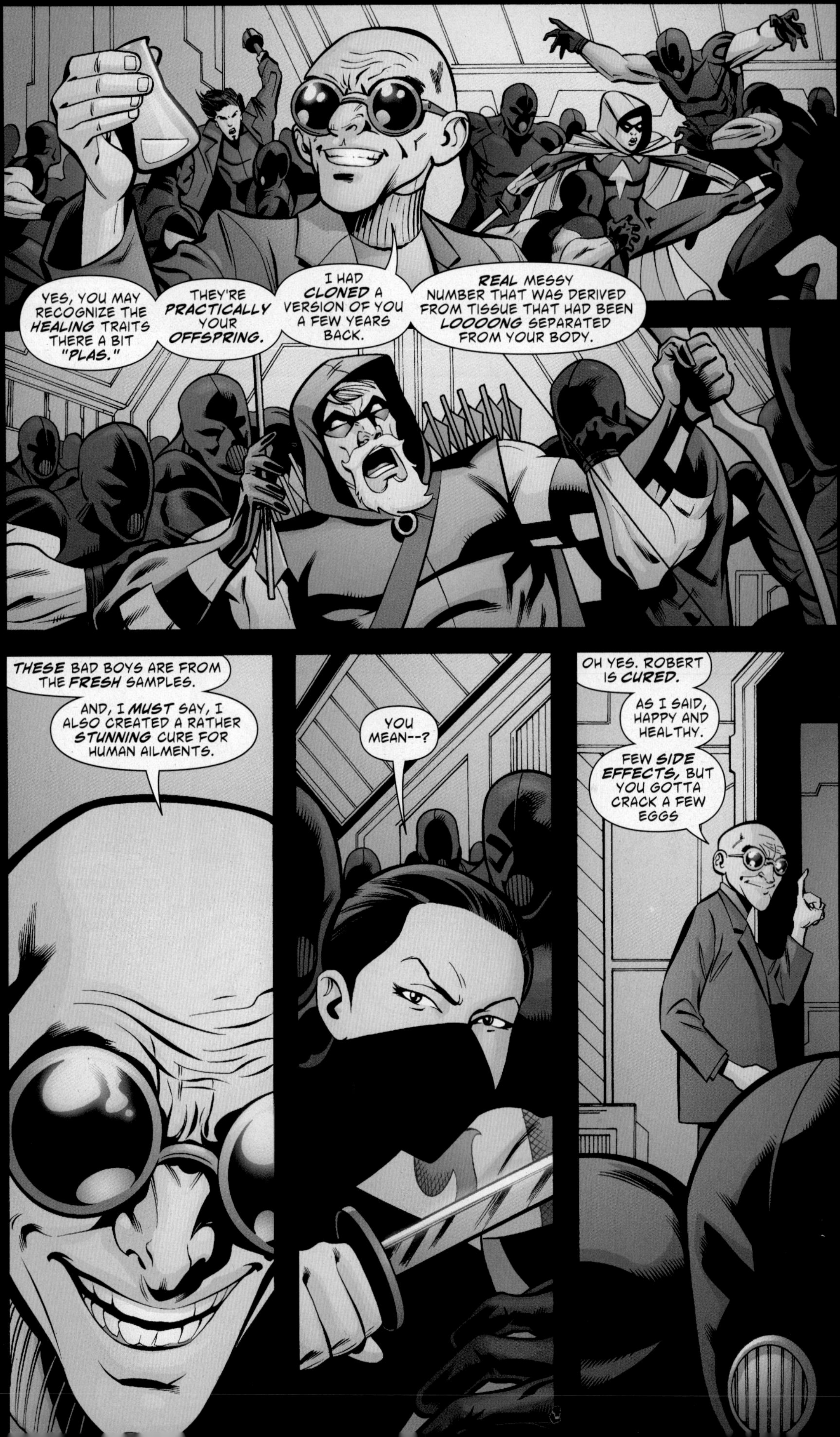
YES, YOU MAY RECOGNIZE THE HEALING TRAITS THERE A BIT "PLAS."
THEY'RE PRACTICALLY YOUR OFFSPRING.
I HAD CLONED A VERSION OF YOU A FEW YEARS BACK.
REAL MESSY NUMBER THAT WAS DERIVED FROM TISSUE THAT HAD BEEN LOOOONG SEPARATED FROM YOUR BODY.
THESE BAD BOYS ARE FROM THE FRESH SAMPLES.
AND, I MUST SAY, I ALSO CREATED A RATHER STUNNING CURE FOR HUMAN AILMENTS.
YOU MEAN--?
OH YES. ROBERT IS CURED.
AS I SAID, HAPPY AND HEALTHY.
FEW SIDE EFFECTS, BUT YOU GOTTA CRACK A FEW EGGS

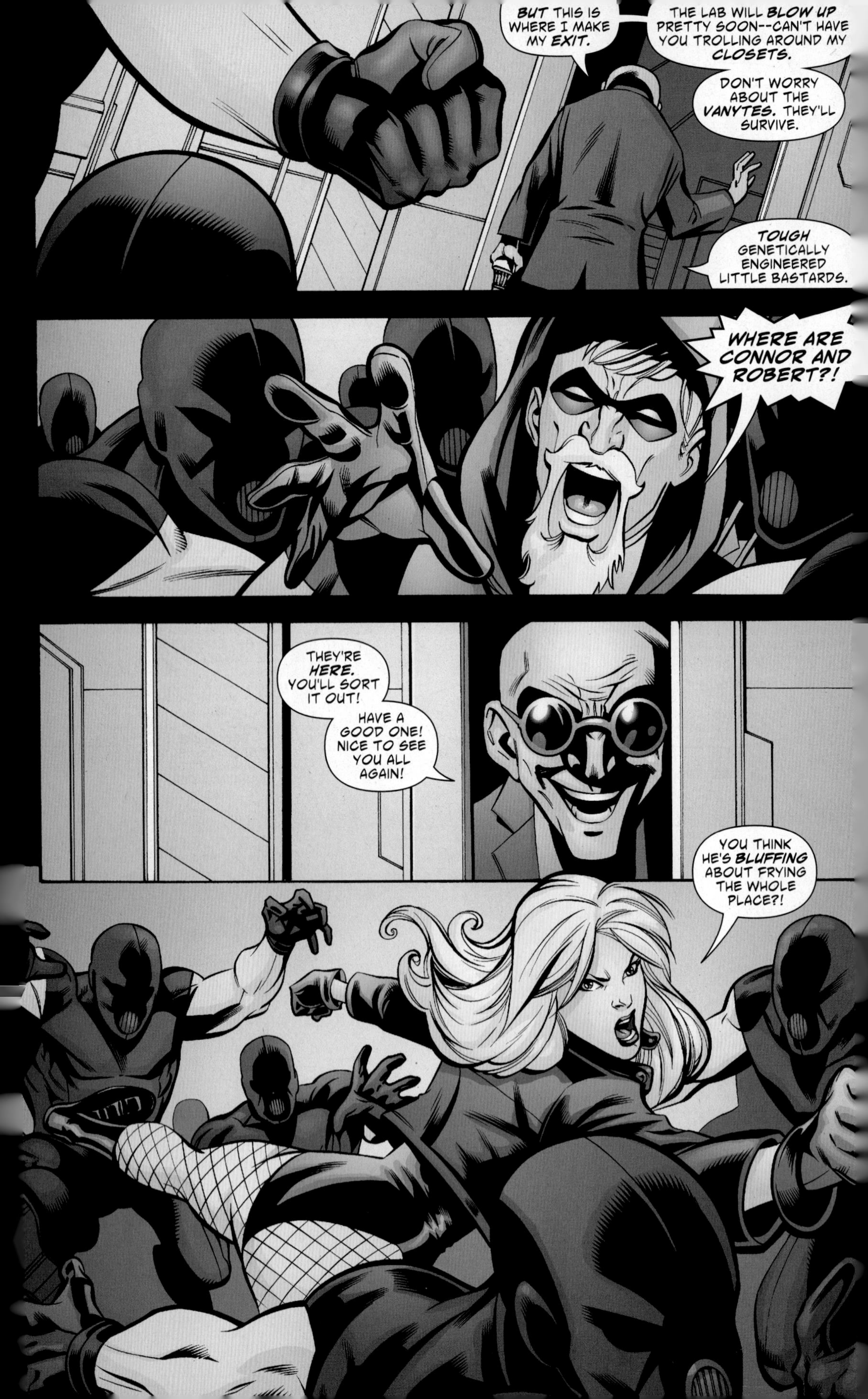
BUT THIS IS WHERE I MAKE MY EXIT.
THE LAB WILL BLOW UP PRETTY SOON--CAN'T HAVE YOU TROLLING AROUND MY CLOSETS.
DON'T WORRY ABOUT THE VANYTES. THEY'LL SURVIVE.
TOUGH GENETICALLY ENGINEERED LITTLE BASTARDS.
WHERE ARE CONNOR AND ROBERT?!
THEY'RE HERE. YOU'LL SORT IT OUT!
HAVE A GOOD ONE! NICE TO SEE YOU ALL AGAIN!
YOU THINK HE'S BLUFFING ABOUT FRYING THE WHOLE PLACE?!

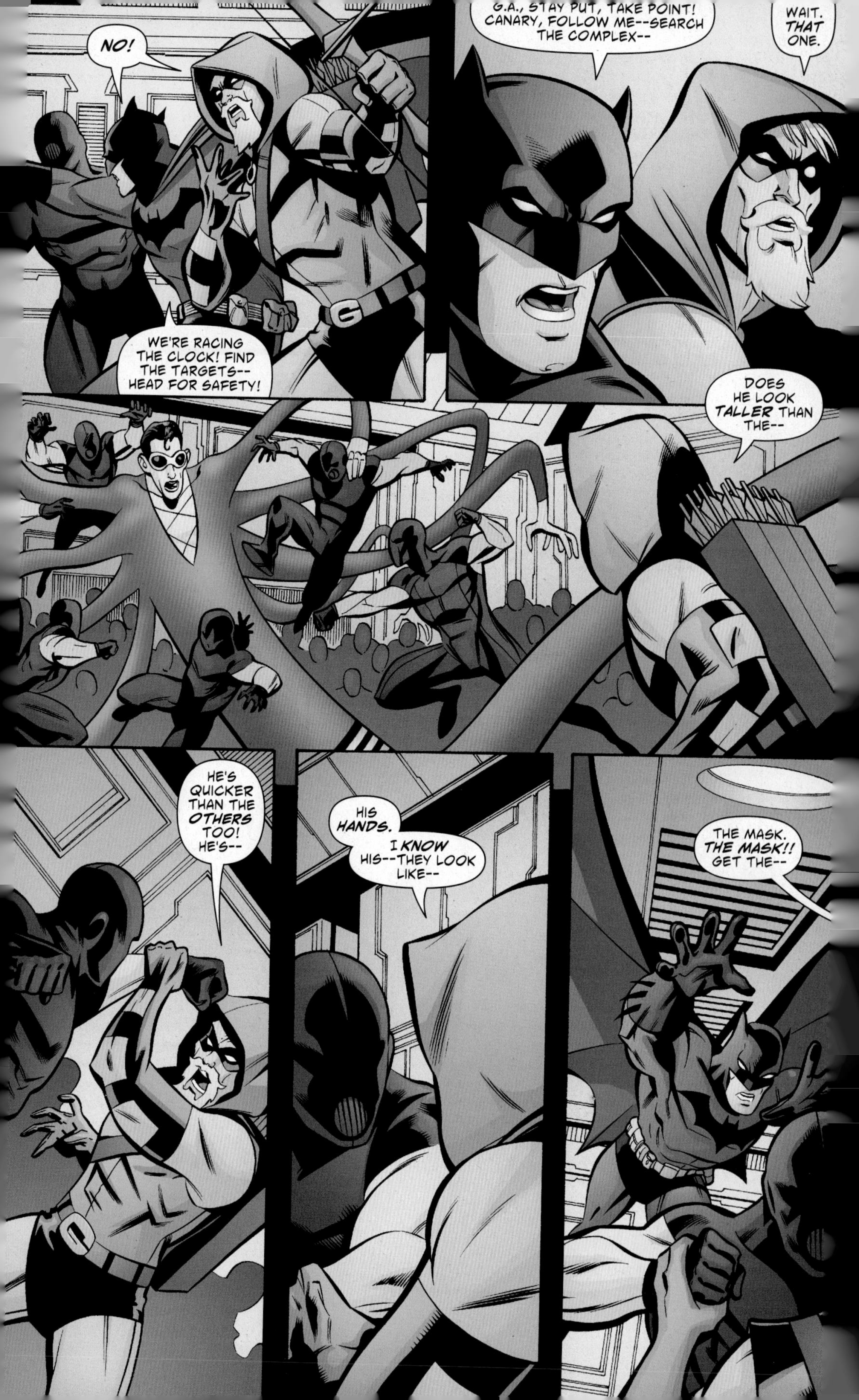

NO!
WE'RE RACING THE CLOCK! FIND THE TARGETS-- HEAD FOR SAFETY!
G.A., STAY PUT, TAKE POINT! CANARY, FOLLOW ME--SEARCH THE COMPLEX--
WAIT. THAT ONE.
DOES HE LOOK TALLER THAN THE--
HE'S QUICKER THAN THE OTHERS TOO! HE'S--
HIS HANDS.
I KNOW HIS--THEY LOOK LIKE--
THE MASK. THE MASK!! GET THE--

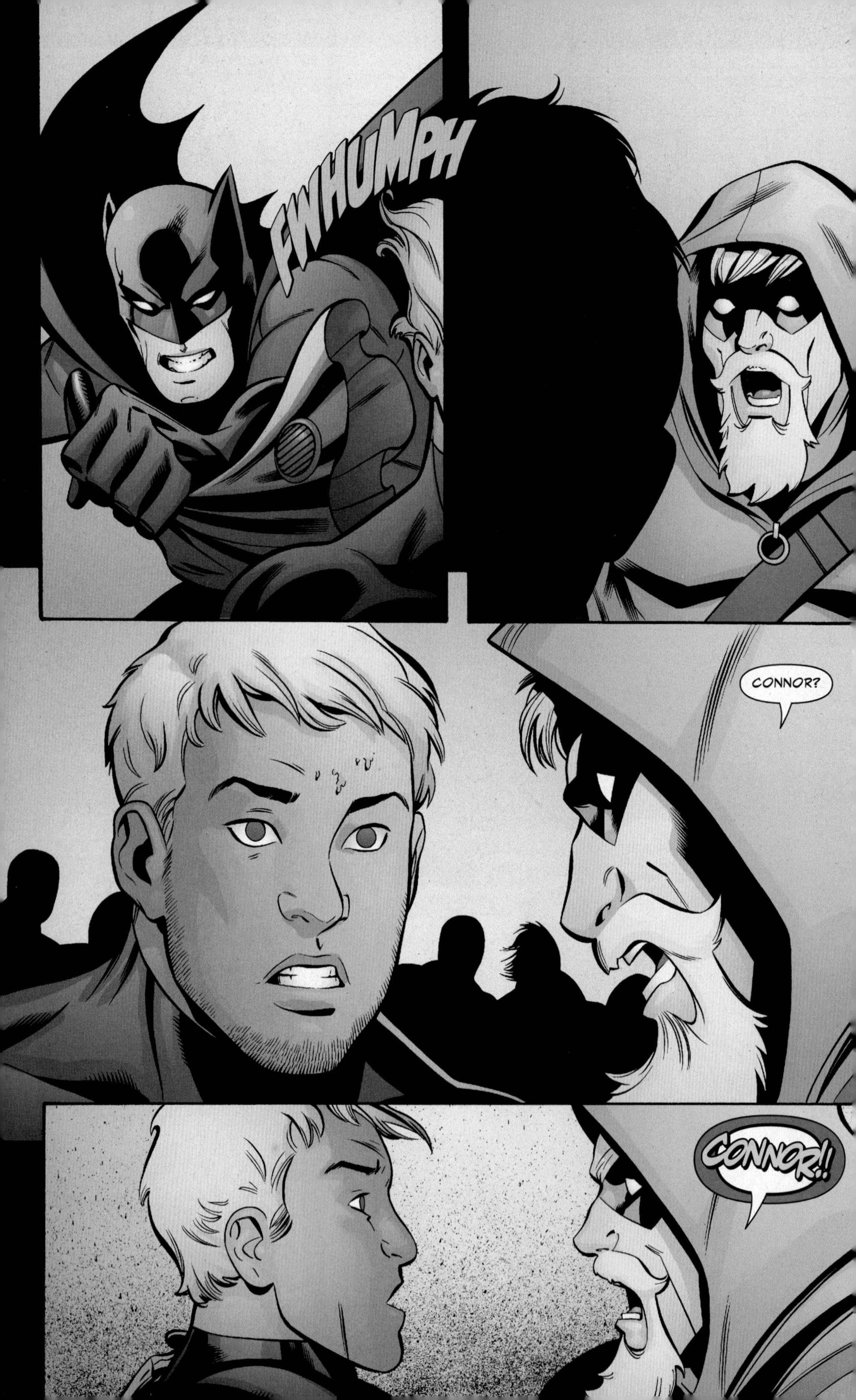
FWHUMPH
CONNOR?
CONNOR!!

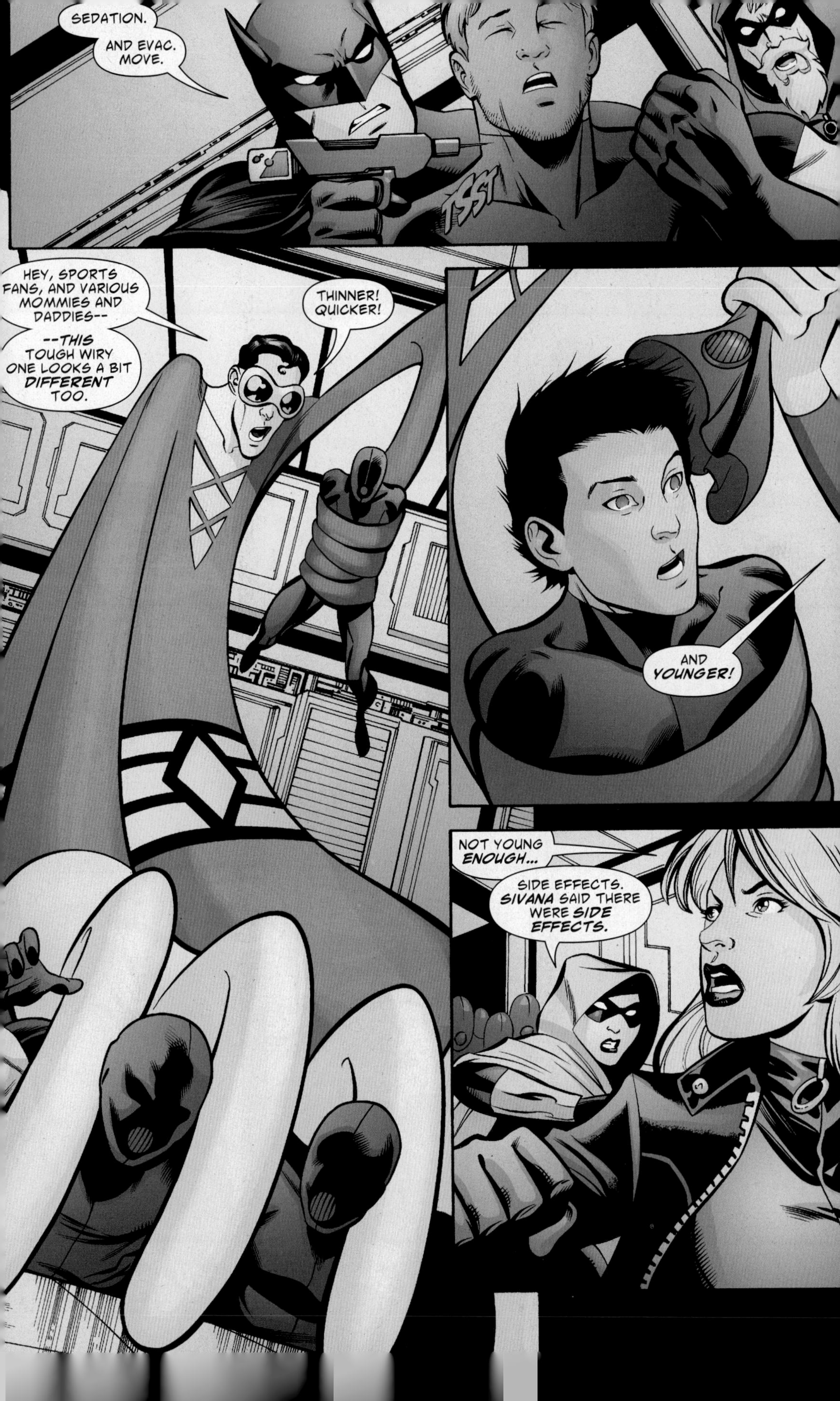
SEDATION.
AND EVAC. MOVE.
TSST
HEY, SPORTS FANS, AND VARIOUS MOMMIES AND DADDIES--
--THIS TOUGH WIRY ONE LOOKS A BIT DIFFERENT TOO.
THINNER! QUICKER!
AND YOUNGER!
NOT YOUNG ENOUGH...
SIDE EFFECTS. SIVANA SAID THERE WERE SIDE EFFECTS.

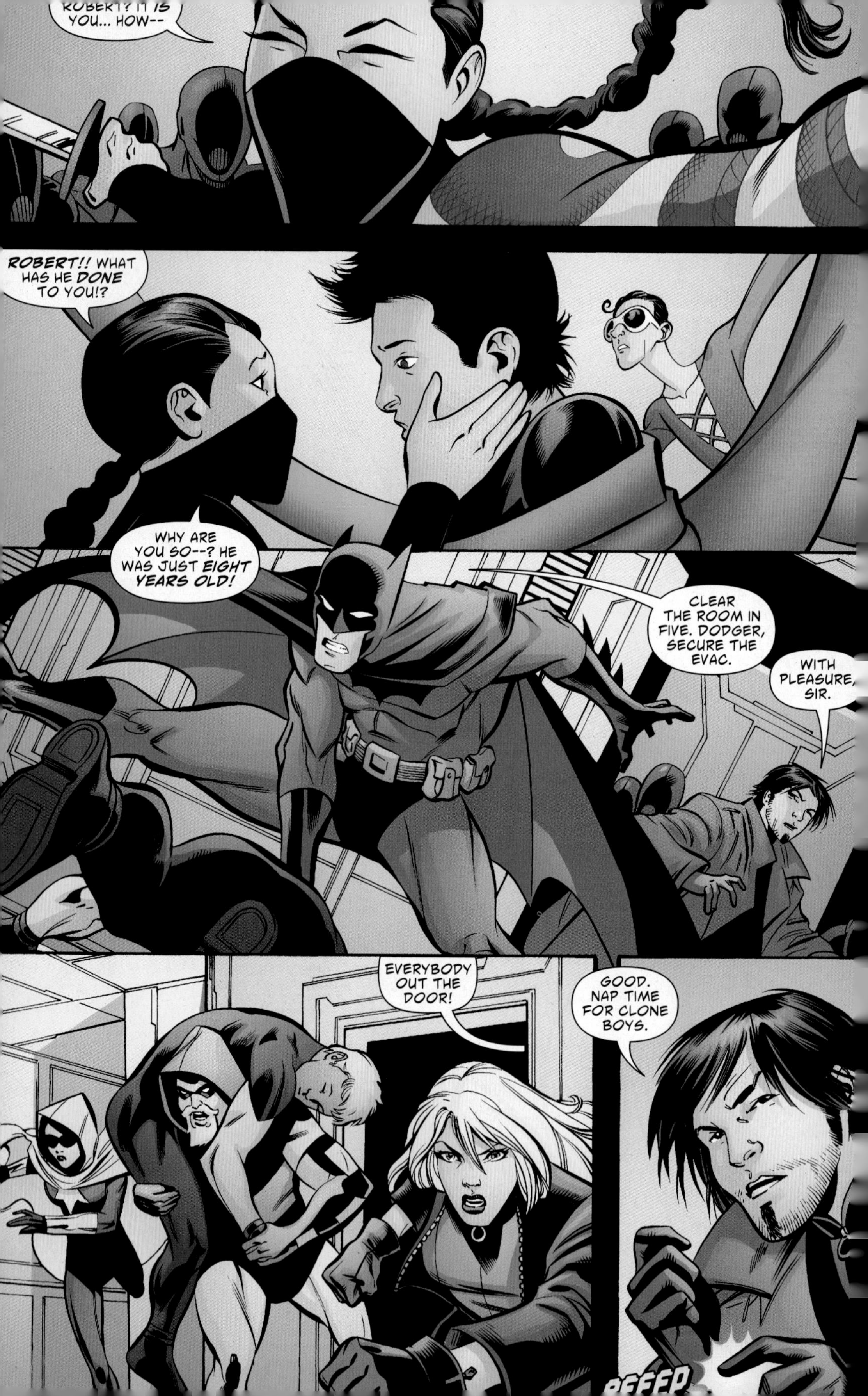

ROBERT? IT IS YOU... HOW--
ROBERT!! WHAT HAS HE DONE TO YOU!?
WHY ARE YOU SO--? HE WAS JUST EIGHT YEARS OLD!
CLEAR THE ROOM IN FIVE. DODGER, SECURE THE EVAC.
WITH PLEASURE, SIR.
EVERYBODY OUT THE DOOR!
GOOD. NAP TIME FOR CLONE BOYS.
BEEEP

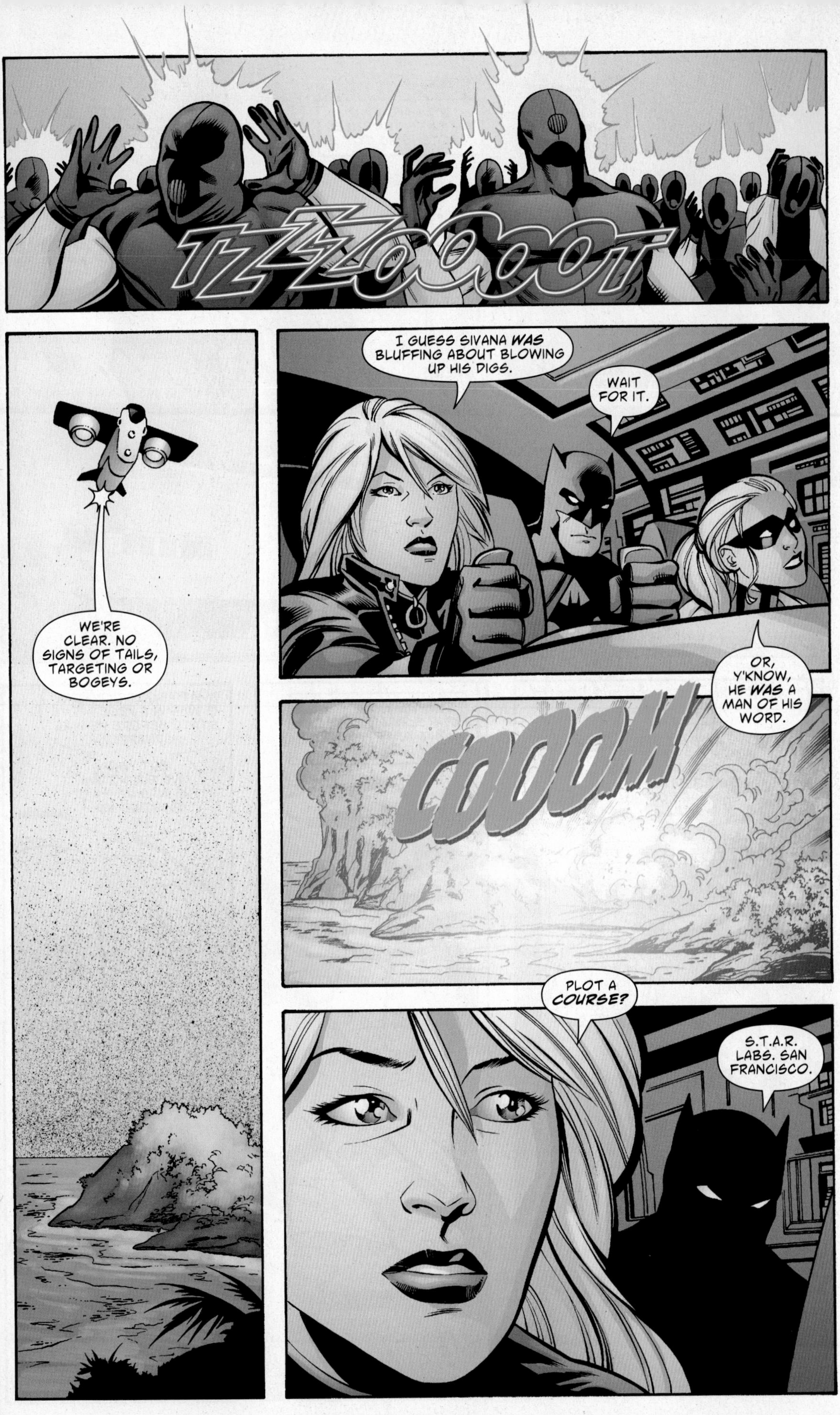
TZZOOOOT
WE'RE CLEAR. NO SIGNS OF TAILS, TARGETING OR BOGEYS.
I GUESS SIVANA WAS BLUFFING ABOUT BLOWING UP HIS DIGS.
WAIT FOR IT.
OR, Y'KNOW, HE WAS A MAN OF HIS WORD.
COOOM
PLOT A COURSE?
S.T.A.R. LABS. SAN FRANCISCO.

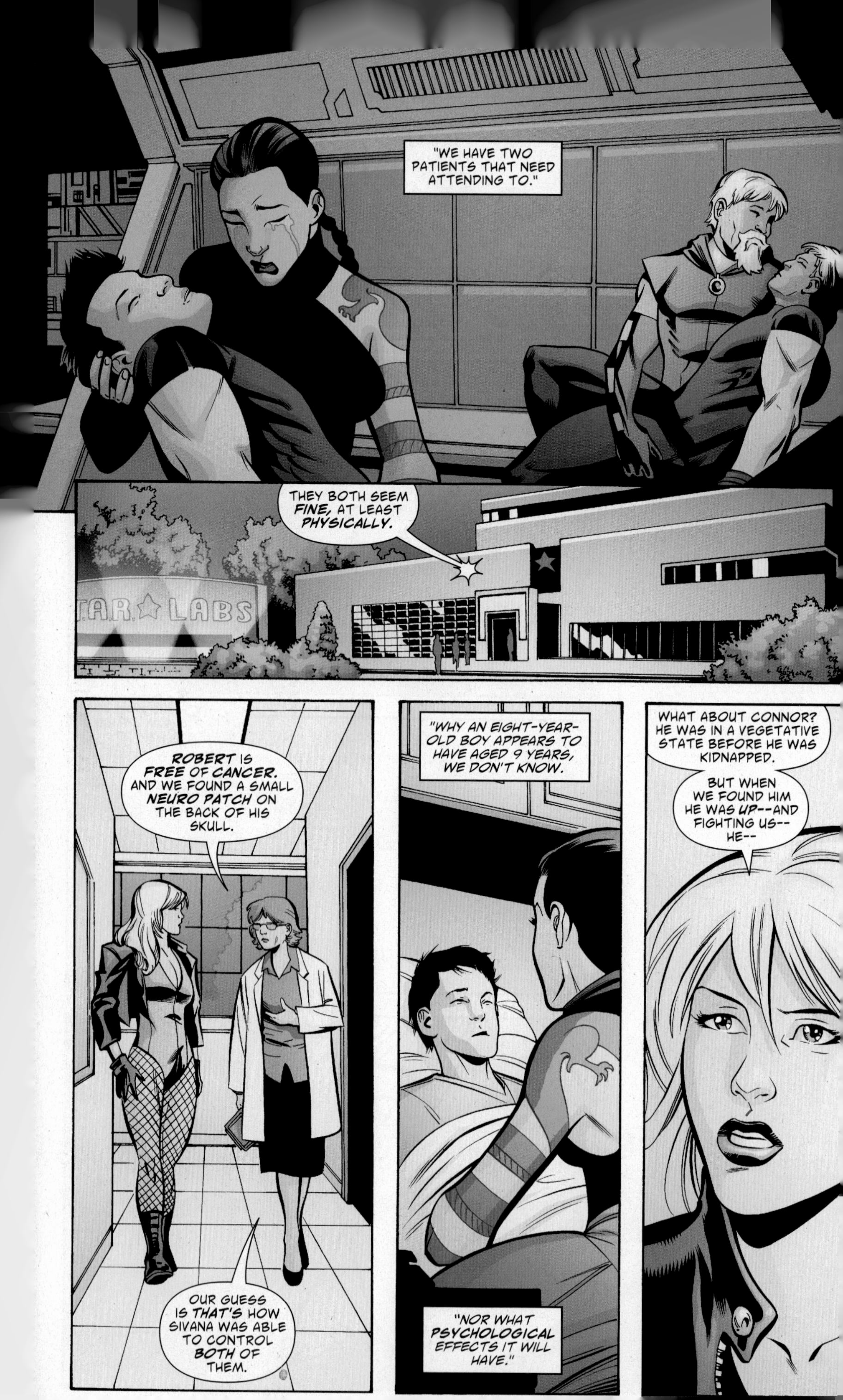
"WE HAVE TWO PATIENTS THAT NEED ATTENDING TO."
THEY BOTH SEEM FINE, AT LEAST PHYSICALLY.
S.T.A.R. LABS
ROBERT IS FREE OF CANCER. AND WE FOUND A SMALL NEURO PATCH ON THE BACK OF HIS SKULL.
OUR GUESS IS THAT'S HOW SIVANA WAS ABLE TO CONTROL BOTH OF THEM.
"WHY AN EIGHT-YEAR-OLD BOY APPEARS TO HAVE AGED 9 YEARS, WE DON'T KNOW.
"NOR WHAT PSYCHOLOGICAL EFFECTS IT WILL HAVE."
WHAT ABOUT CONNOR? HE WAS IN A VEGETATIVE STATE BEFORE HE WAS KIDNAPPED.
BUT WHEN WE FOUND HIM HE WAS UP--AND FIGHTING US--HE--

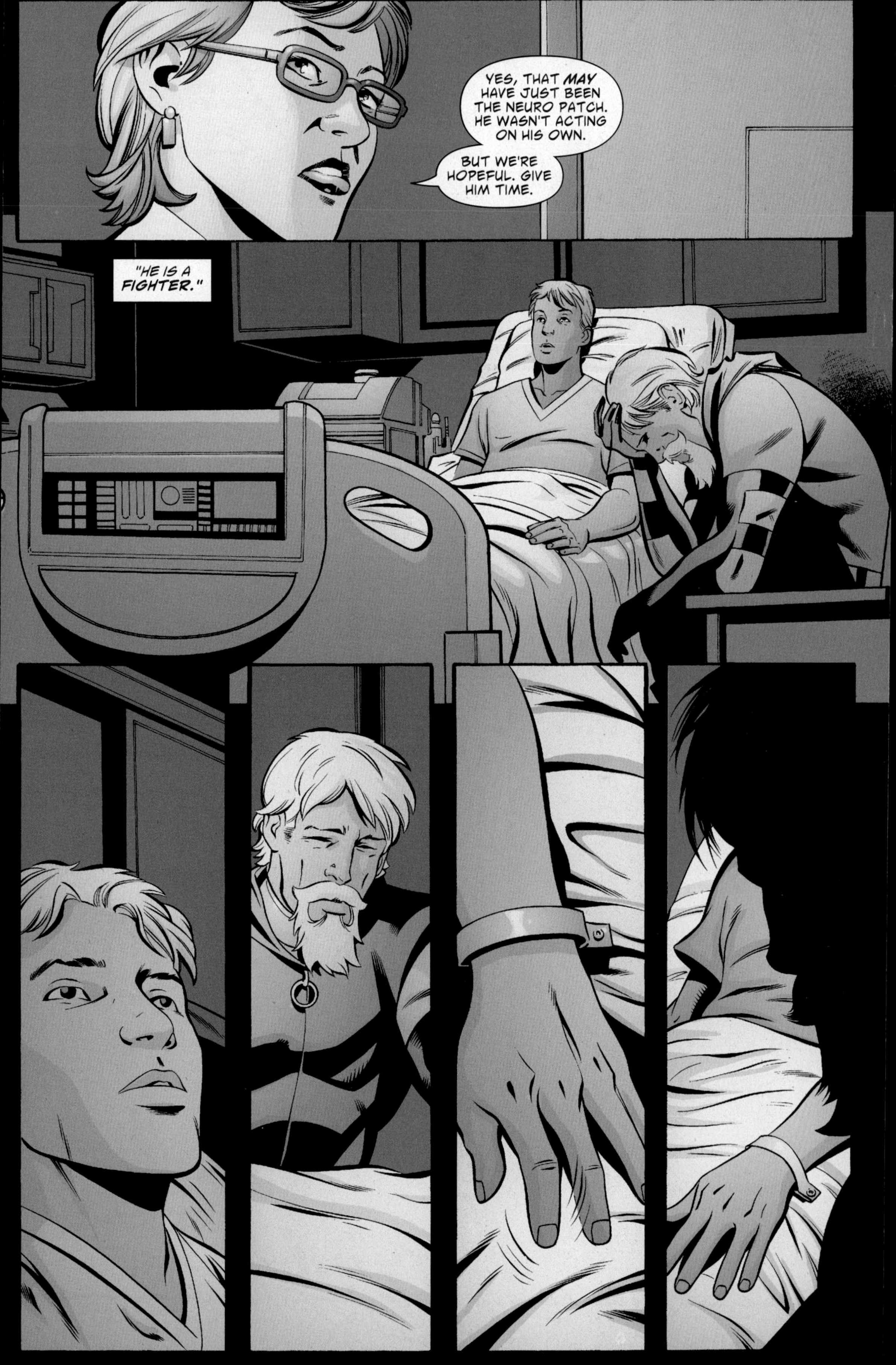
YES, THAT MAY HAVE JUST BEEN THE NEURO PATCH. HE WASN'T ACTING ON HIS OWN.
BUT WE'RE HOPEFUL. GIVE HIM TIME.
"HE IS A FIGHTER."

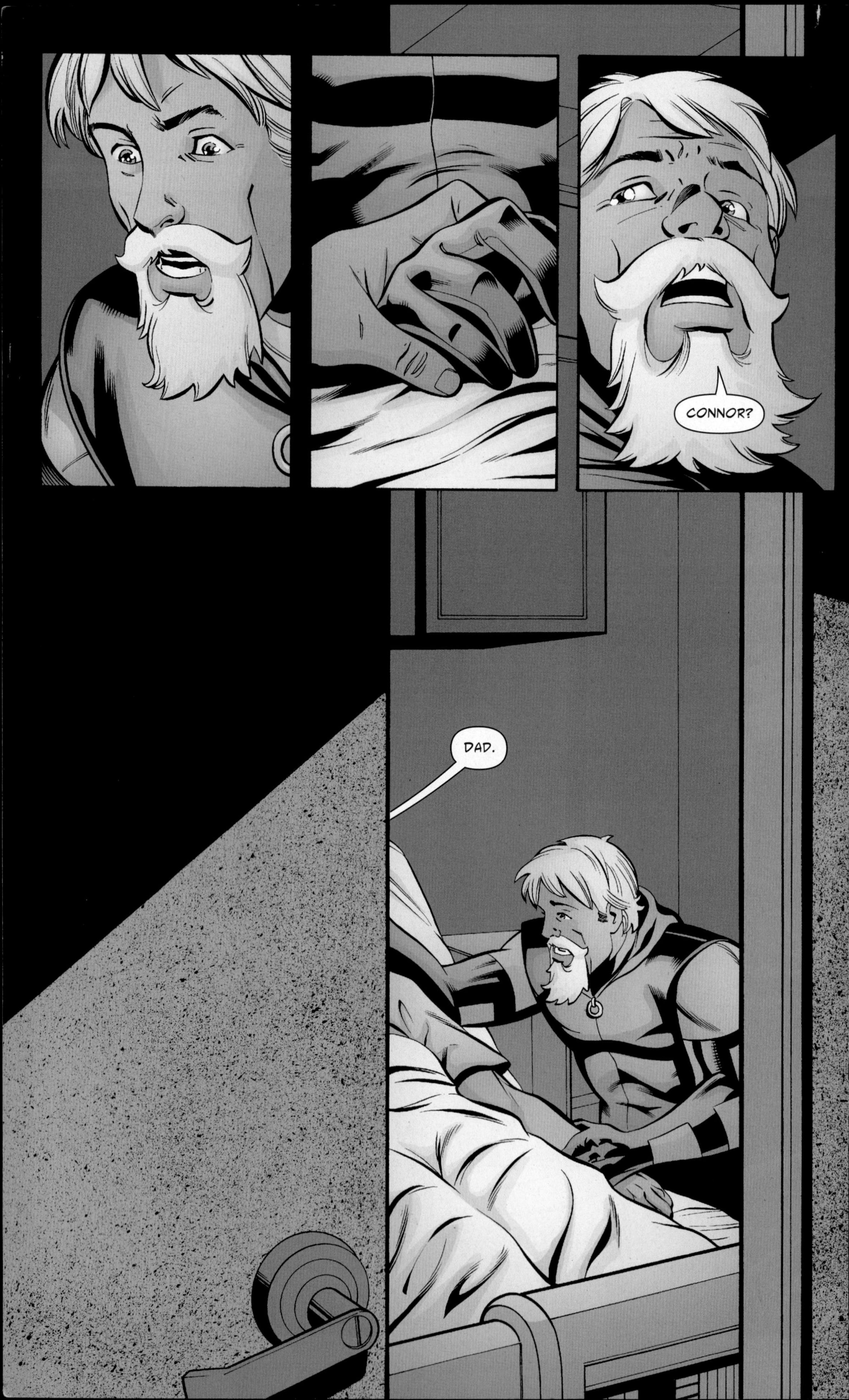
CONNOR?
DAD.

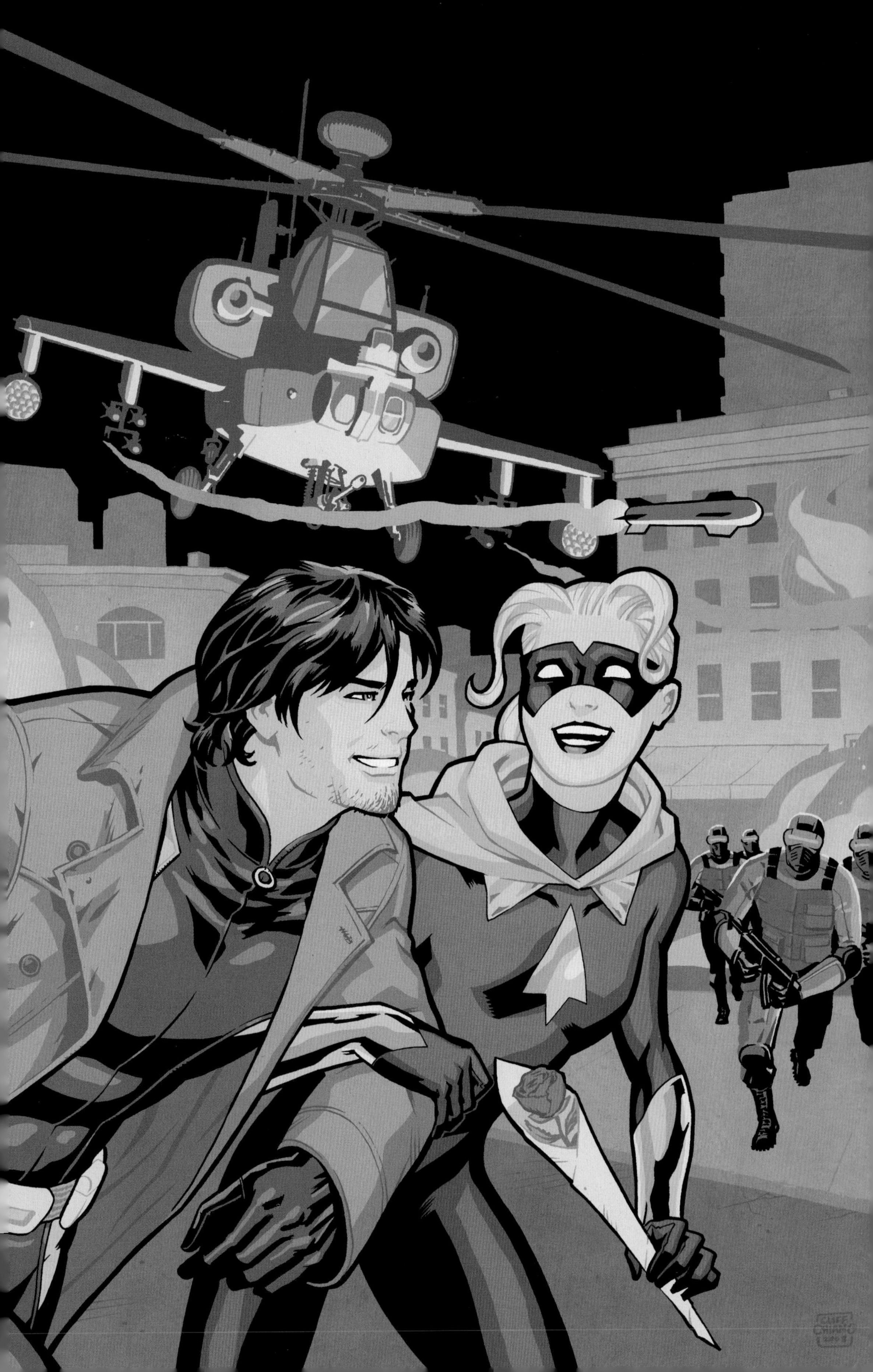

A LEAGUE OF THEIR OWN:

HOME AGAIN, HOME AGAIN

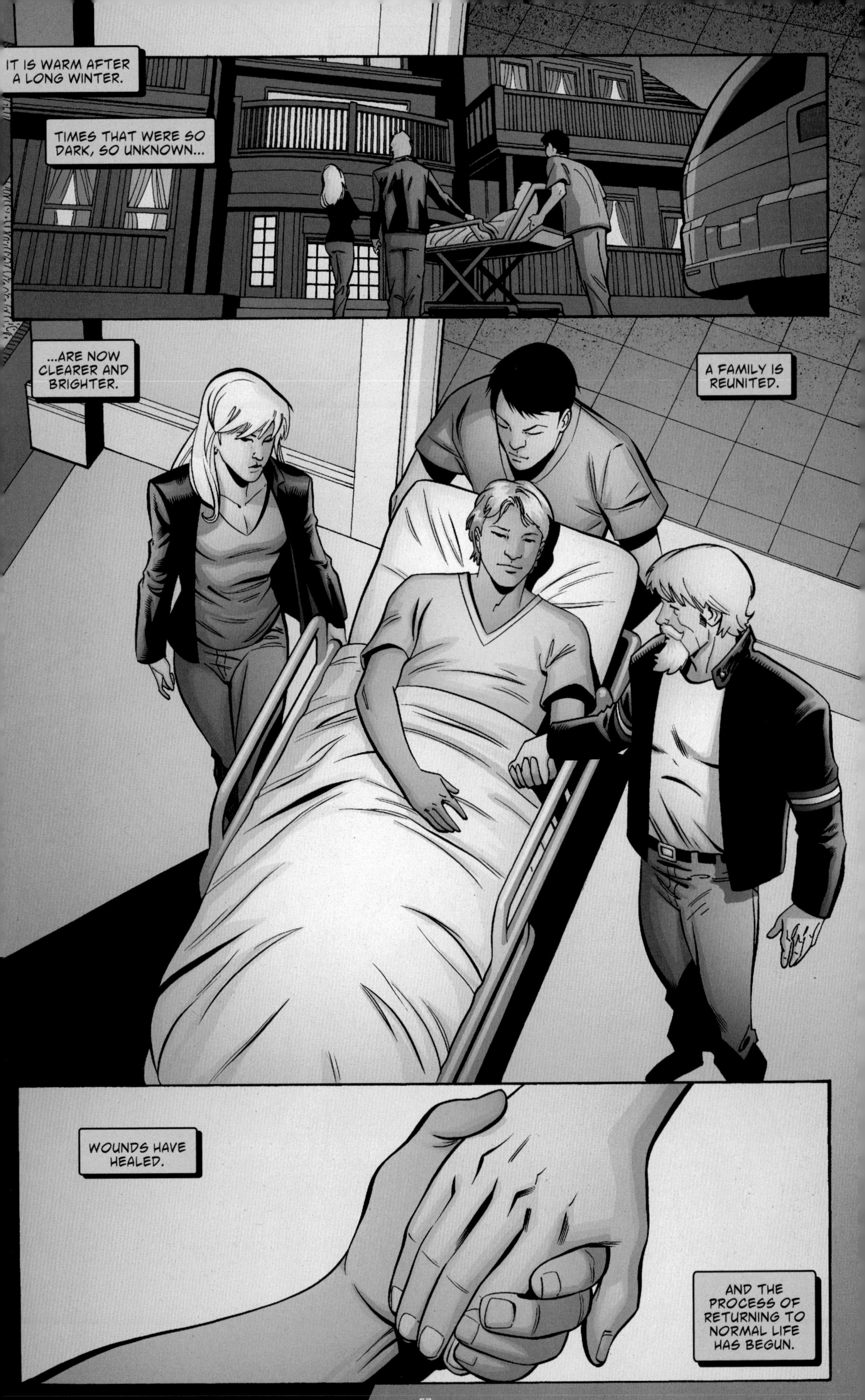
IT IS WARM AFTER A LONG WINTER.
TIMES THAT WERE SO DARK, SO UNKNOWN...
...ARE NOW CLEARER AND BRIGHTER.
A FAMILY IS REUNITED.
WOUNDS HAVE HEALED.
AND THE PROCESS OF RETURNING TO NORMAL LIFE HAS BEGUN.

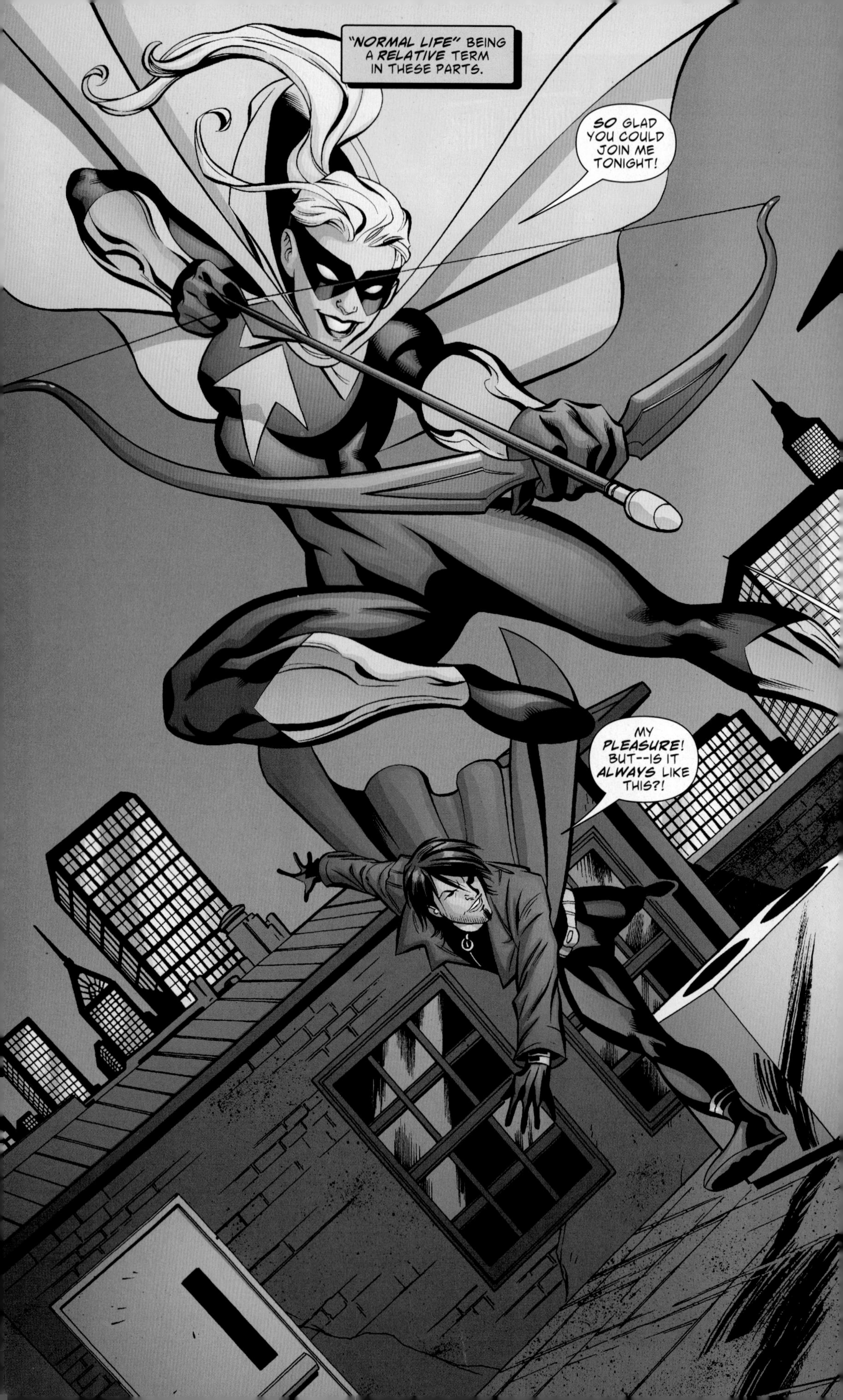
"NORMAL LIFE" BEING A RELATIVE TERM IN THESE PARTS.
SO GLAD YOU COULD JOIN ME TONIGHT!
MY PLEASURE! BUT--IS IT ALWAYS LIKE THIS?!

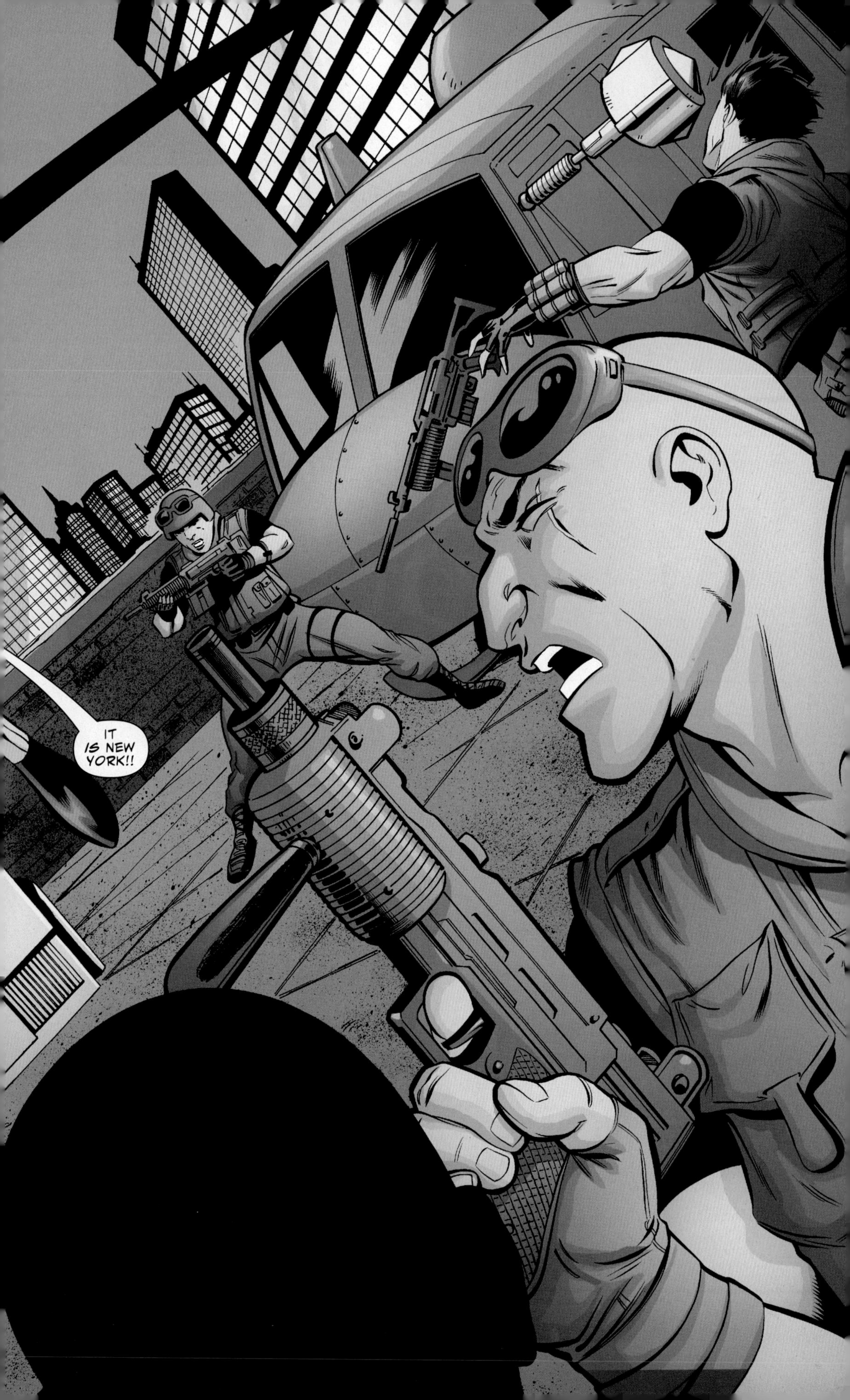
IT IS NEW YORK!!

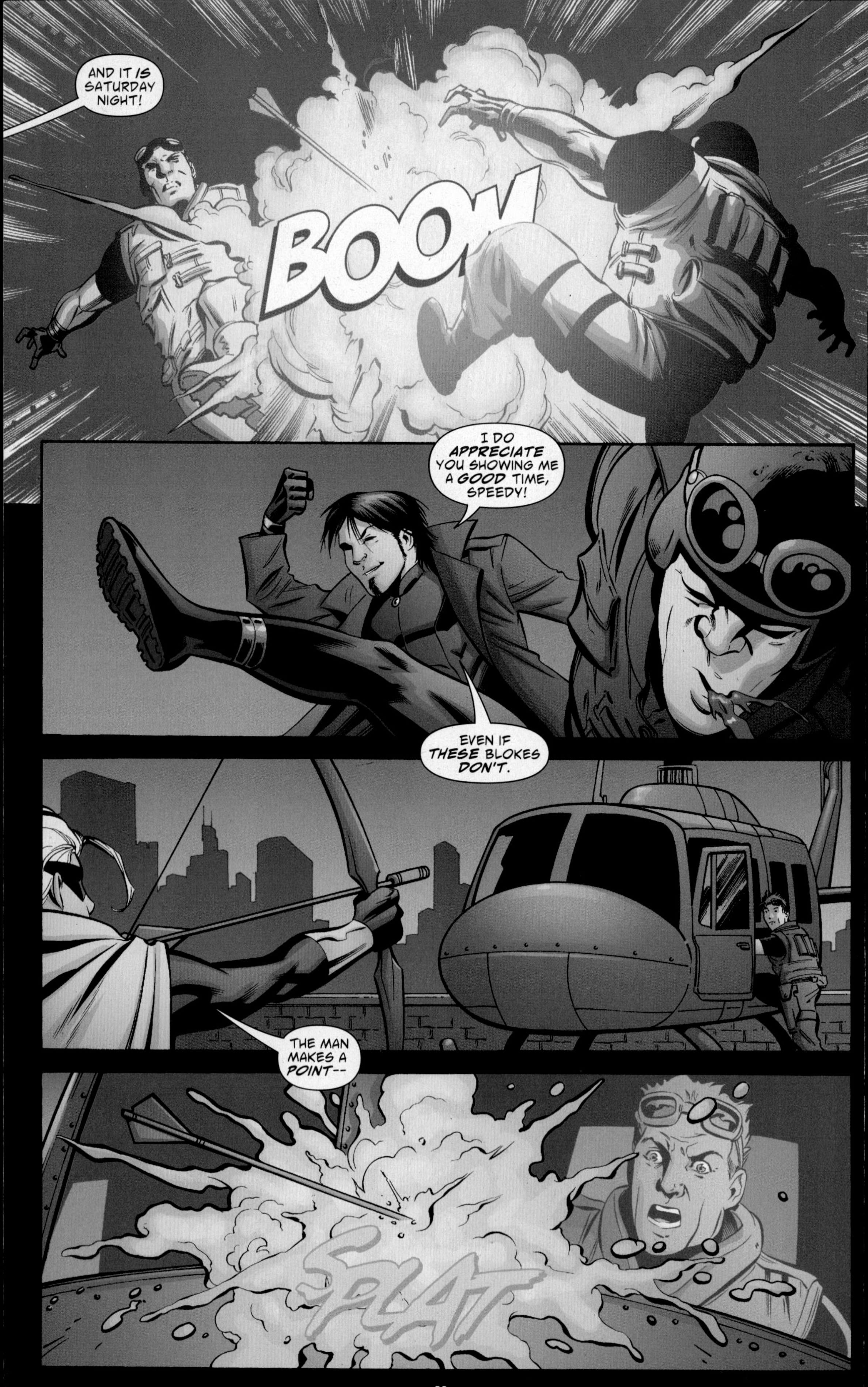
AND IT IS SATURDAY NIGHT!
BOOM
I DO APPRECIATE YOU SHOWING ME A GOOD TIME, SPEEDY!
EVEN IF THESE BLOKES DON'T.
THE MAN MAKES A POINT--
SPLAT

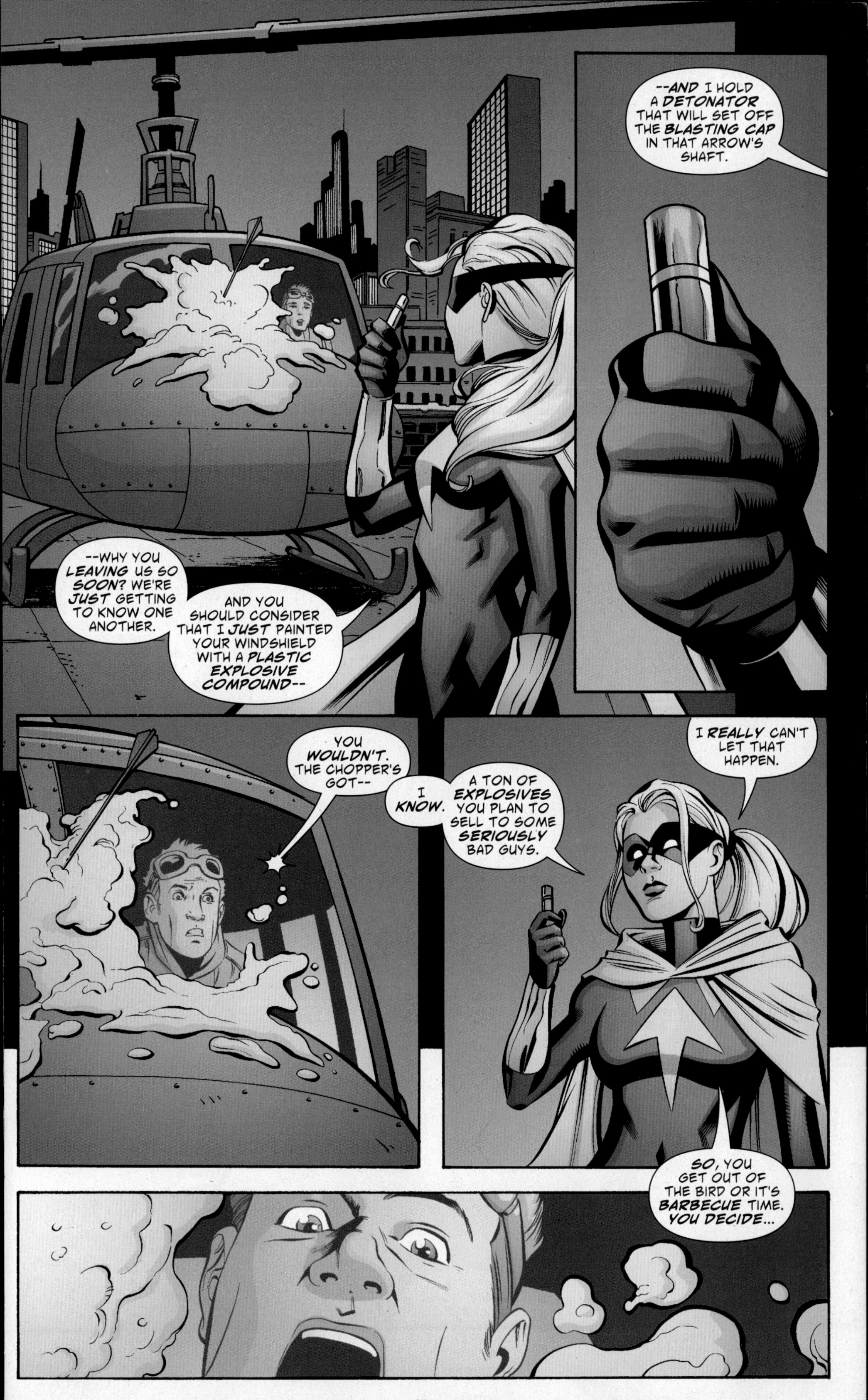
--WHY YOU LEAVING US SO SOON? WE'RE JUST GETTING TO KNOW ONE ANOTHER.
AND YOU SHOULD CONSIDER THAT I JUST PAINTED YOUR WINDSHIELD WITH A PLASTIC EXPLOSIVE COMPOUND--
--AND I HOLD A DETONATOR THAT WILL SET OFF THE BLASTING CAP IN THAT ARROW'S SHAFT.
YOU WOULDN'T. THE CHOPPER'S GOT--
I KNOW.
A TON OF EXPLOSIVES YOU PLAN TO SELL TO SOME SERIOUSLY BAD GUYS.
I REALLY CAN'T LET THAT HAPPEN.
SO, YOU GET OUT OF THE BIRD OR IT'S BARBECUE TIME. YOU DECIDE...

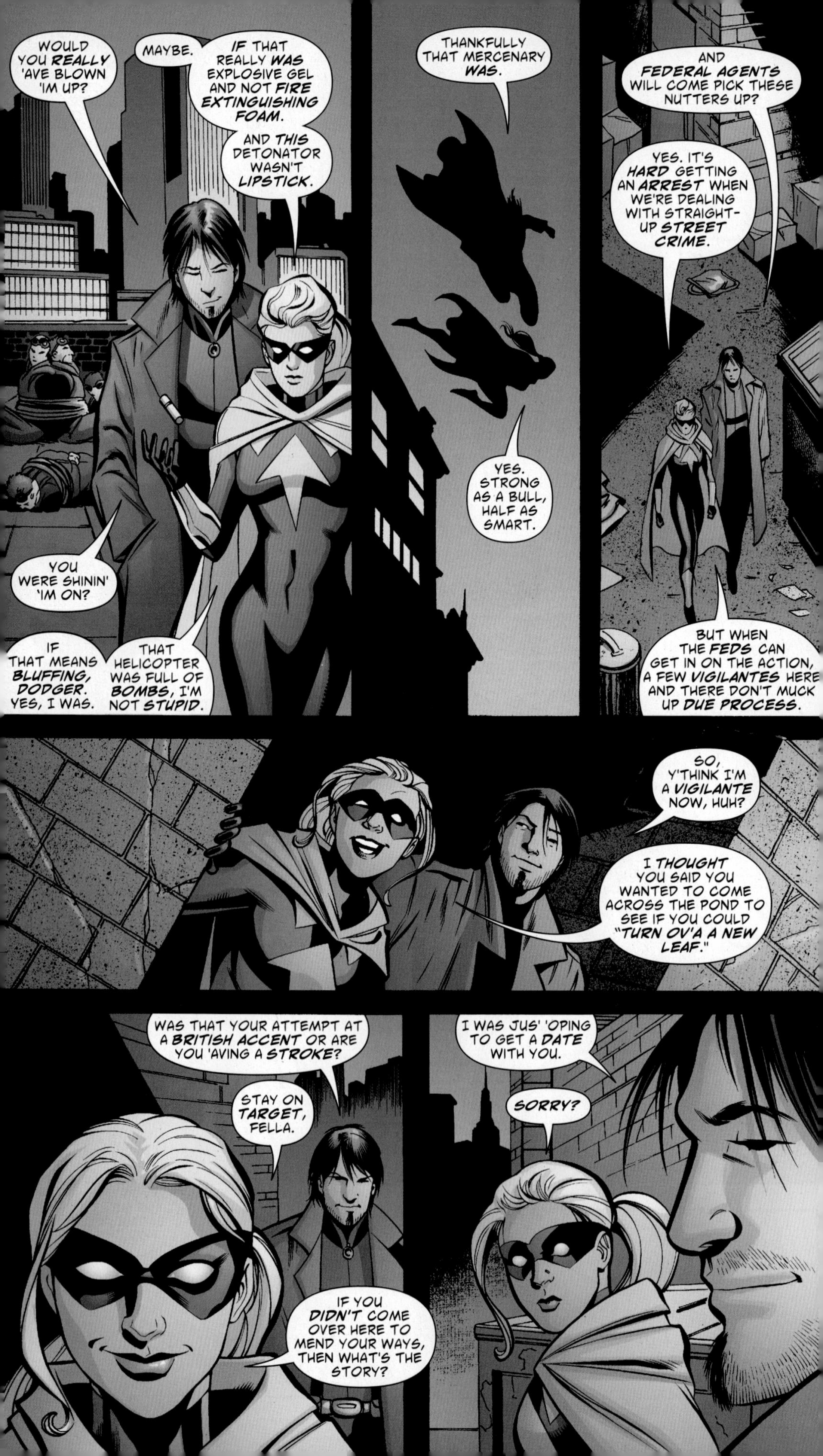
WOULD YOU REALLY 'AVE BLOWN 'IM UP?
MAYBE.
IF THAT REALLY WAS EXPLOSIVE GEL AND NOT FIRE EXTINGUISHING FOAM.
AND THIS DETONATOR WASN'T LIPSTICK.
YOU WERE SHININ' 'IM ON?
IF THAT MEANS BLUFFING, DODGER. YES, I WAS.
THAT HELICOPTER WAS FULL OF BOMBS, I'M NOT STUPID.
THANKFULLY THAT MERCENARY WAS.
YES. STRONG AS A BULL, HALF AS SMART.
AND FEDERAL AGENTS WILL COME PICK THESE NUTTERS UP?
YES. IT'S HARD GETTING AN ARREST WHEN WE'RE DEALING WITH STRAIGHT-UP STREET CRIME.
BUT WHEN THE FEDS CAN GET IN ON THE ACTION, A FEW VIGILANTES HERE AND THERE DON'T MUCK UP DUE PROCESS.
SO, Y'THINK I'M A VIGILANTE NOW, HUH?
I THOUGHT YOU SAID YOU WANTED TO COME ACROSS THE POND TO SEE IF YOU COULD "TURN OV'A A NEW LEAF."
WAS THAT YOUR ATTEMPT AT A BRITISH ACCENT OR ARE YOU 'AVING A STROKE?
STAY ON TARGET, FELLA.
IF YOU DIDN'T COME OVER HERE TO MEND YOUR WAYS, THEN WHAT'S THE STORY?
I WAS JUS' 'OPING TO GET A DATE WITH YOU.
SORRY?

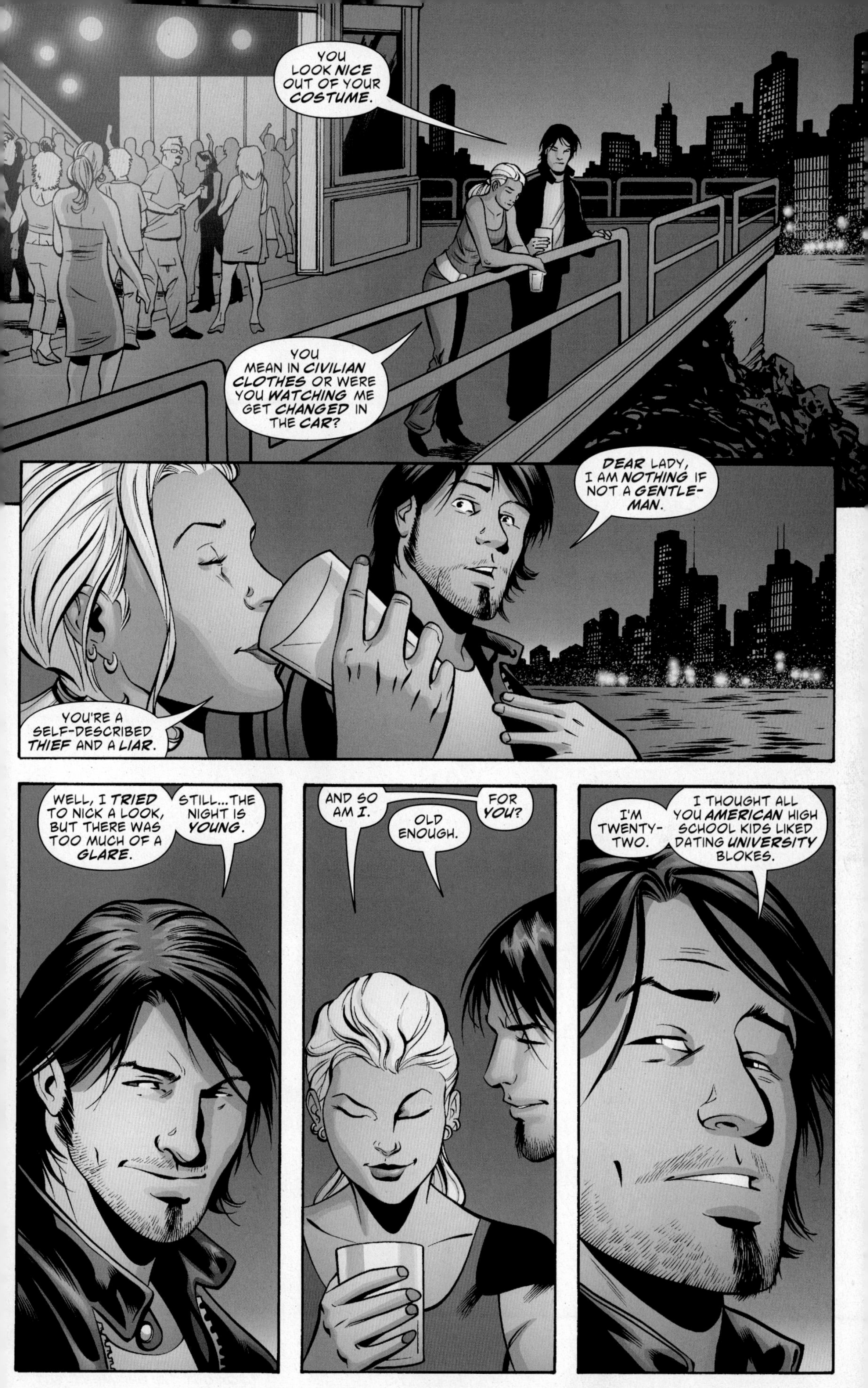
YOU LOOK NICE OUT OF YOUR COSTUME.
YOU MEAN IN CIVILIAN CLOTHES OR WERE YOU WATCHING ME GET CHANGED IN THE CAR?
DEAR LADY, I AM NOTHING IF NOT A GENTLE-MAN.
YOU'RE A SELF-DESCRIBED THIEF AND A LIAR.
WELL, I TRIED TO NICK A LOOK, BUT THERE WAS TOO MUCH OF A GLARE.
STILL...THE NIGHT IS YOUNG.
AND SO AM I.
FOR YOU?
OLD ENOUGH.
I'M TWENTY-TWO.
I THOUGHT ALL YOU AMERICAN HIGH SCHOOL KIDS LIKED DATING UNIVERSITY BLOKES.

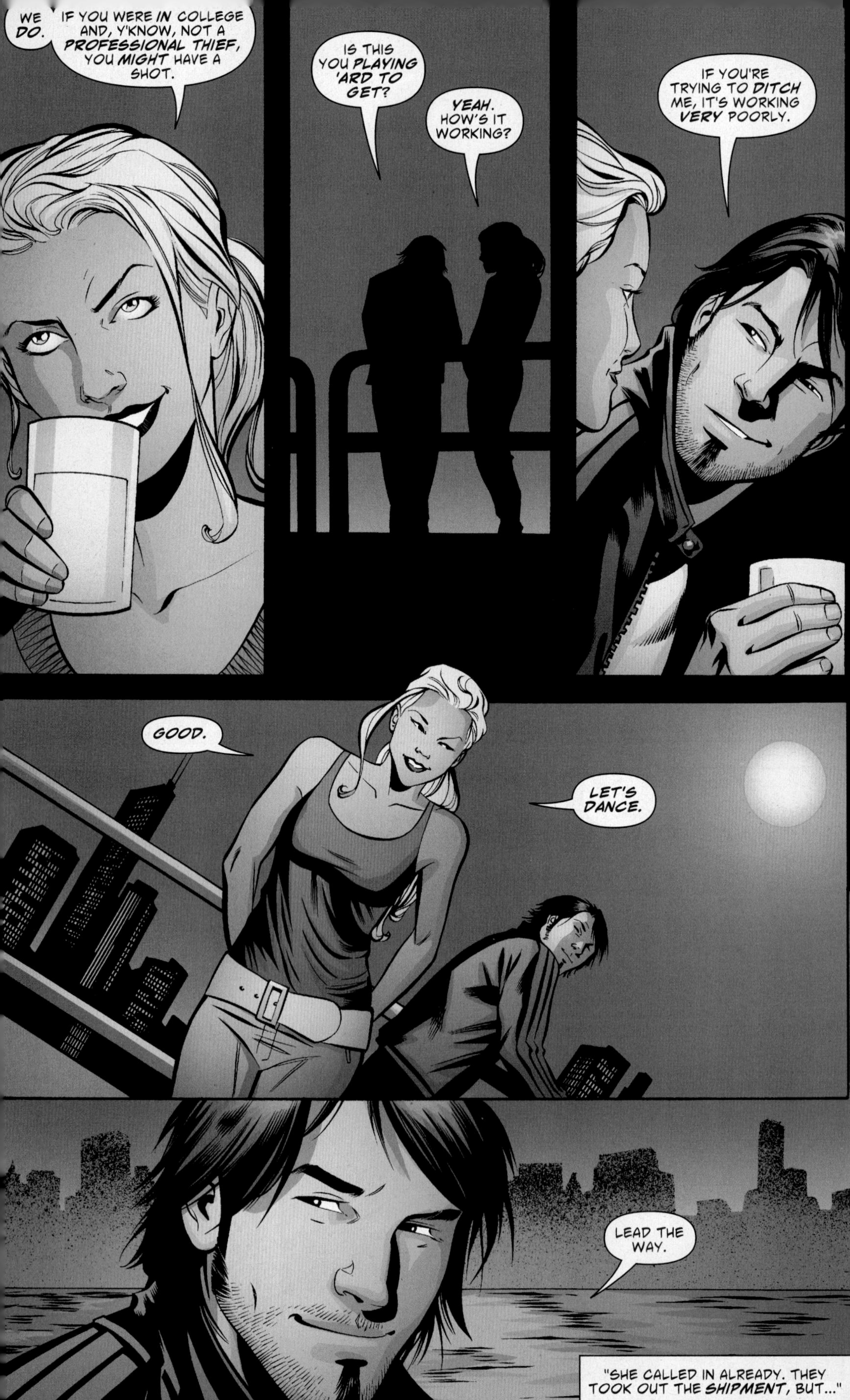
WE DO.
IF YOU WERE IN COLLEGE AND, Y'KNOW, NOT A PROFESSIONAL THIEF, YOU MIGHT HAVE A SHOT.
IS THIS YOU PLAYING 'ARD TO GET?
YEAH. HOW'S IT WORKING?
IF YOU'RE TRYING TO DITCH ME, IT'S WORKING VERY POORLY.
GOOD.
LET'S DANCE.
LEAD THE WAY.
"SHE CALLED IN ALREADY. THEY TOOK OUT THE SHIPMENT, BUT..."

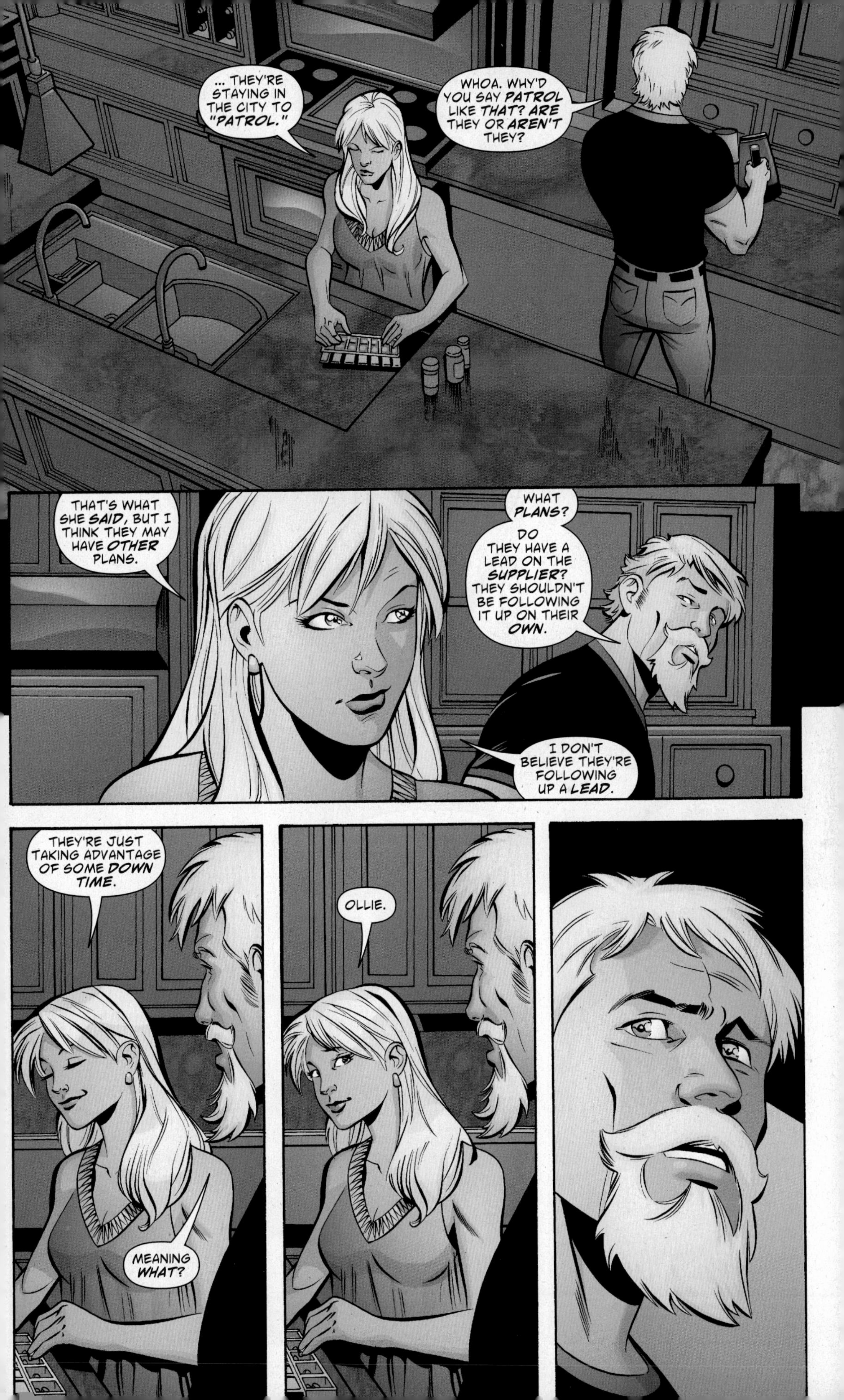
... THEY'RE STAYING IN THE CITY TO "PATROL."
WHOA. WHY'D YOU SAY PATROL LIKE THAT? ARE THEY OR AREN'T THEY?
THAT'S WHAT SHE SAID, BUT I THINK THEY MAY HAVE OTHER PLANS.
WHAT PLANS?
DO THEY HAVE A LEAD ON THE SUPPLIER? THEY SHOULDN'T BE FOLLOWING IT UP ON THEIR OWN.
I DON'T BELIEVE THEY'RE FOLLOWING UP A LEAD.
THEY'RE JUST TAKING ADVANTAGE OF SOME DOWN TIME.
MEANING WHAT?
OLLIE.

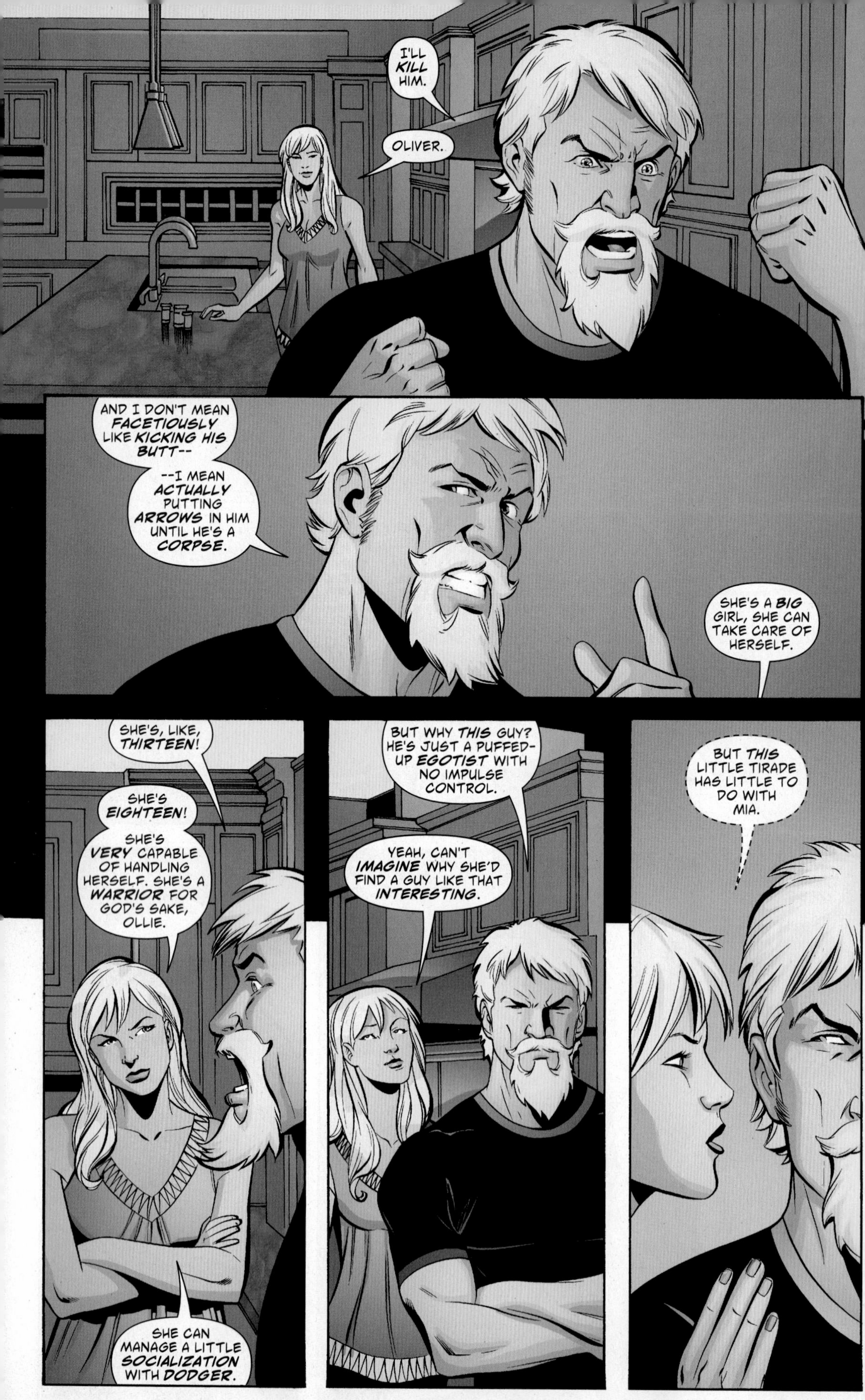
I'LL KILL HIM.
OLIVER.
AND I DON'T MEAN FACETIOUSLY LIKE KICKING HIS BUTT--
--I MEAN ACTUALLY PUTTING ARROWS IN HIM UNTIL HE'S A CORPSE.
SHE'S A BIG GIRL, SHE CAN TAKE CARE OF HERSELF.
SHE'S, LIKE, THIRTEEN!
SHE'S EIGHTEEN!
SHE'S VERY CAPABLE OF HANDLING HERSELF. SHE'S A WARRIOR FOR GOD'S SAKE, OLLIE.
SHE CAN MANAGE A LITTLE SOCIALIZATION WITH DODGER.
BUT WHY THIS GUY? HE'S JUST A PUFFED-UP EGOTIST WITH NO IMPULSE CONTROL.
YEAH, CAN'T IMAGINE WHY SHE'D FIND A GUY LIKE THAT INTERESTING.
BUT THIS LITTLE TIRADE HAS LITTLE TO DO WITH MIA.

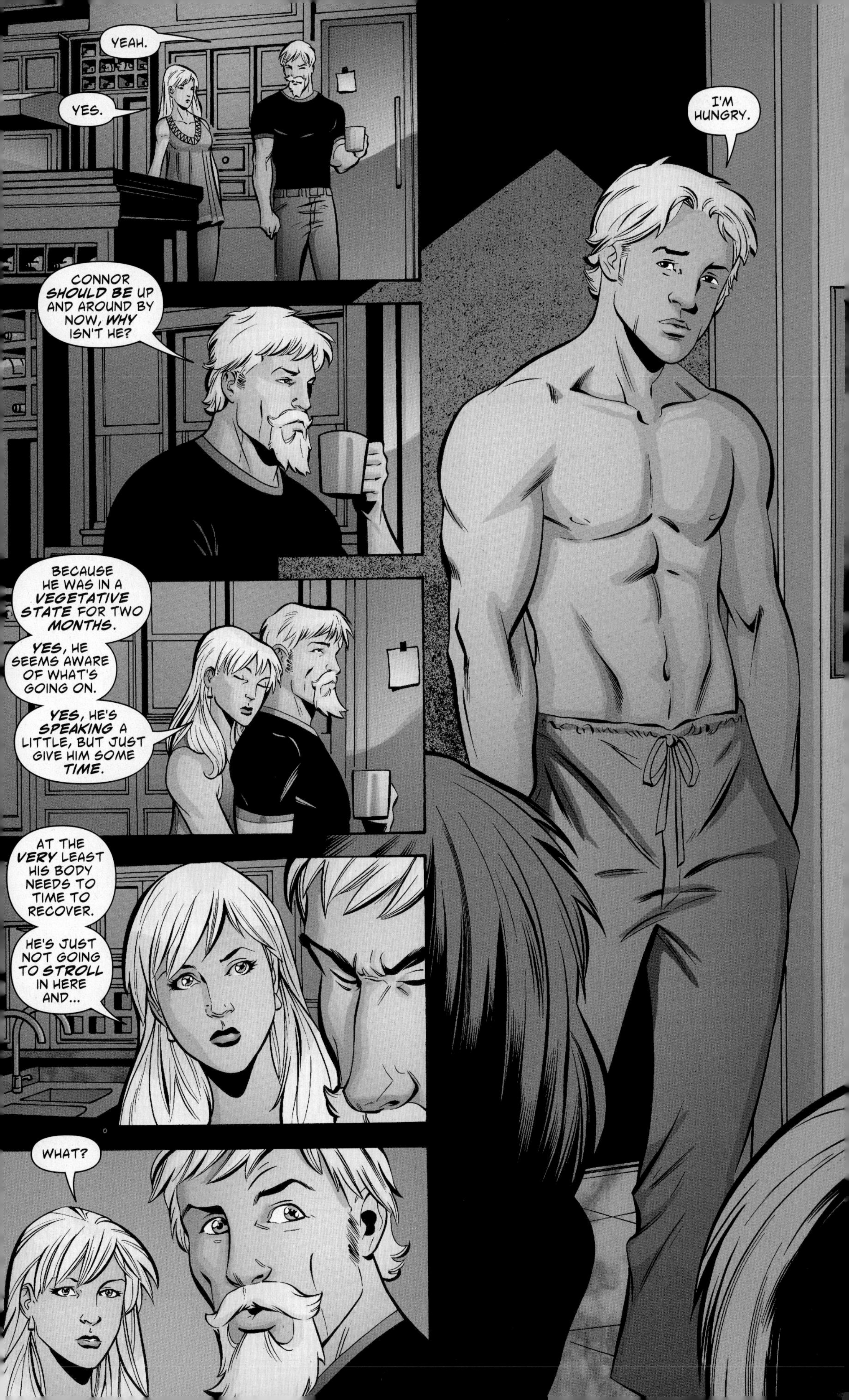
YEAH.
YES.
I'M HUNGRY.
CONNOR SHOULD BE UP AND AROUND BY NOW, WHY ISN'T HE?
BECAUSE HE WAS IN A VEGETATIVE STATE FOR TWO MONTHS.
YES, HE SEEMS AWARE OF WHAT'S GOING ON.
YES, HE'S SPEAKING A LITTLE, BUT JUST GIVE HIM SOME TIME.
AT THE VERY LEAST HIS BODY NEEDS TO TIME TO RECOVER.
HE'S JUST NOT GOING TO STROLL IN HERE AND...
WHAT?

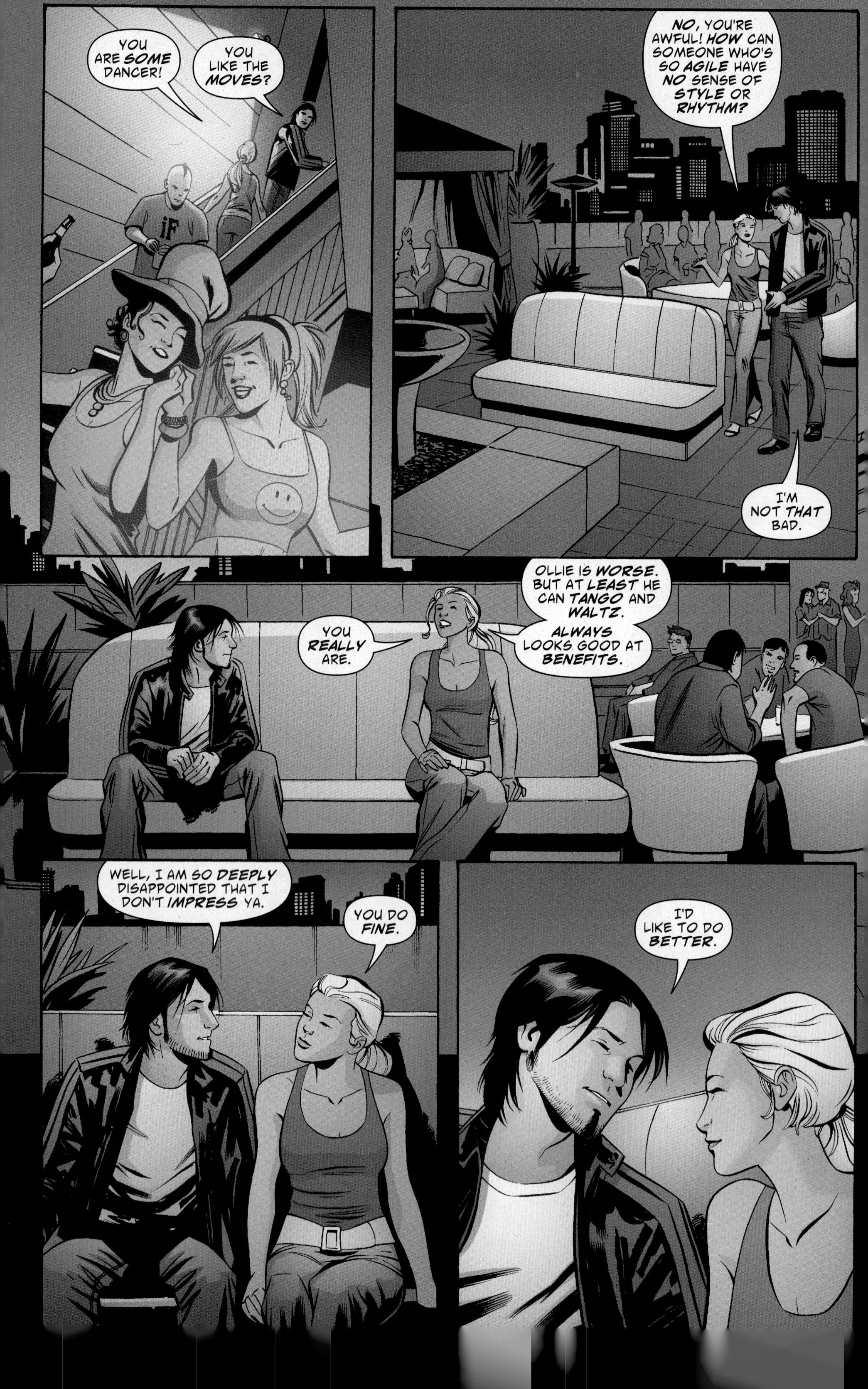
YOU ARE SOME DANCER!
YOU LIKE THE MOVES?
NO, YOU'RE AWFUL! HOW CAN SOMEONE WHO'S SO AGILE HAVE NO SENSE OF STYLE OR RHYTHM?
I'M NOT THAT BAD.
YOU REALLY ARE.
OLLIE IS WORSE. BUT AT LEAST HE CAN TANGO AND WALTZ.
ALWAYS LOOKS GOOD AT BENEFITS.
WELL, I AM SO DEEPLY DISAPPOINTED THAT I DON'T IMPRESS YA.
YOU DO FINE.
I'D LIKE TO DO BETTER.

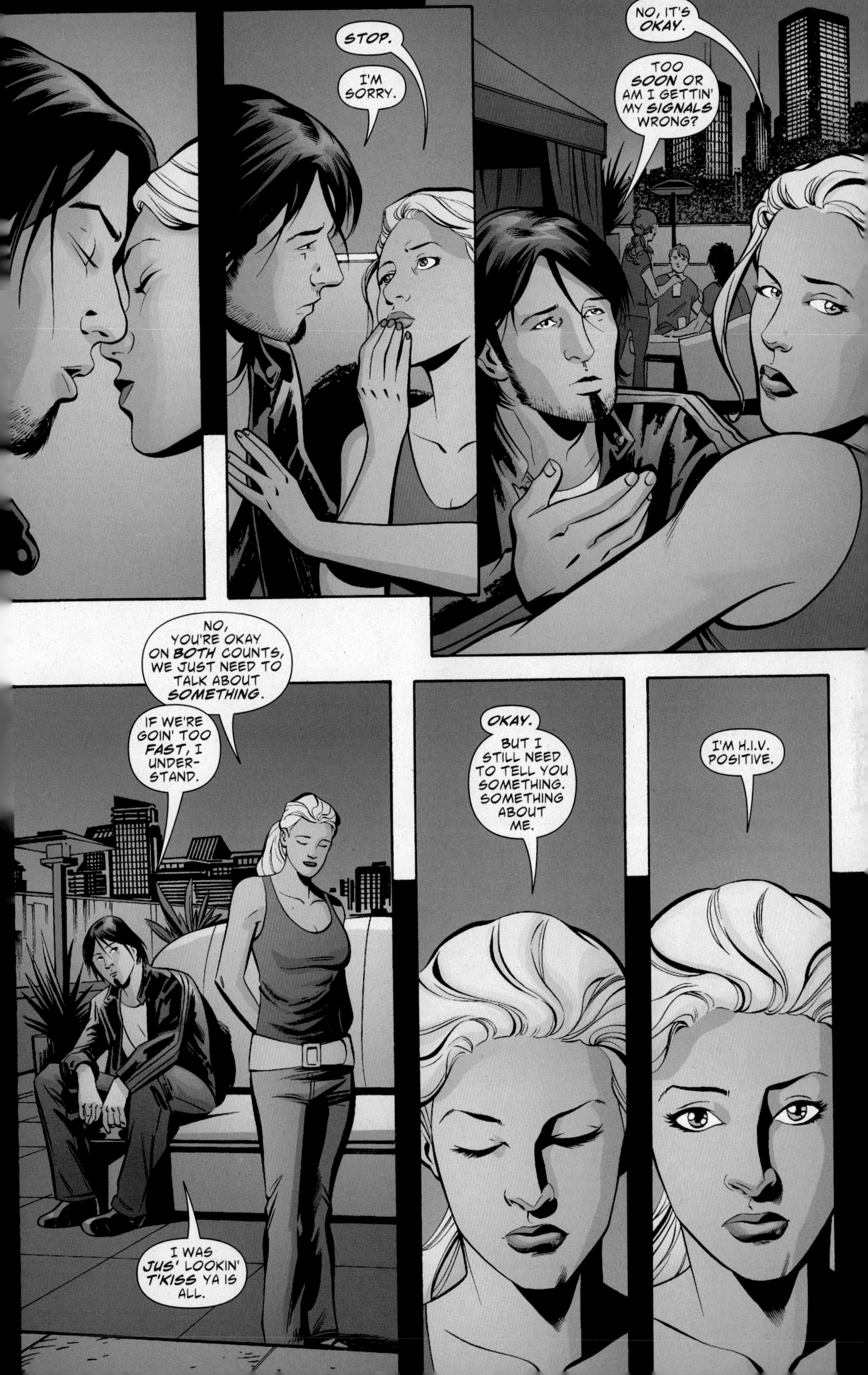
STOP.
I'M SORRY.
NO, IT'S OKAY.
TOO SOON OR AM I GETTIN' MY SIGNALS WRONG?
NO, YOU'RE OKAY ON BOTH COUNTS, WE JUST NEED TO TALK ABOUT SOMETHING.
IF WE'RE GOIN' TOO FAST, I UNDER-STAND.
I WAS JUS' LOOKIN' T'KISS YA IS ALL.
OKAY.
BUT I STILL NEED TO TELL YOU SOMETHING. SOMETHING ABOUT ME.
I'M H.I.V. POSITIVE.

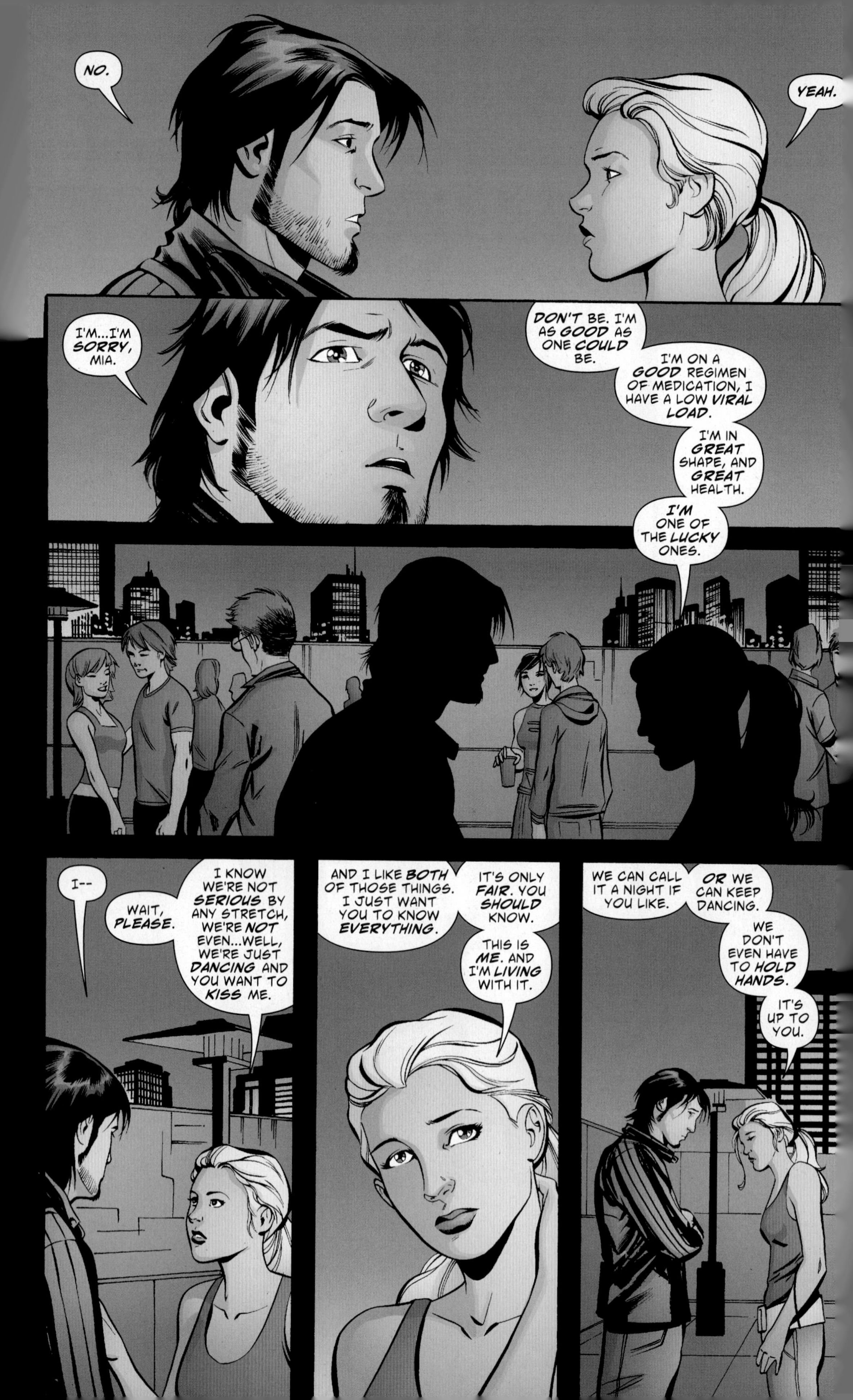
NO.
YEAH.
I'M...I'M SORRY, MIA.
DON'T BE. I'M AS GOOD AS ONE COULD BE.
I'M ON A GOOD REGIMEN OF MEDICATION, I HAVE A LOW VIRAL LOAD.
I'M IN GREAT SHAPE, AND GREAT HEALTH.
I'M ONE OF THE LUCKY ONES.
I--
WAIT, PLEASE.
I KNOW WE'RE NOT SERIOUS BY ANY STRETCH, WE'RE NOT EVEN...WELL, WE'RE JUST DANCING AND YOU WANT TO KISS ME.
AND I LIKE BOTH OF THOSE THINGS. I JUST WANT YOU TO KNOW EVERYTHING.
IT'S ONLY FAIR. YOU SHOULD KNOW.
THIS IS ME. AND I'M LIVING WITH IT.
WE CAN CALL IT A NIGHT IF YOU LIKE.
OR WE CAN KEEP DANCING.
WE DON'T EVEN HAVE TO HOLD HANDS.
IT'S UP TO YOU.

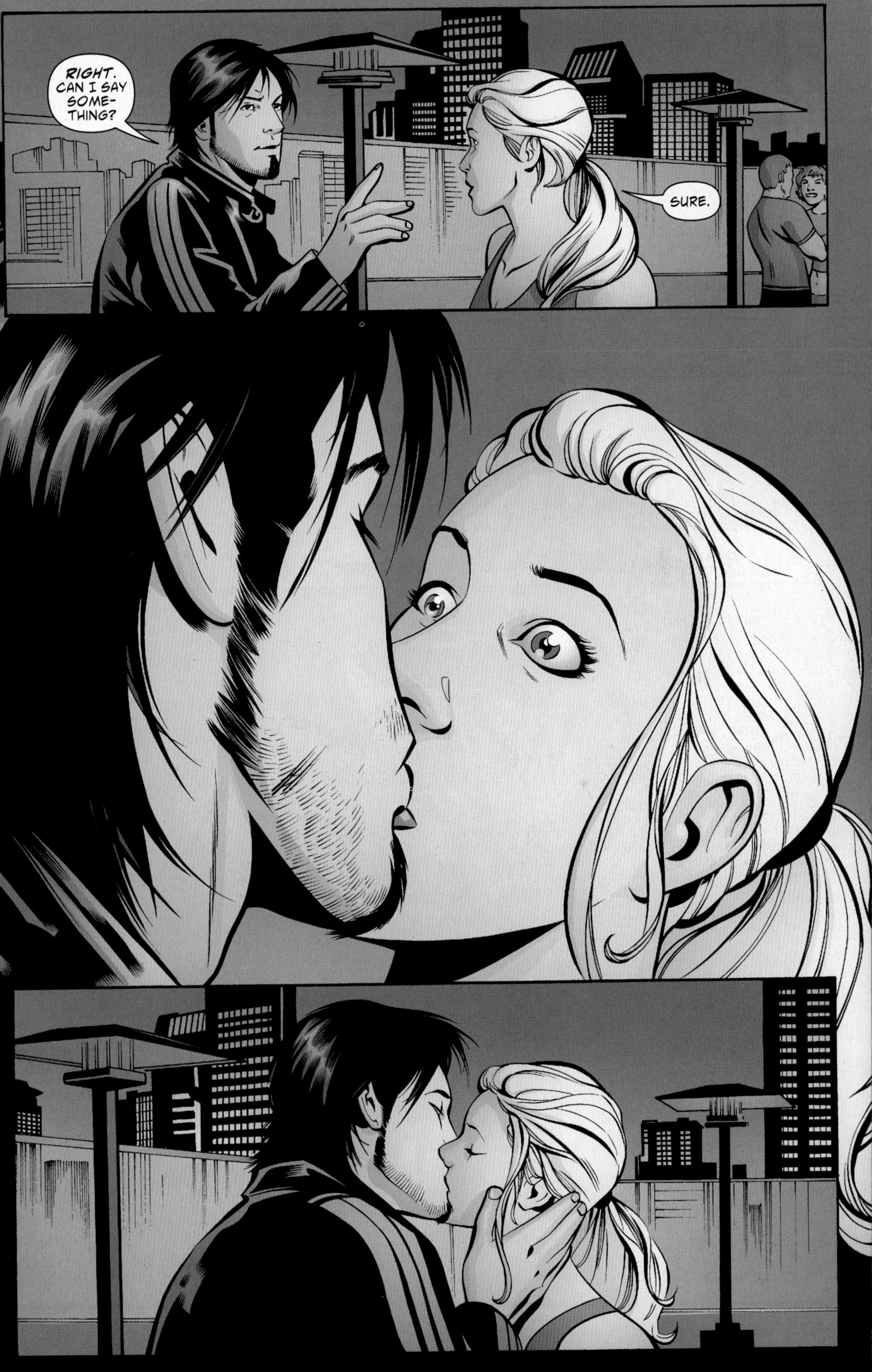
RIGHT. CAN I SAY SOME-THING?
SURE.

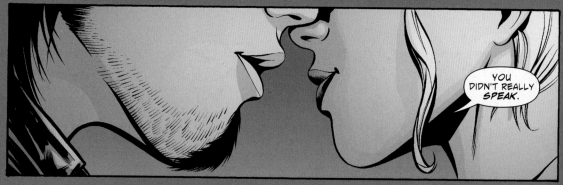

YOU DIDN'T REALLY *SPEAK.*

NO. I DIDN'T.

YOU *ALWAYS TALK* THIS MUCH?

YOU'RE OKAY WITH THIS?

ALWAYS.

WE'LL HAVE TO WORK ON THAT.

"WHY ARE YOU SO *WORRIED?* THIS IS *WONDERFUL.*"

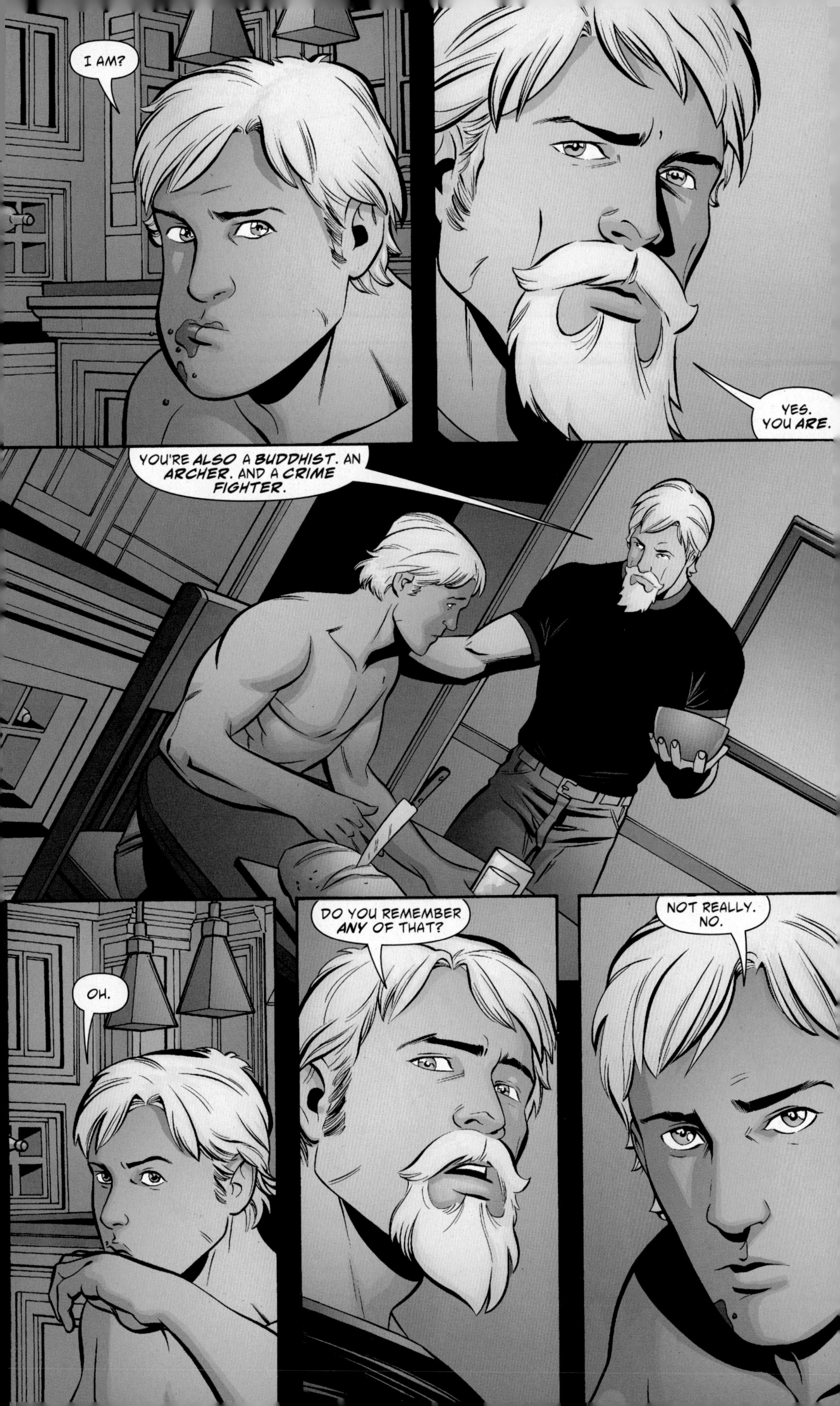
I AM?
YES. YOU ARE.
YOU'RE ALSO A BUDDHIST. AN ARCHER. AND A CRIME FIGHTER.
OH.
DO YOU REMEMBER ANY OF THAT?
NOT REALLY. NO.

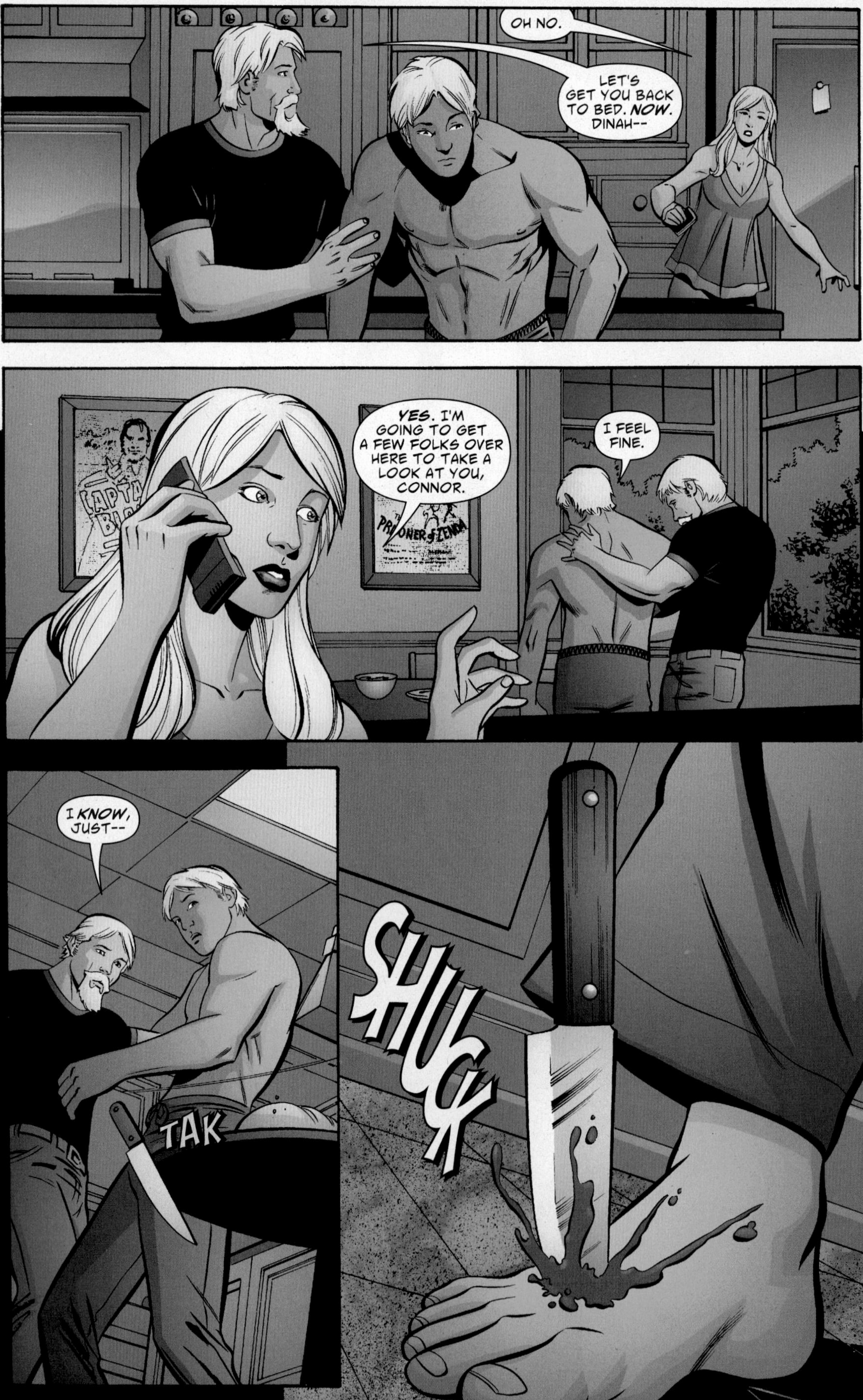
OH NO.
LET'S GET YOU BACK TO BED. NOW. DINAH--
YES. I'M GOING TO GET A FEW FOLKS OVER HERE TO TAKE A LOOK AT YOU, CONNOR.
I FEEL FINE.
I KNOW, JUST--
TAK
SHUCK

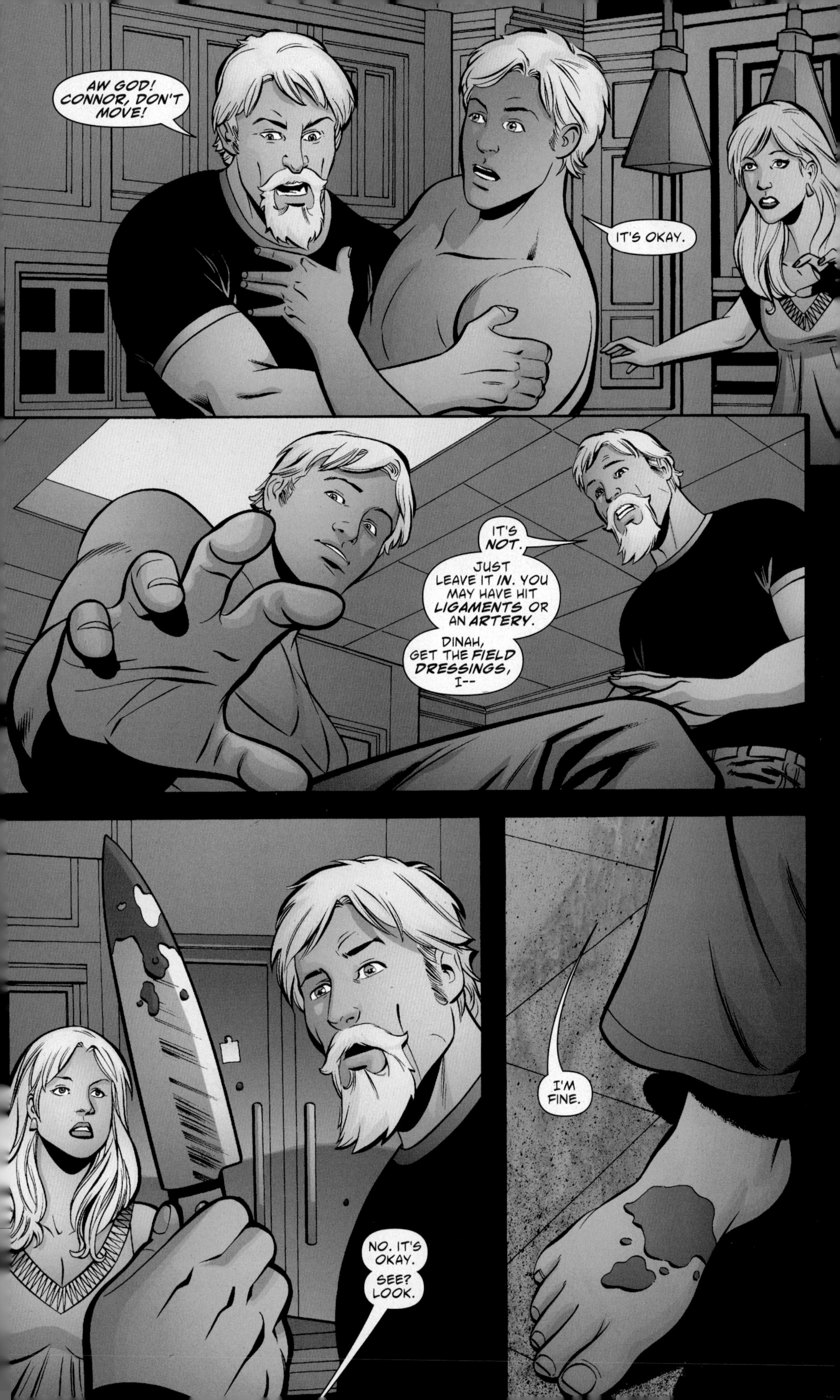
AW GOD! CONNOR, DON'T MOVE!
IT'S OKAY.
IT'S NOT.
JUST LEAVE IT IN. YOU MAY HAVE HIT LIGAMENTS OR AN ARTERY.
DINAH, GET THE FIELD DRESSINGS, I--
NO. IT'S OKAY.
SEE? LOOK.
I'M FINE.

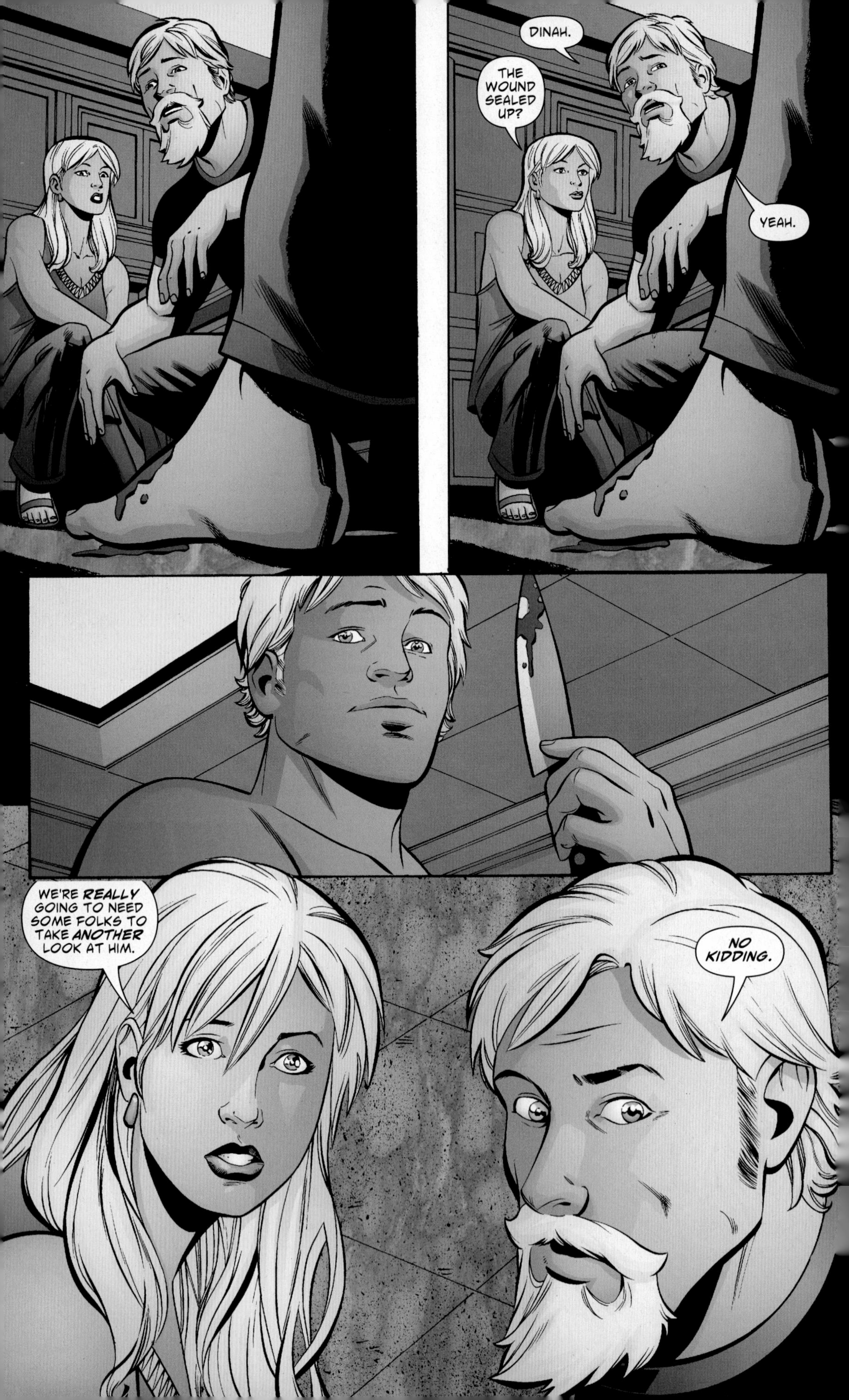
DINAH.
THE WOUND SEALED UP?
YEAH.
WE'RE REALLY GOING TO NEED SOME FOLKS TO TAKE ANOTHER LOOK AT HIM.
NO KIDDING.

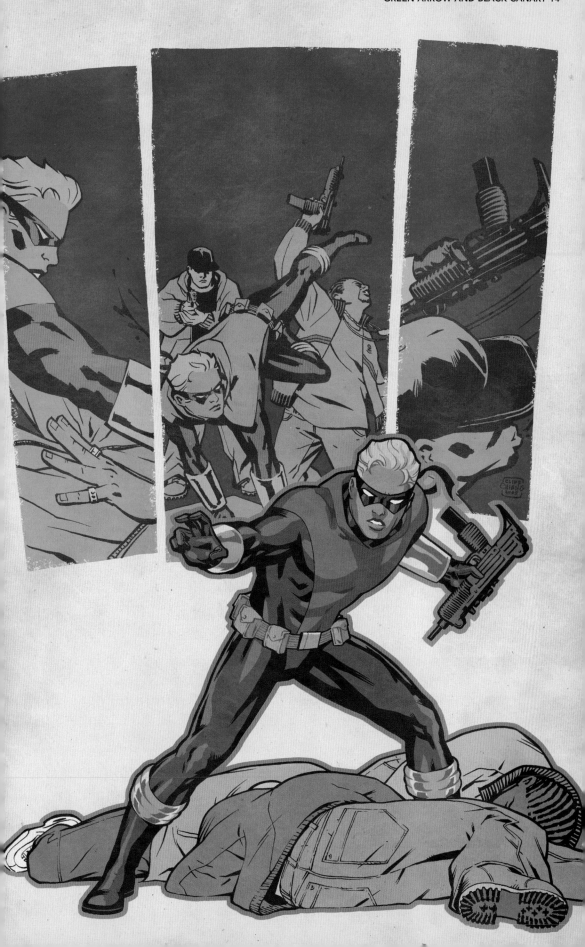

A LEAGUE OF THEIR OWN:

ONE DOOR CLOSES,
ANOTHER OPENS

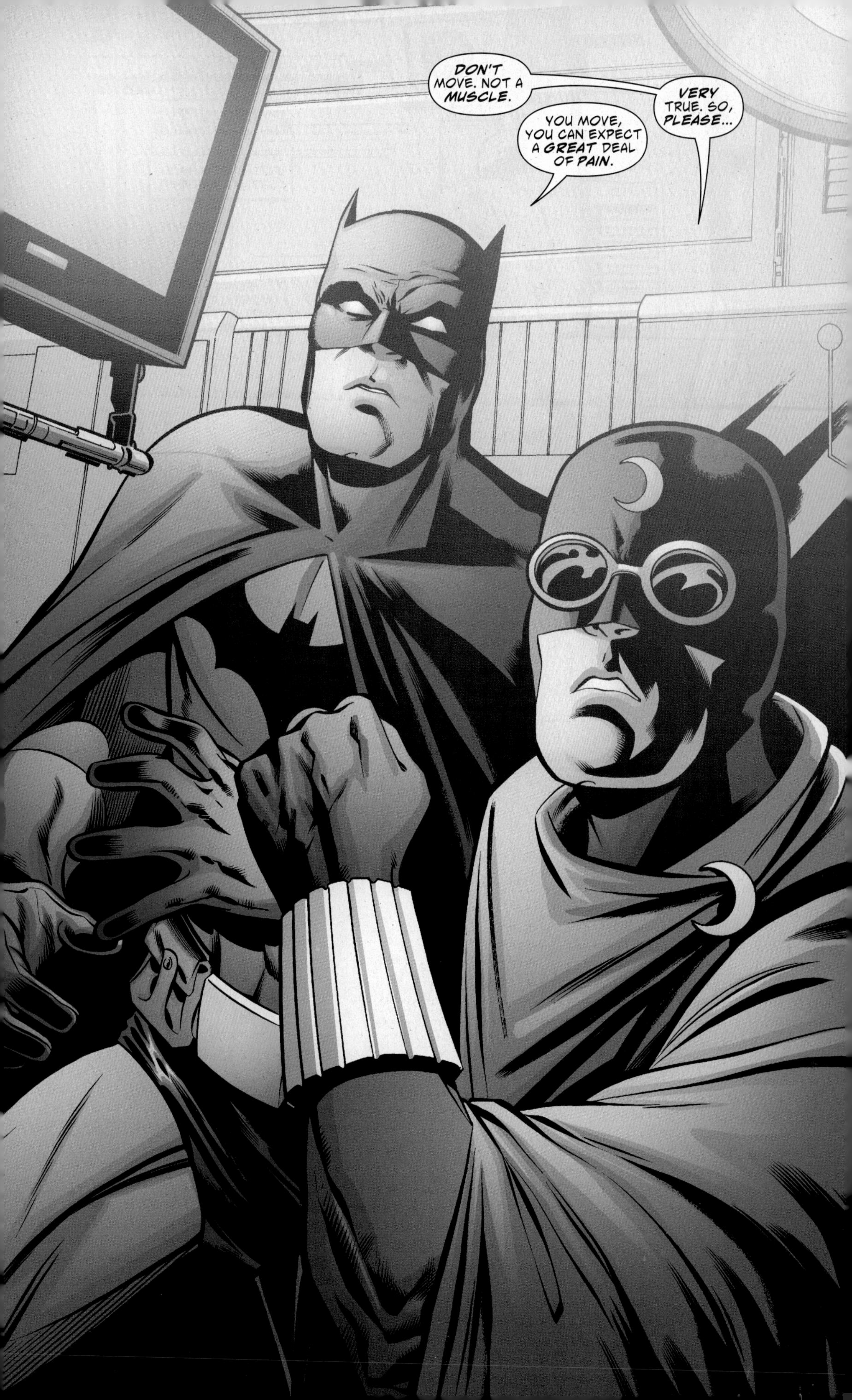
DON'T MOVE. NOT A MUSCLE.
YOU MOVE, YOU CAN EXPECT A GREAT DEAL OF PAIN.
VERY TRUE. SO, PLEASE...

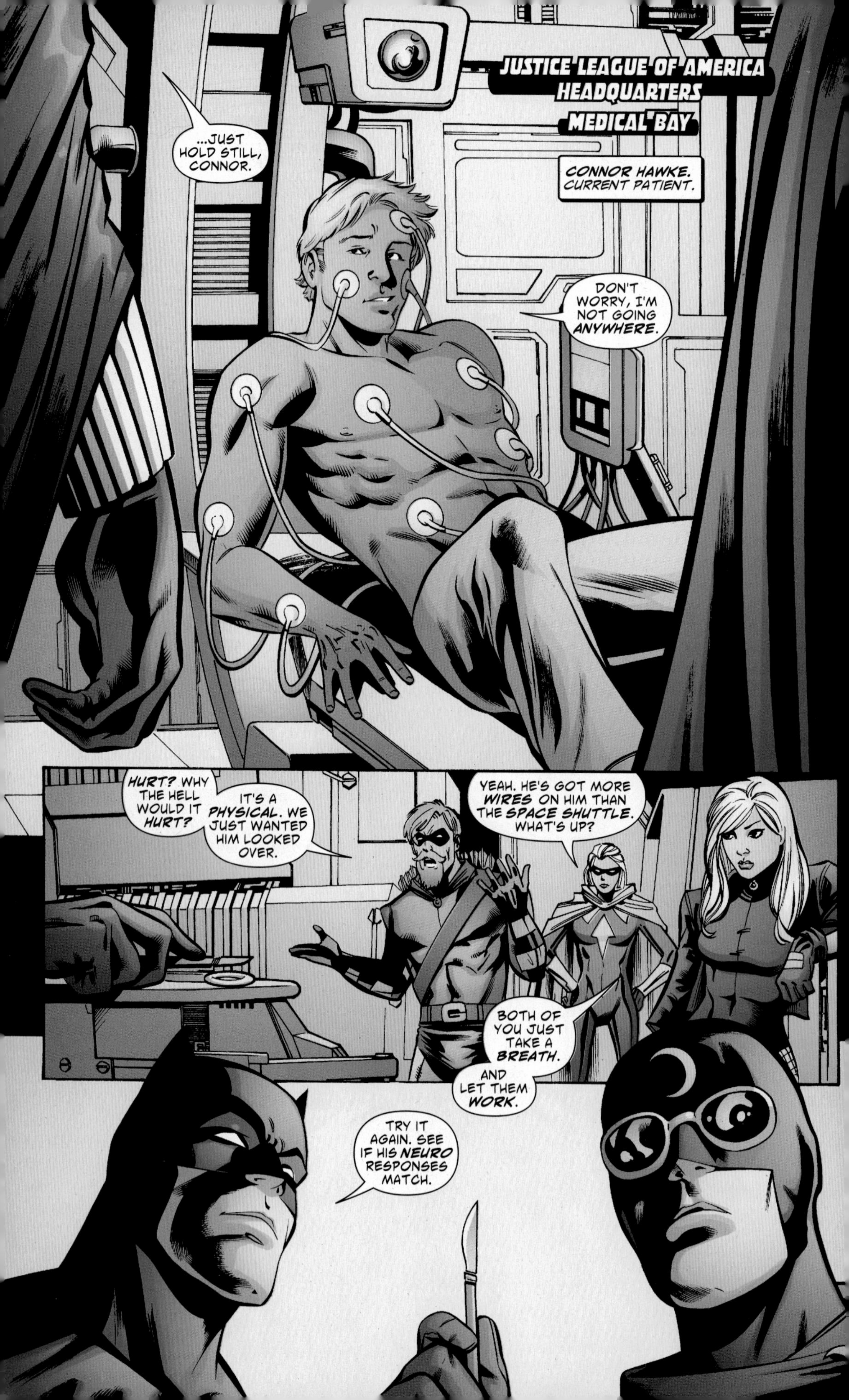
JUSTICE LEAGUE OF AMERICA HEADQUARTERS
MEDICAL BAY
...JUST HOLD STILL, CONNOR.
CONNOR HAWKE. CURRENT PATIENT.
DON'T WORRY, I'M NOT GOING ANYWHERE.
HURT? WHY THE HELL WOULD IT HURT?
IT'S A PHYSICAL. WE JUST WANTED HIM LOOKED OVER.
YEAH. HE'S GOT MORE WIRES ON HIM THAN THE SPACE SHUTTLE. WHAT'S UP?
BOTH OF YOU JUST TAKE A BREATH.
AND LET THEM WORK.
TRY IT AGAIN. SEE IF HIS NEURO RESPONSES MATCH.

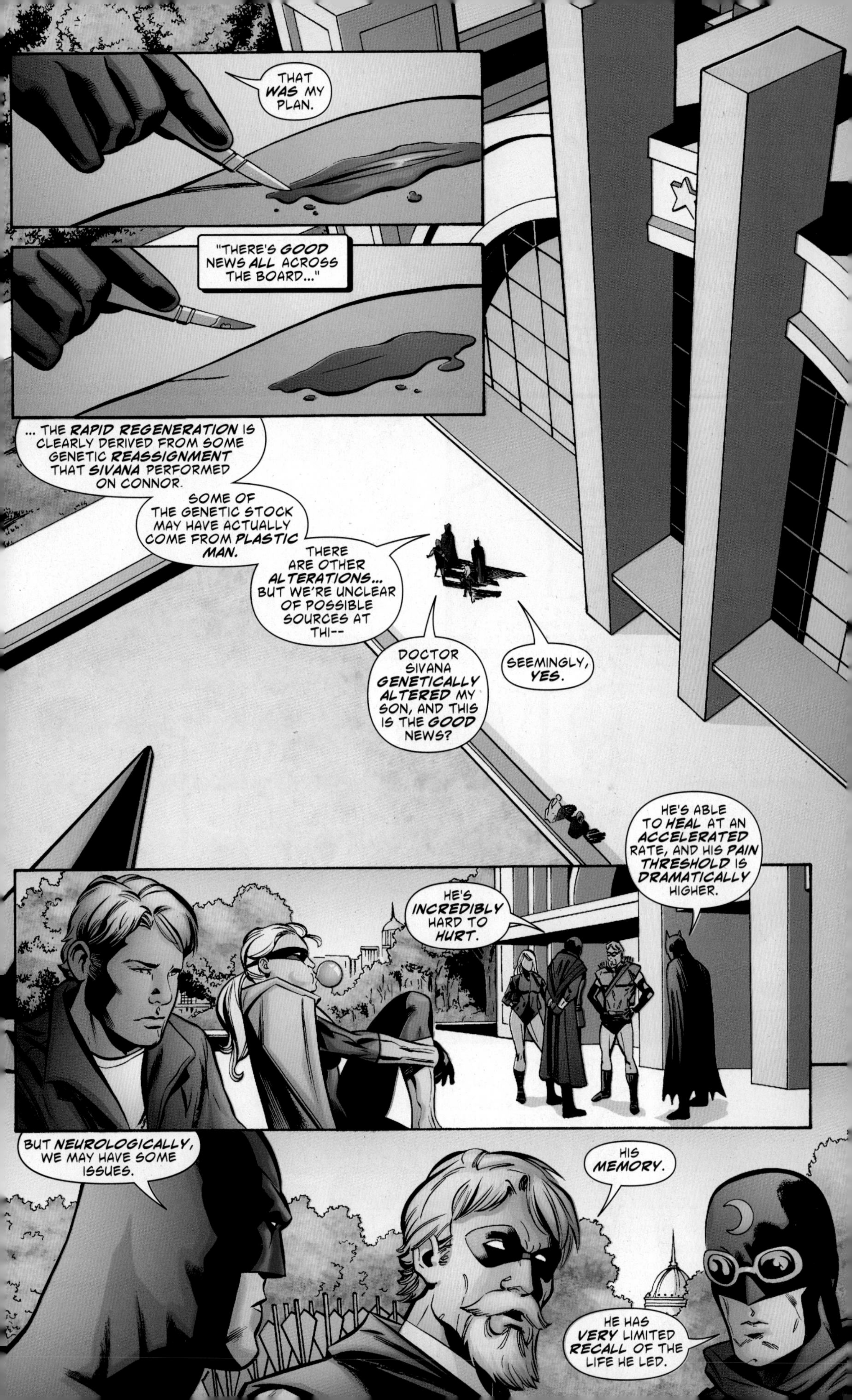
THAT WAS MY PLAN.
"THERE'S GOOD NEWS ALL ACROSS THE BOARD..."
... THE RAPID REGENERATION IS CLEARLY DERIVED FROM SOME GENETIC REASSIGNMENT THAT SIVANA PERFORMED ON CONNOR.
SOME OF THE GENETIC STOCK MAY HAVE ACTUALLY COME FROM PLASTIC MAN.
THERE ARE OTHER ALTERATIONS... BUT WE'RE UNCLEAR OF POSSIBLE SOURCES AT THI--
DOCTOR SIVANA GENETICALLY ALTERED MY SON, AND THIS IS THE GOOD NEWS?
SEEMINGLY, YES.
HE'S ABLE TO HEAL AT AN ACCELERATED RATE, AND HIS PAIN THRESHOLD IS DRAMATICALLY HIGHER.
HE'S INCREDIBLY HARD TO HURT.
BUT NEUROLOGICALLY, WE MAY HAVE SOME ISSUES.
HIS MEMORY.
HE HAS VERY LIMITED RECALL OF THE LIFE HE LED.

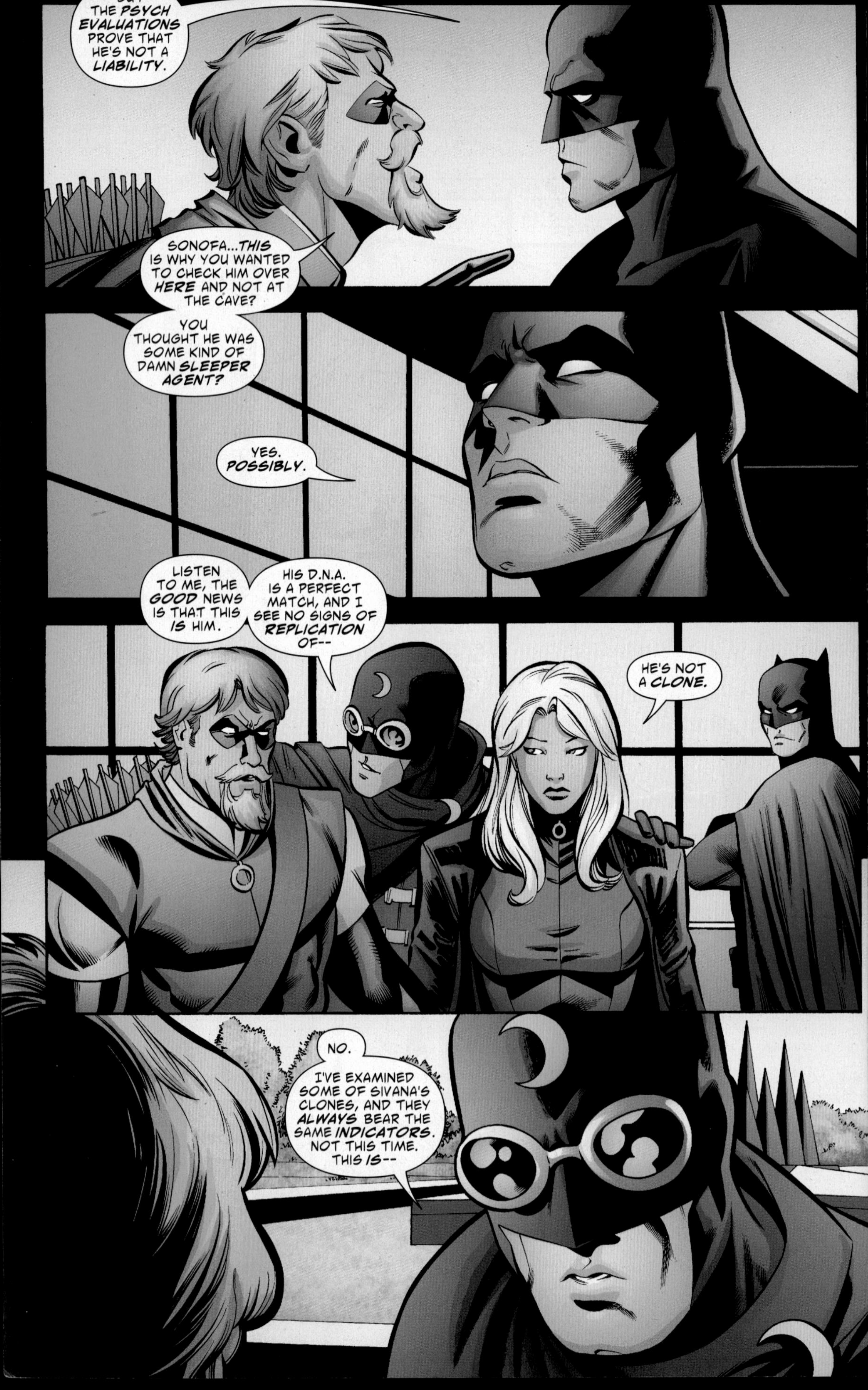
BUT THE PSYCH EVALUATIONS PROVE THAT HE'S NOT A LIABILITY.
SONOFA...THIS IS WHY YOU WANTED TO CHECK HIM OVER HERE AND NOT AT THE CAVE?
YOU THOUGHT HE WAS SOME KIND OF DAMN SLEEPER AGENT?
YES. POSSIBLY.
LISTEN TO ME, THE GOOD NEWS IS THAT THIS IS HIM.
HIS D.N.A. IS A PERFECT MATCH, AND I SEE NO SIGNS OF REPLICATION OF--
HE'S NOT A CLONE.
NO.
I'VE EXAMINED SOME OF SIVANA'S CLONES, AND THEY ALWAYS BEAR THE SAME INDICATORS. NOT THIS TIME. THIS IS--

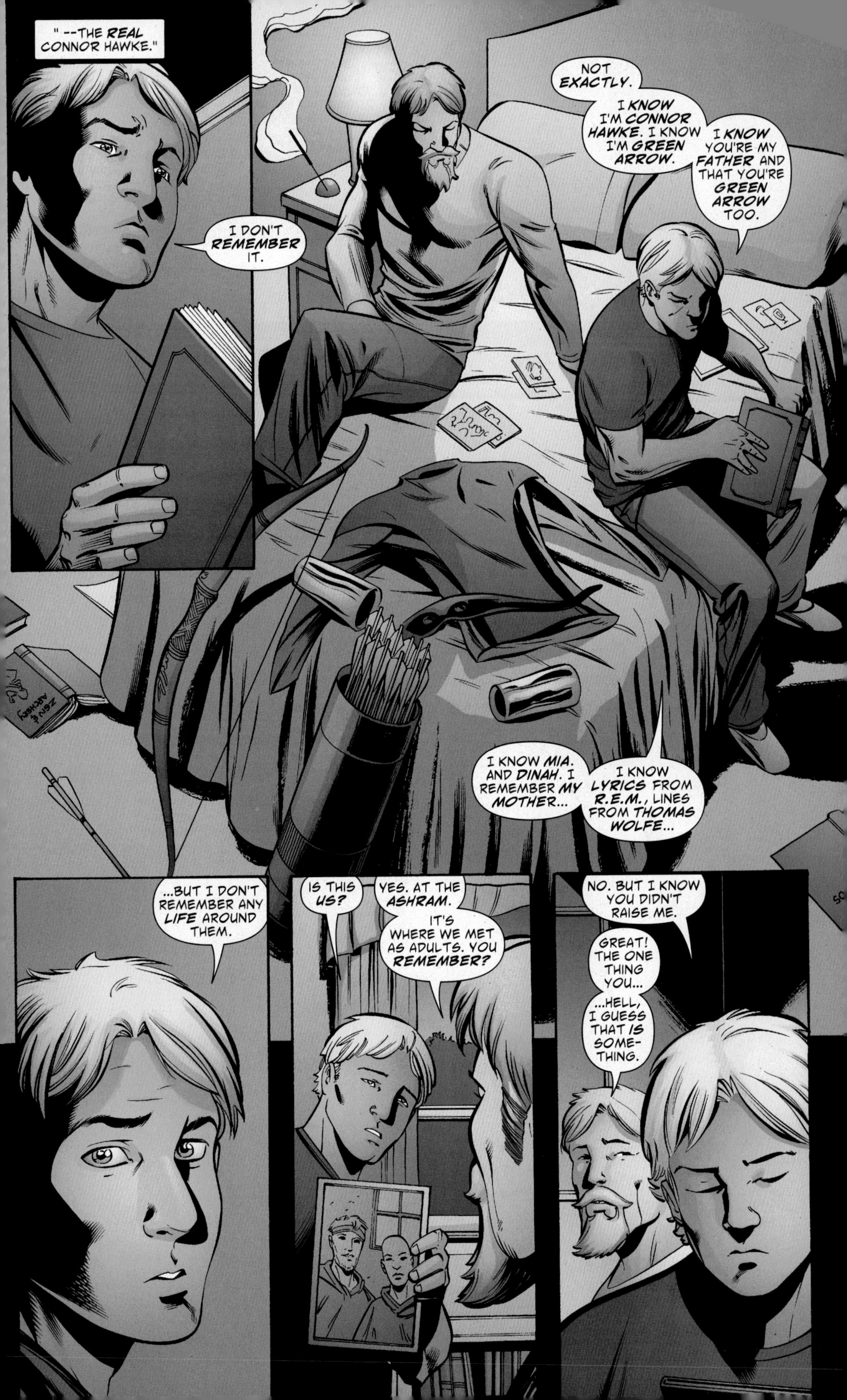
" --THE REAL CONNOR HAWKE."
I DON'T REMEMBER IT.
NOT EXACTLY.
I KNOW I'M CONNOR HAWKE. I KNOW I'M GREEN ARROW.
I KNOW YOU'RE MY FATHER AND THAT YOU'RE GREEN ARROW TOO.
ZEN & ARCHERY
I KNOW MIA. AND DINAH. I REMEMBER MY MOTHER...
I KNOW LYRICS FROM R.E.M., LINES FROM THOMAS WOLFE...
...BUT I DON'T REMEMBER ANY LIFE AROUND THEM.
IS THIS US?
YES. AT THE ASHRAM.
IT'S WHERE WE MET AS ADULTS. YOU REMEMBER?
NO. BUT I KNOW YOU DIDN'T RAISE ME.
GREAT! THE ONE THING YOU...
...HELL, I GUESS THAT IS SOME-THING.

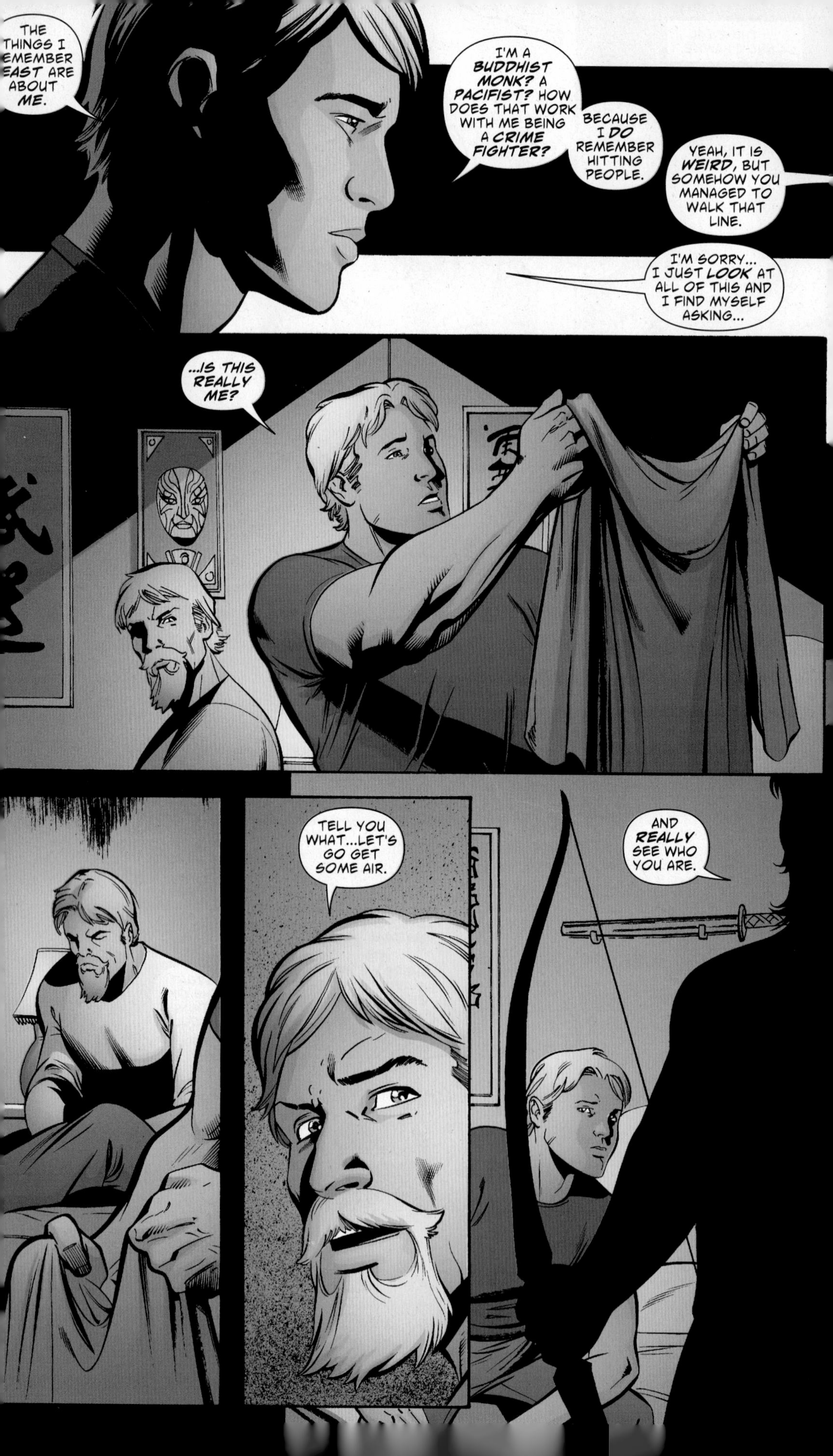
THE THINGS I REMEMBER LEAST ARE ABOUT ME.
I'M A BUDDHIST MONK? A PACIFIST? HOW DOES THAT WORK WITH ME BEING A CRIME FIGHTER?
BECAUSE I DO REMEMBER HITTING PEOPLE.
YEAH, IT IS WEIRD, BUT SOMEHOW YOU MANAGED TO WALK THAT LINE.
I'M SORRY... I JUST LOOK AT ALL OF THIS AND I FIND MYSELF ASKING...
...IS THIS REALLY ME?
TELL YOU WHAT...LET'S GO GET SOME AIR.
AND REALLY SEE WHO YOU ARE.

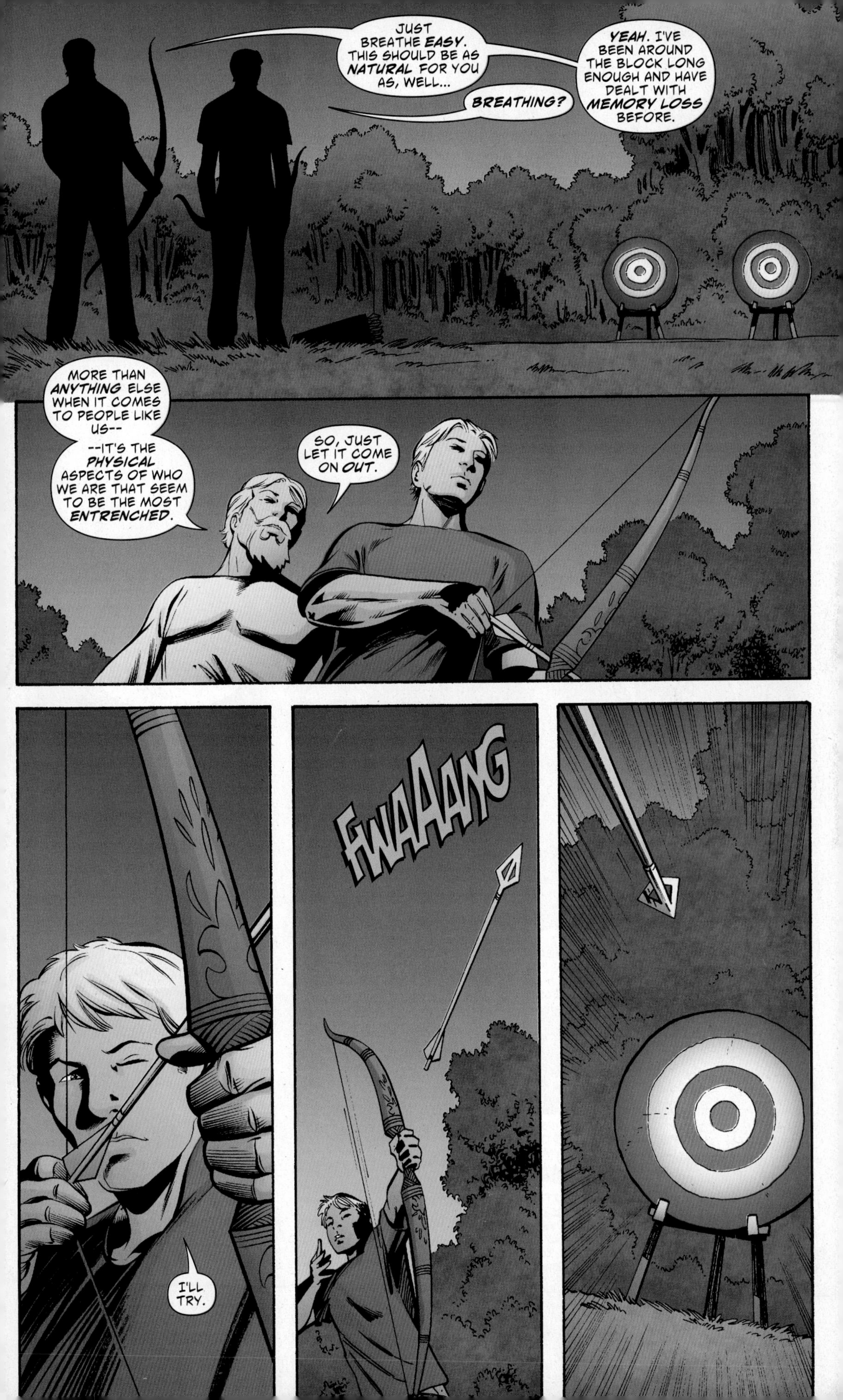
JUST BREATHE EASY. THIS SHOULD BE AS NATURAL FOR YOU AS, WELL...
BREATHING?
YEAH. I'VE BEEN AROUND THE BLOCK LONG ENOUGH AND HAVE DEALT WITH MEMORY LOSS BEFORE.
MORE THAN ANYTHING ELSE WHEN IT COMES TO PEOPLE LIKE US--
--IT'S THE PHYSICAL ASPECTS OF WHO WE ARE THAT SEEM TO BE THE MOST ENTRENCHED.
SO, JUST LET IT COME ON OUT.
I'LL TRY.
FWAAANG

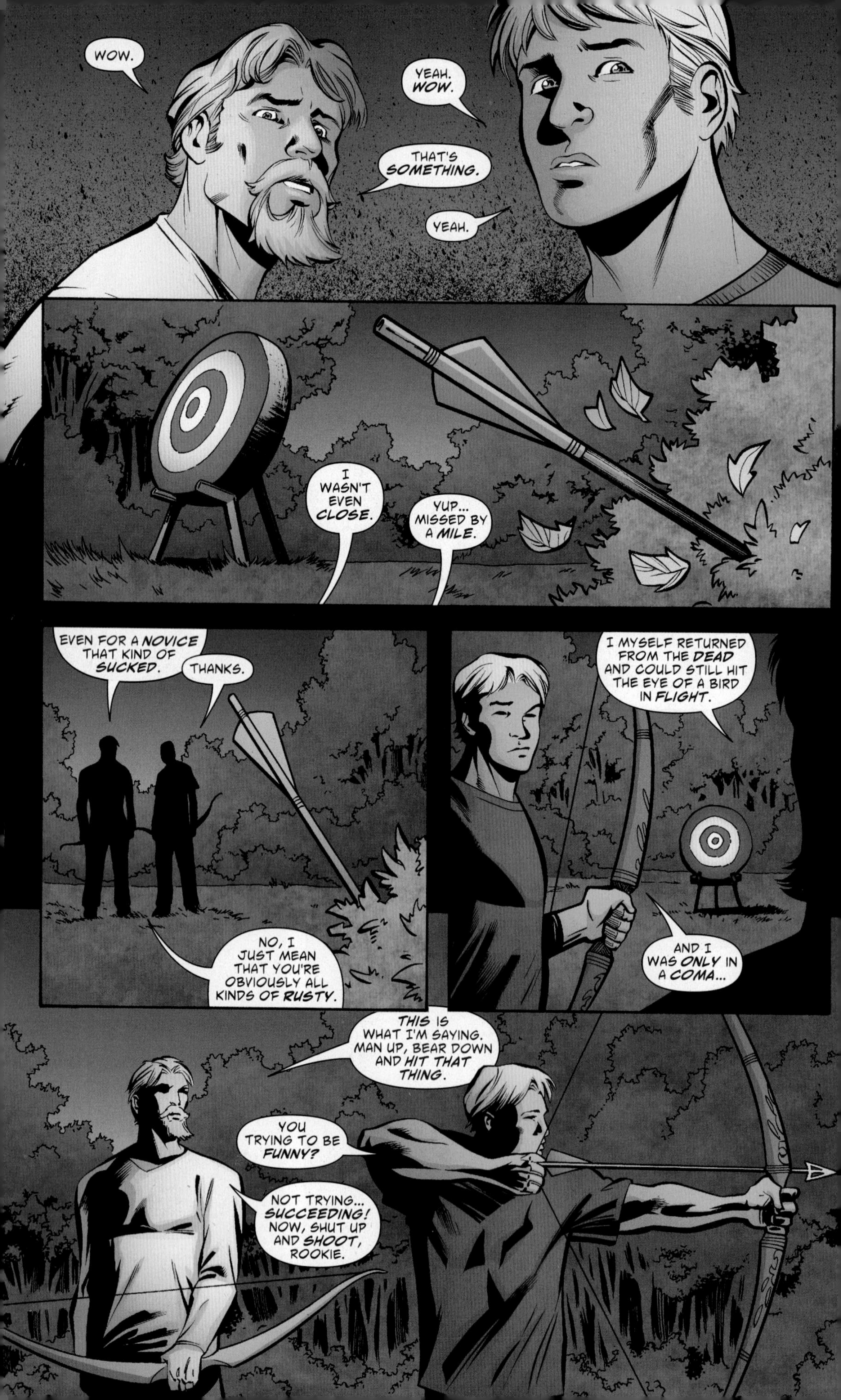

WOW.
YEAH. WOW.
THAT'S SOMETHING.
YEAH.
I WASN'T EVEN CLOSE.
YUP... MISSED BY A MILE.
EVEN FOR A NOVICE THAT KIND OF SUCKED.
THANKS.
NO, I JUST MEAN THAT YOU'RE OBVIOUSLY ALL KINDS OF RUSTY.
I MYSELF RETURNED FROM THE DEAD AND COULD STILL HIT THE EYE OF A BIRD IN FLIGHT.
AND I WAS ONLY IN A COMA...
THIS IS WHAT I'M SAYING. MAN UP, BEAR DOWN AND HIT THAT THING.
YOU TRYING TO BE FUNNY?
NOT TRYING... SUCCEEDING! NOW, SHUT UP AND SHOOT, ROOKIE.

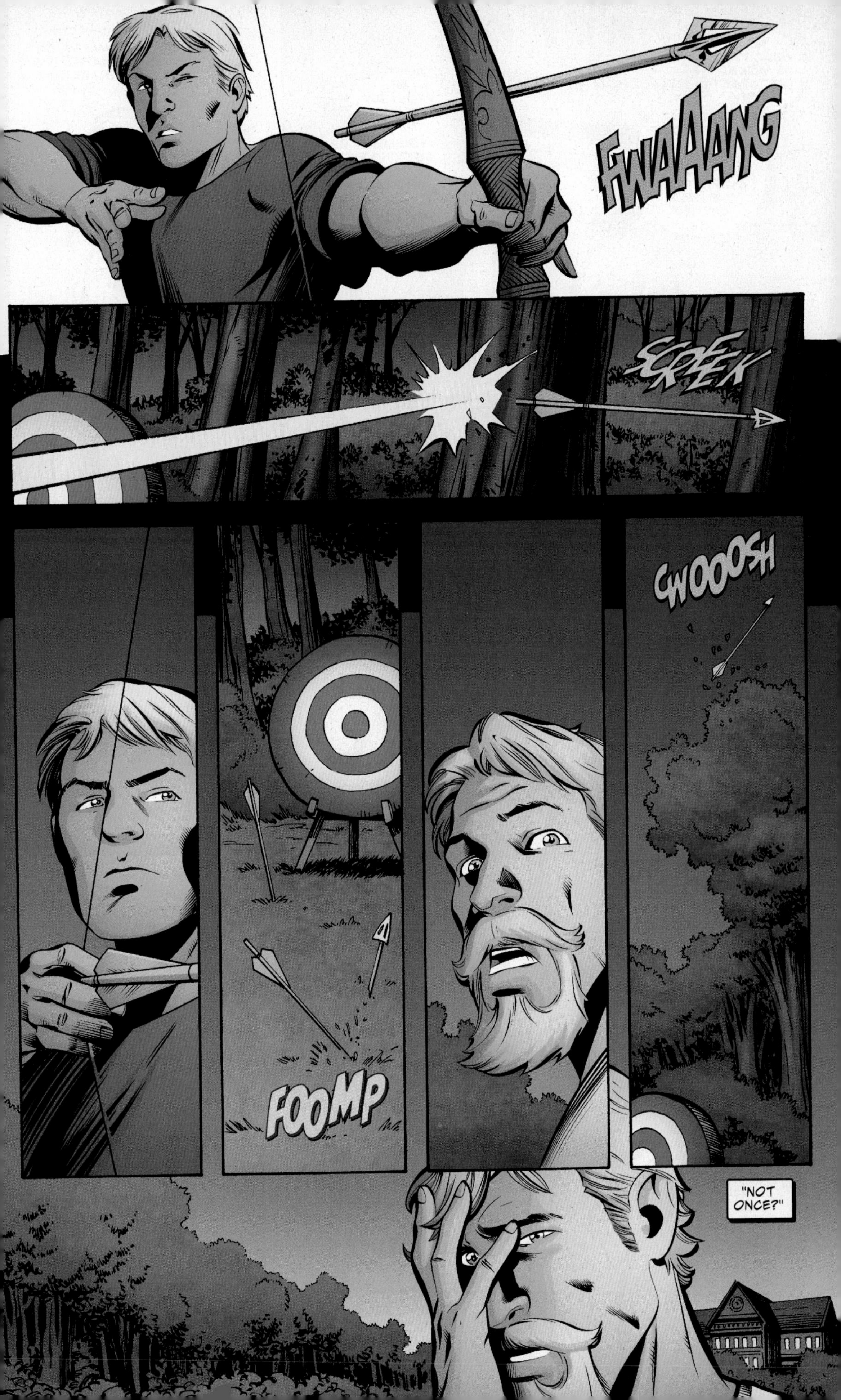
FWAAANG
SCREEK
FOOMP
GWOOOSH
"NOT ONCE?"

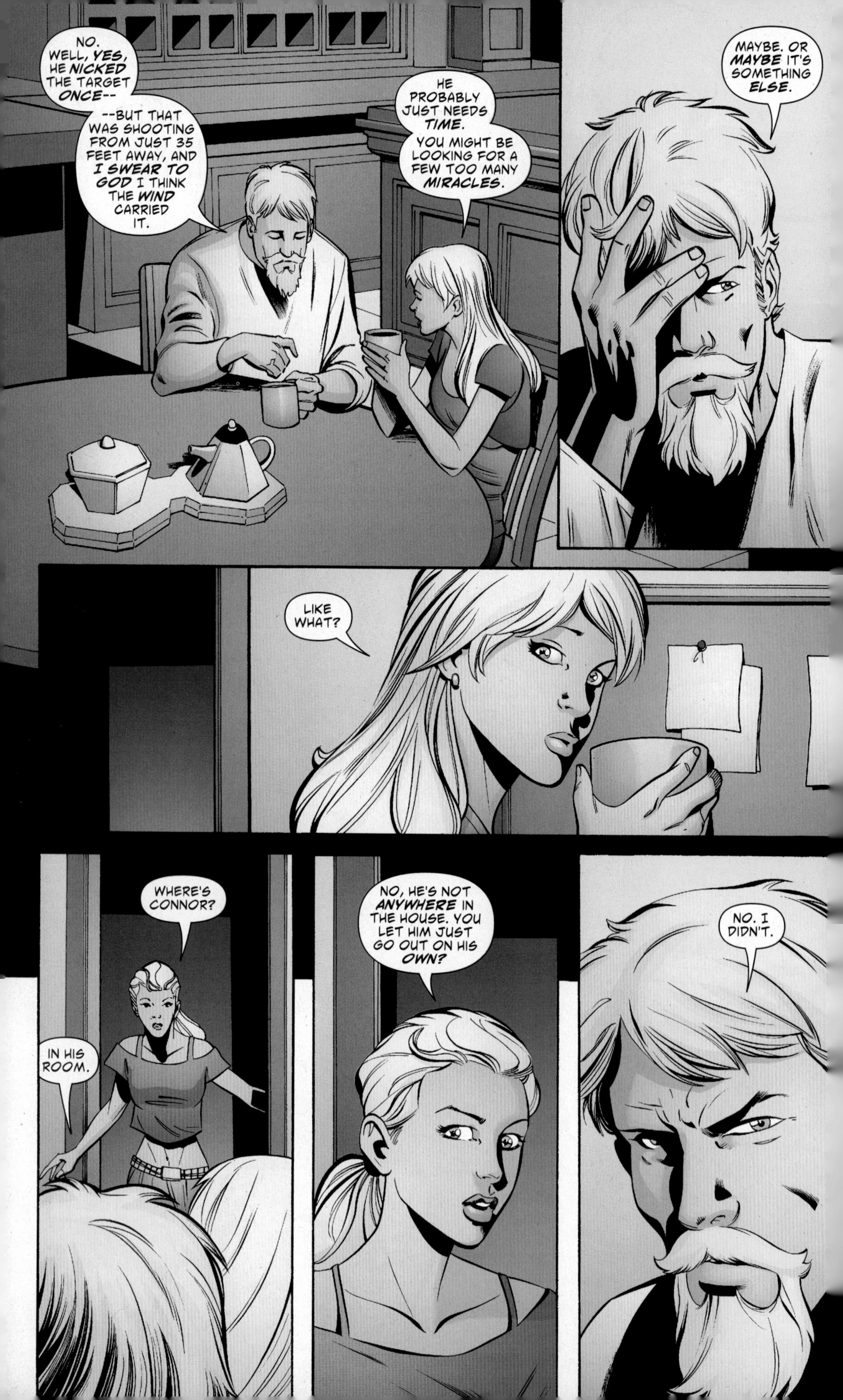
NO.
WELL, YES, HE NICKED THE TARGET ONCE--
--BUT THAT WAS SHOOTING FROM JUST 35 FEET AWAY, AND I SWEAR TO GOD I THINK THE WIND CARRIED IT.
HE PROBABLY JUST NEEDS TIME.
YOU MIGHT BE LOOKING FOR A FEW TOO MANY MIRACLES.
MAYBE. OR MAYBE IT'S SOMETHING ELSE.
LIKE WHAT?
WHERE'S CONNOR?
IN HIS ROOM.
NO, HE'S NOT ANYWHERE IN THE HOUSE. YOU LET HIM JUST GO OUT ON HIS OWN?
NO. I DIDN'T.

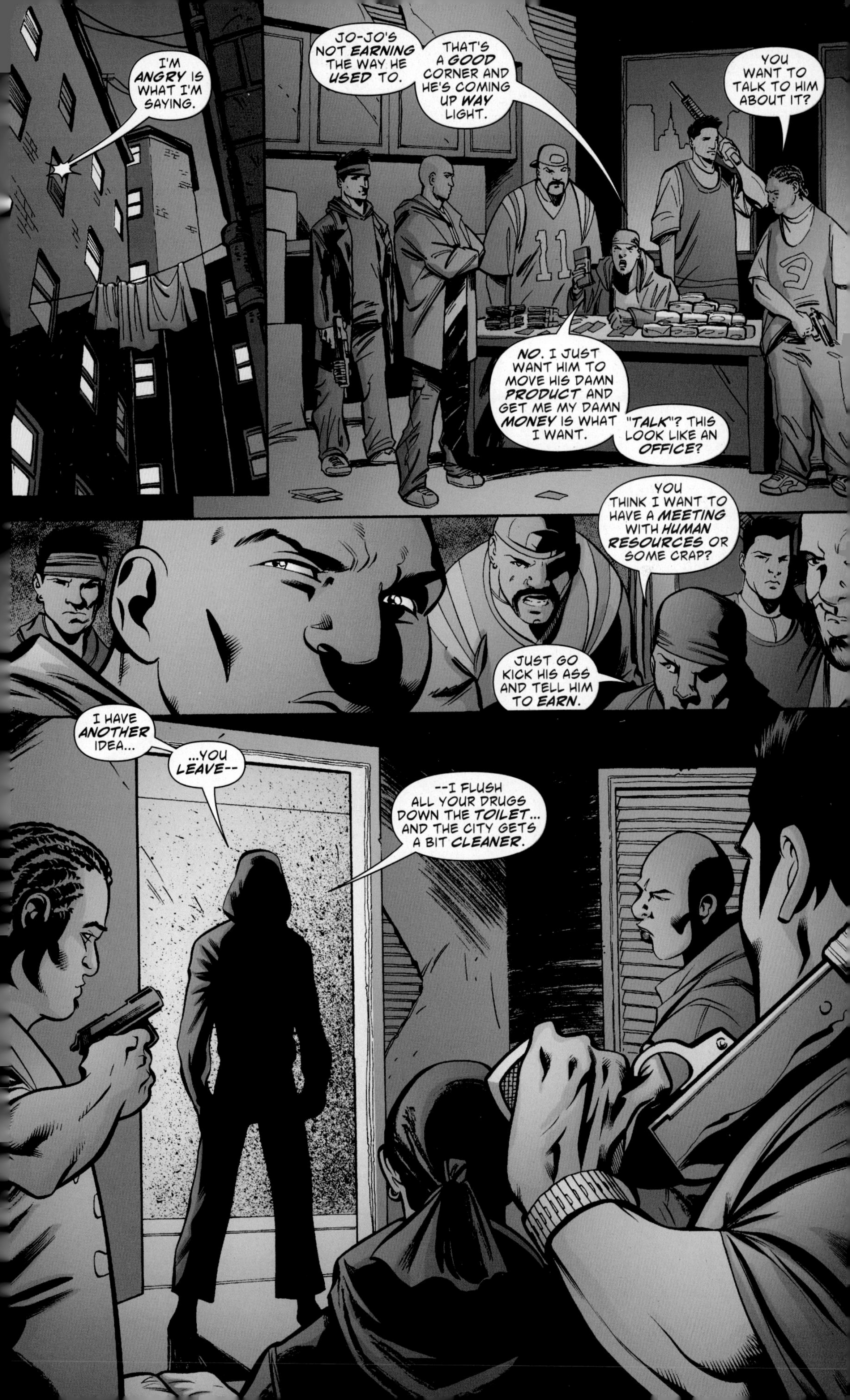
I'M ANGRY IS WHAT I'M SAYING.
JO-JO'S NOT EARNING THE WAY HE USED TO.
THAT'S A GOOD CORNER AND HE'S COMING UP WAY LIGHT.
YOU WANT TO TALK TO HIM ABOUT IT?
NO. I JUST WANT HIM TO MOVE HIS DAMN PRODUCT AND GET ME MY DAMN MONEY IS WHAT I WANT.
"TALK"? THIS LOOK LIKE AN OFFICE?
YOU THINK I WANT TO HAVE A MEETING WITH HUMAN RESOURCES OR SOME CRAP?
JUST GO KICK HIS ASS AND TELL HIM TO EARN.
I HAVE ANOTHER IDEA...
...YOU LEAVE--
--I FLUSH ALL YOUR DRUGS DOWN THE TOILET... AND THE CITY GETS A BIT CLEANER.

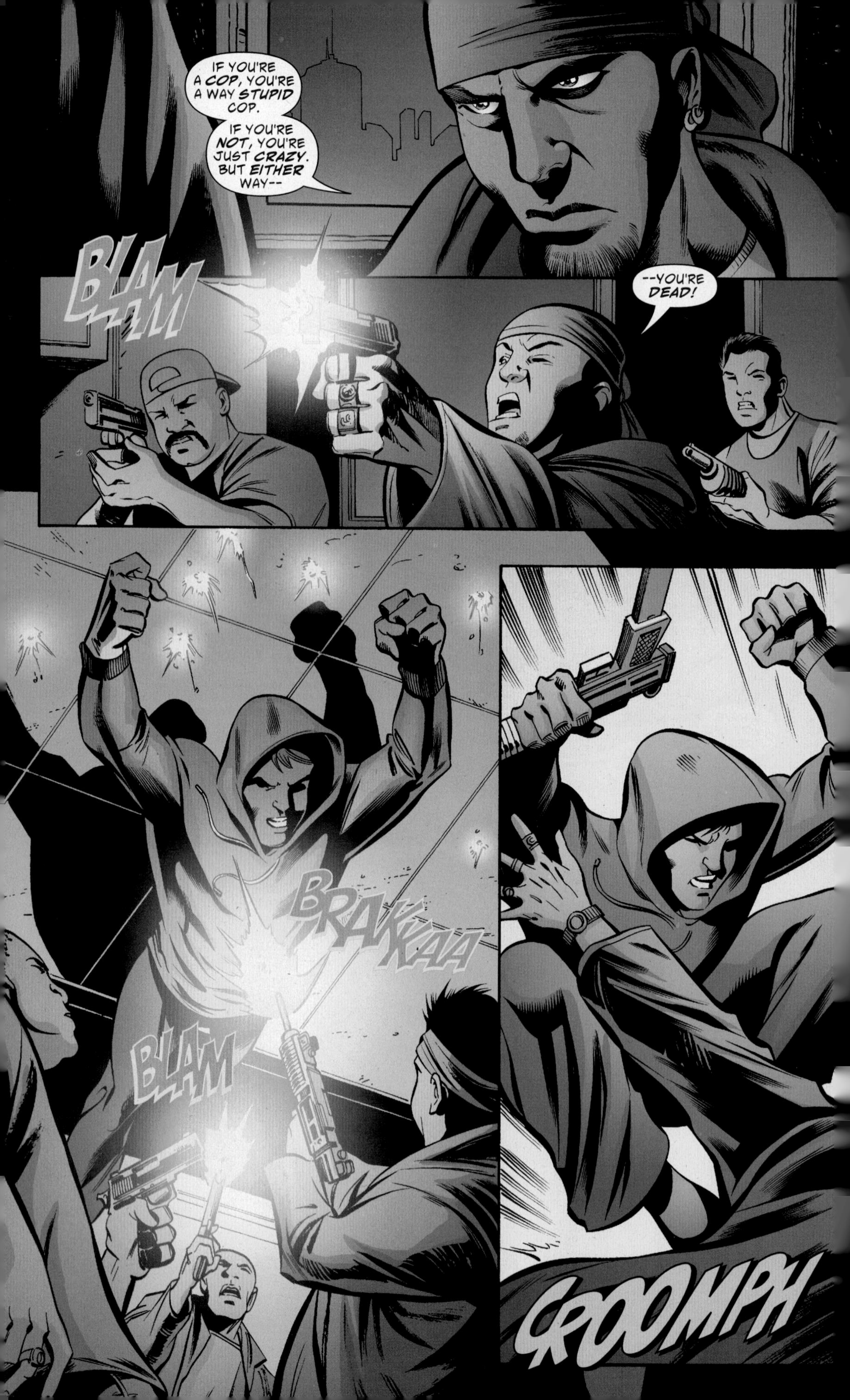
IF YOU'RE A COP, YOU'RE A WAY STUPID COP.
IF YOU'RE NOT, YOU'RE JUST CRAZY. BUT EITHER WAY--
BLAM
--YOU'RE DEAD!
BRAKKAA
BLAM
GROOMPH

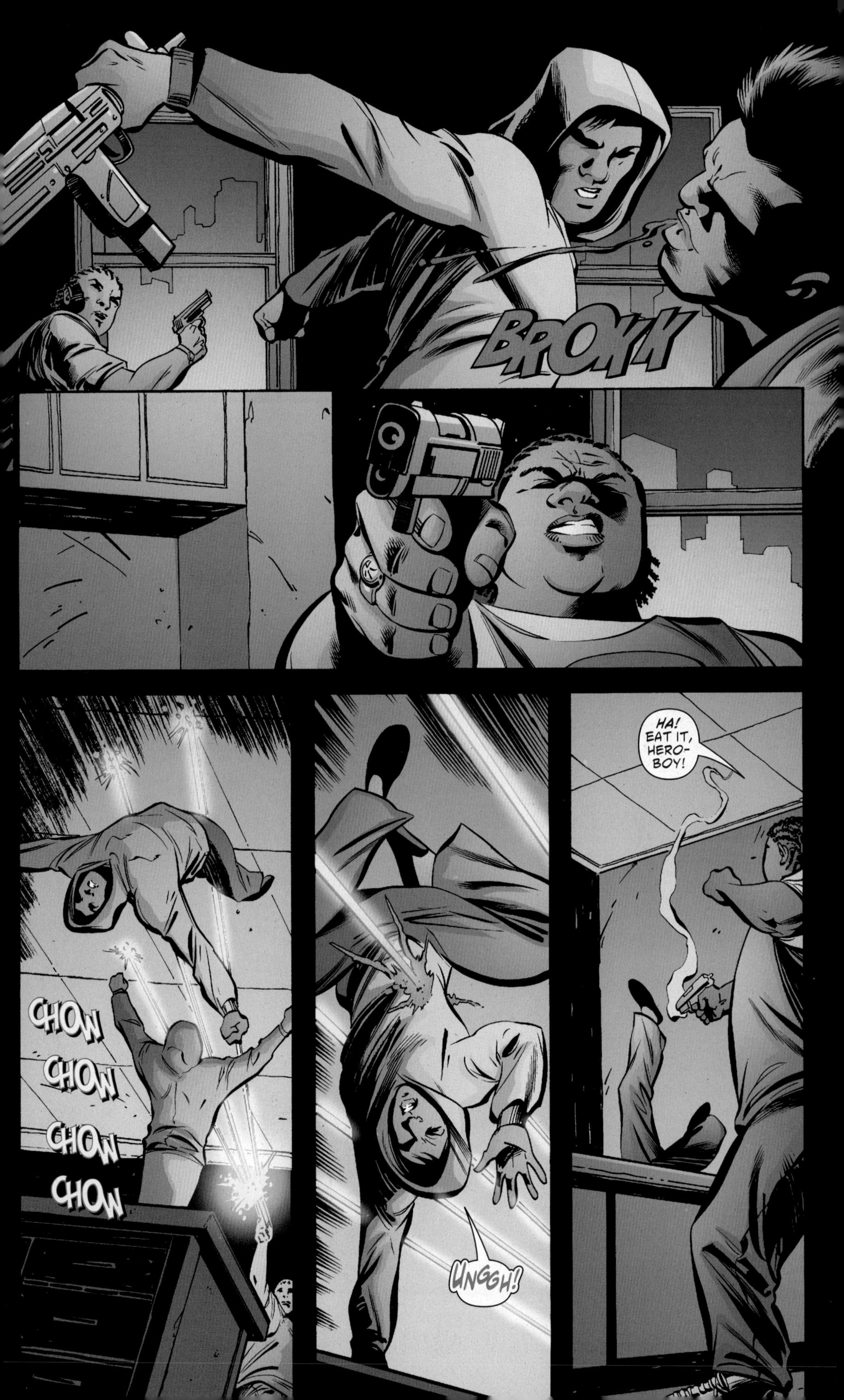
BROKK
CHOW
CHOW
CHOW
CHOW
UNGGH!
HA! EAT IT, HERO-BOY!

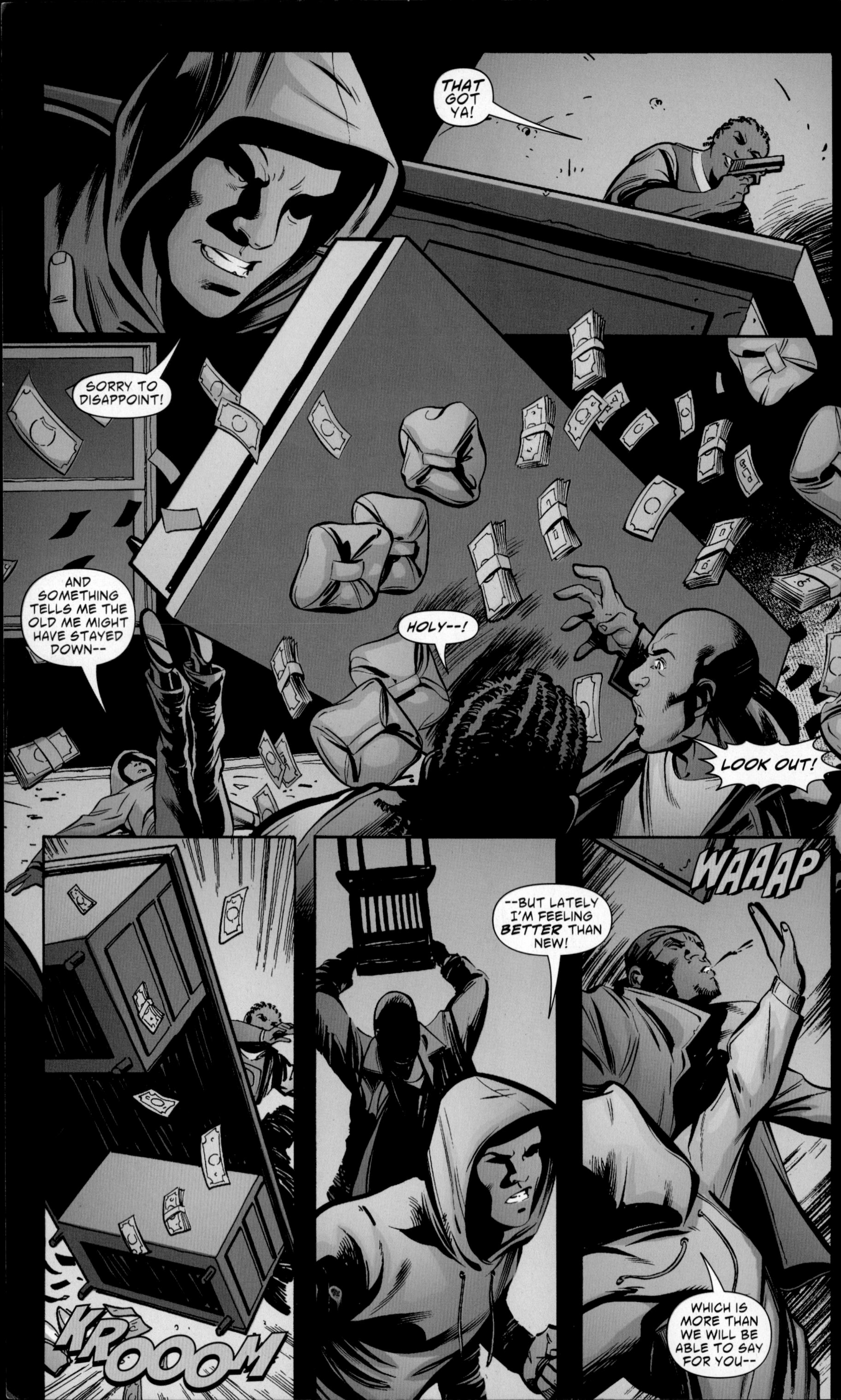
THAT GOT YA!
SORRY TO DISAPPOINT!
AND SOMETHING TELLS ME THE OLD ME MIGHT HAVE STAYED DOWN--
HOLY--!
LOOK OUT!
KROOOM
--BUT LATELY I'M FEELING BETTER THAN NEW!
WAAAP
WHICH IS MORE THAN WE WILL BE ABLE TO SAY FOR YOU--

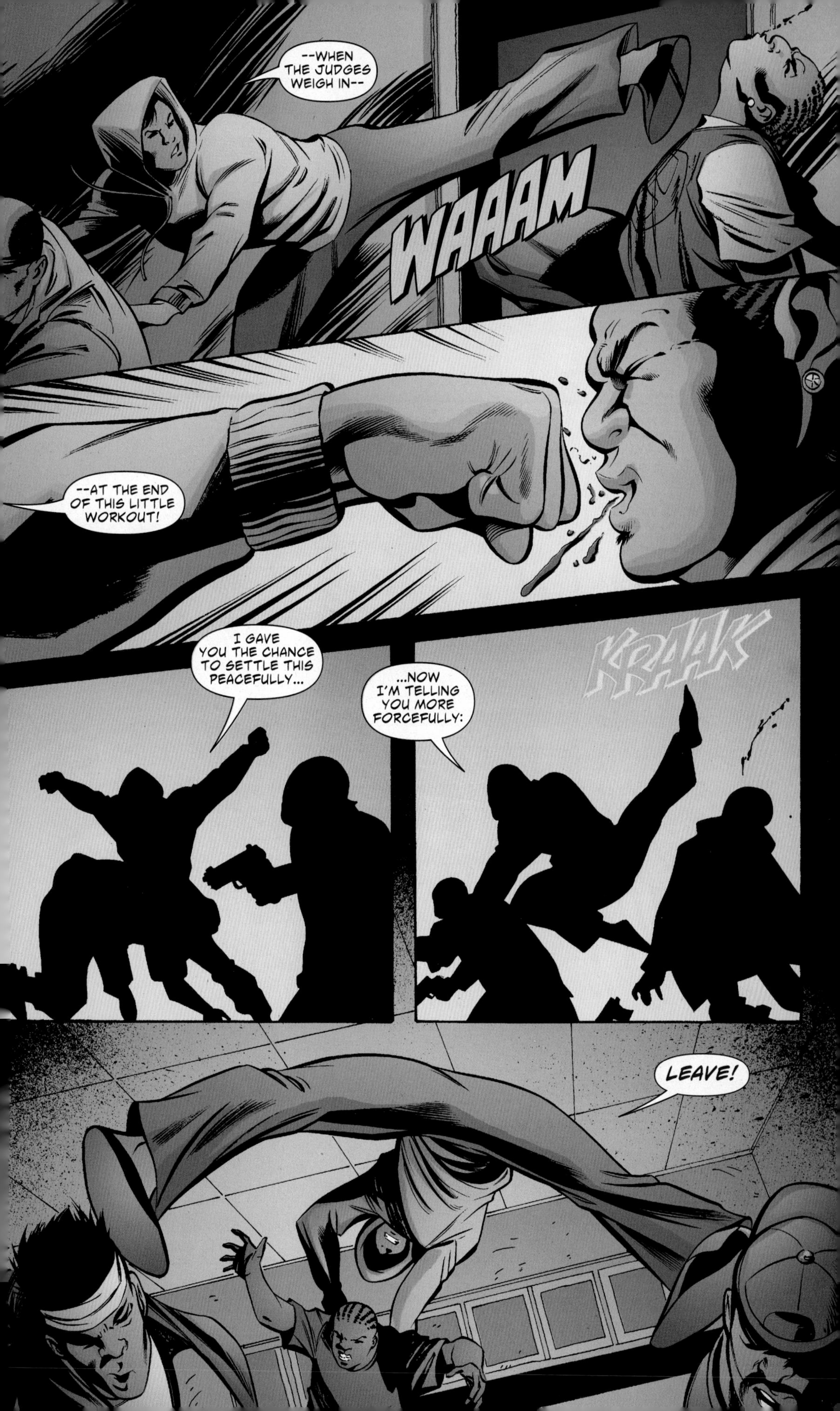
--WHEN THE JUDGES WEIGH IN--
WAAAM
--AT THE END OF THIS LITTLE WORKOUT!
I GAVE YOU THE CHANCE TO SETTLE THIS PEACEFULLY...
KRAAK
...NOW I'M TELLING YOU MORE FORCEFULLY:
LEAVE!

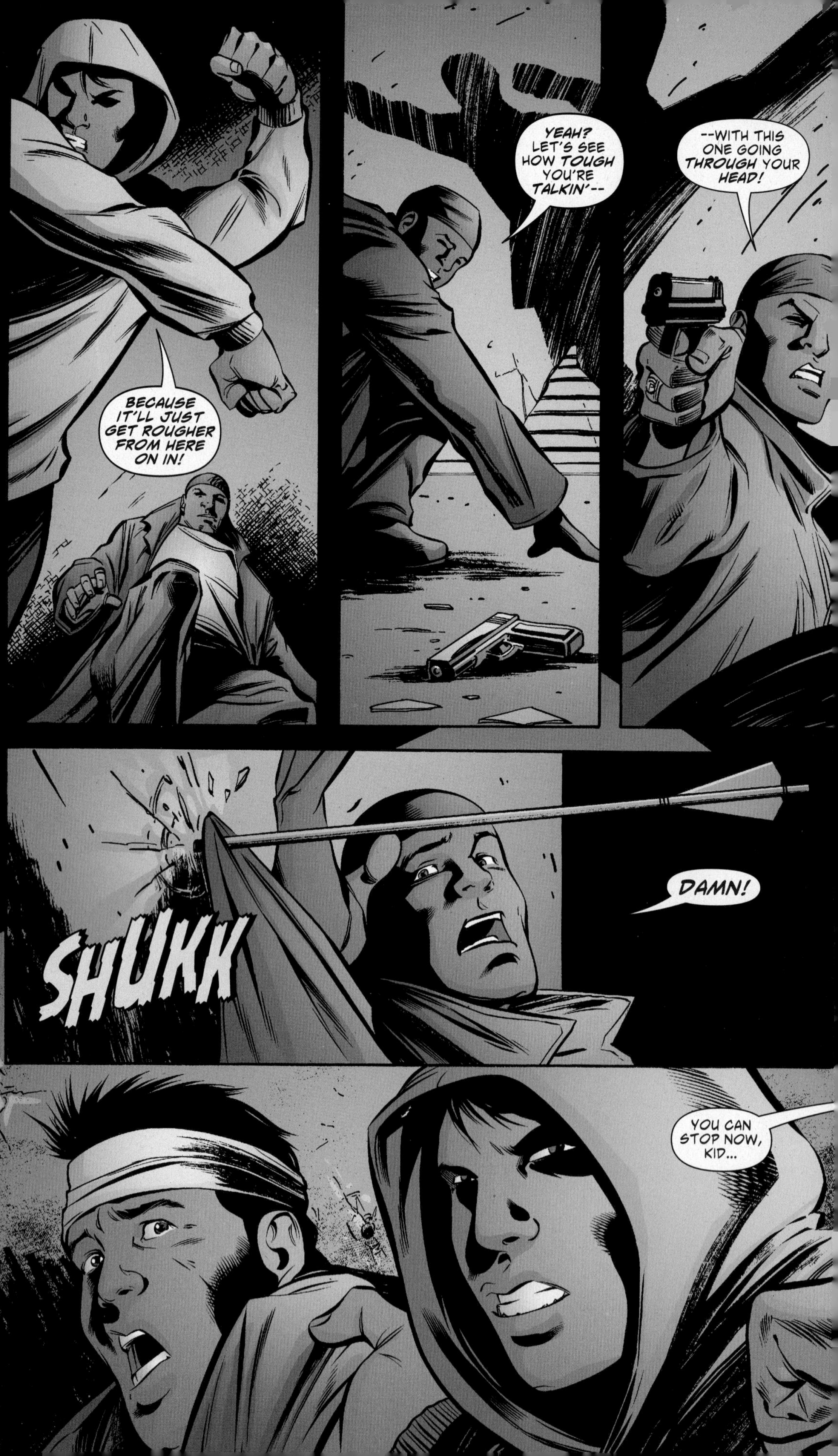
BECAUSE IT'LL JUST GET ROUGHER FROM HERE ON IN!
YEAH? LET'S SEE HOW TOUGH YOU'RE TALKIN'--
--WITH THIS ONE GOING THROUGH YOUR HEAD!
SHUKK
DAMN!
YOU CAN STOP NOW, KID...

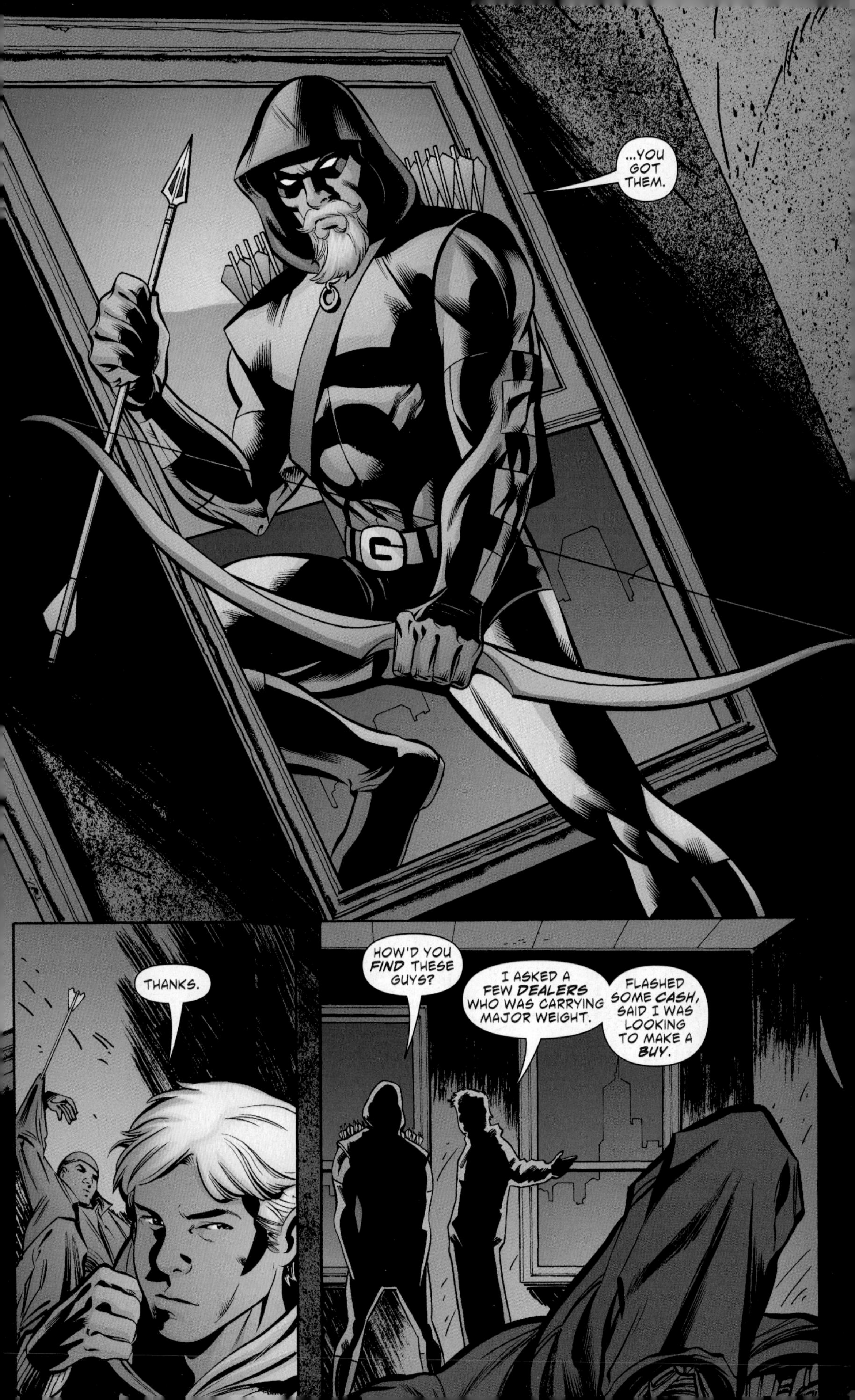

...YOU GOT THEM.
THANKS.
HOW'D YOU FIND THESE GUYS?
I ASKED A FEW DEALERS WHO WAS CARRYING MAJOR WEIGHT.
FLASHED SOME CASH, SAID I WAS LOOKING TO MAKE A BUY.

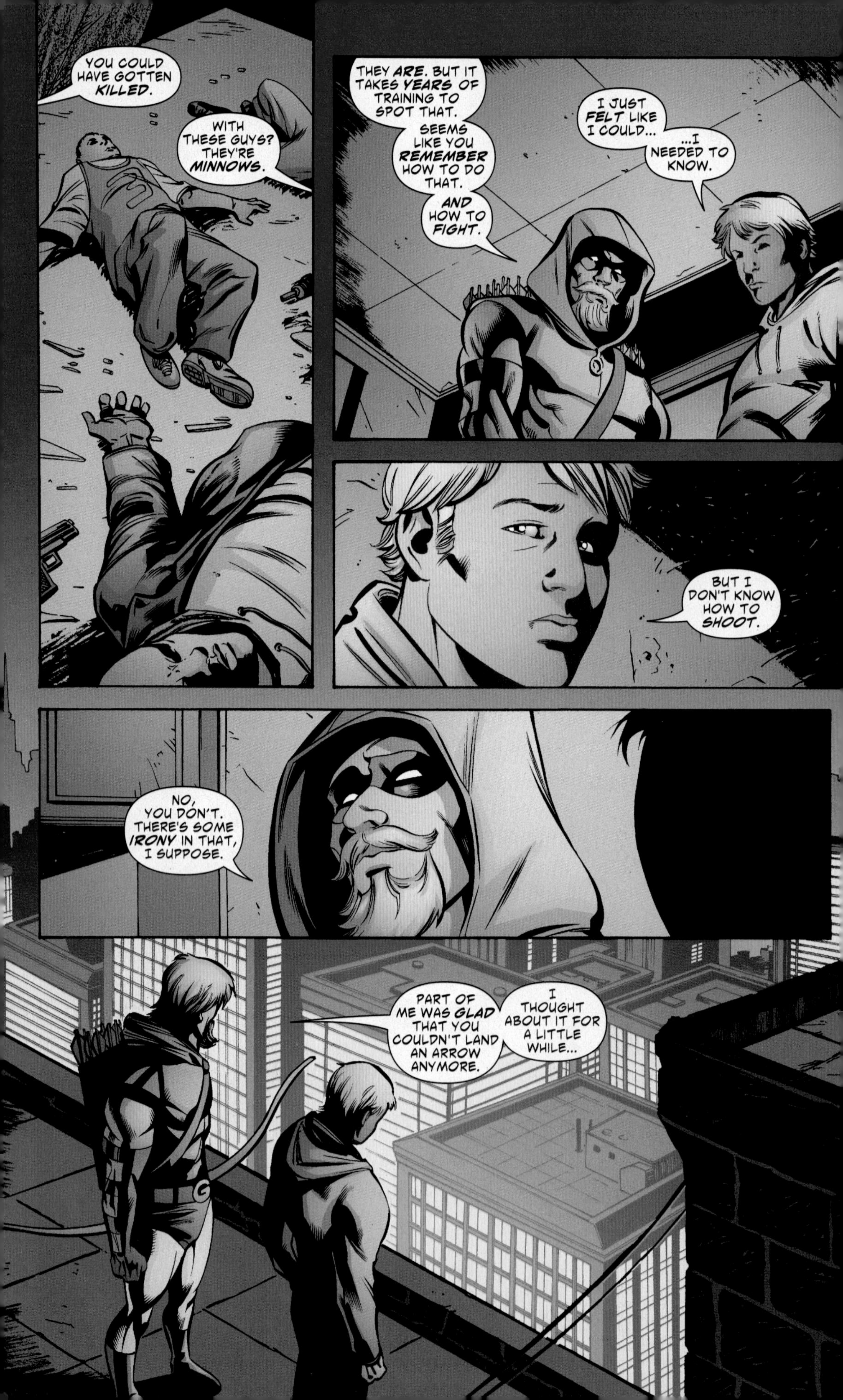
YOU COULD HAVE GOTTEN KILLED.
WITH THESE GUYS? THEY'RE MINNOWS.
THEY ARE. BUT IT TAKES YEARS OF TRAINING TO SPOT THAT.
SEEMS LIKE YOU REMEMBER HOW TO DO THAT.
AND HOW TO FIGHT.
I JUST FELT LIKE I COULD...
...I NEEDED TO KNOW.
BUT I DON'T KNOW HOW TO SHOOT.
NO, YOU DON'T. THERE'S SOME IRONY IN THAT, I SUPPOSE.
I THOUGHT ABOUT IT FOR A LITTLE WHILE...
PART OF ME WAS GLAD THAT YOU COULDN'T LAND AN ARROW ANYMORE.

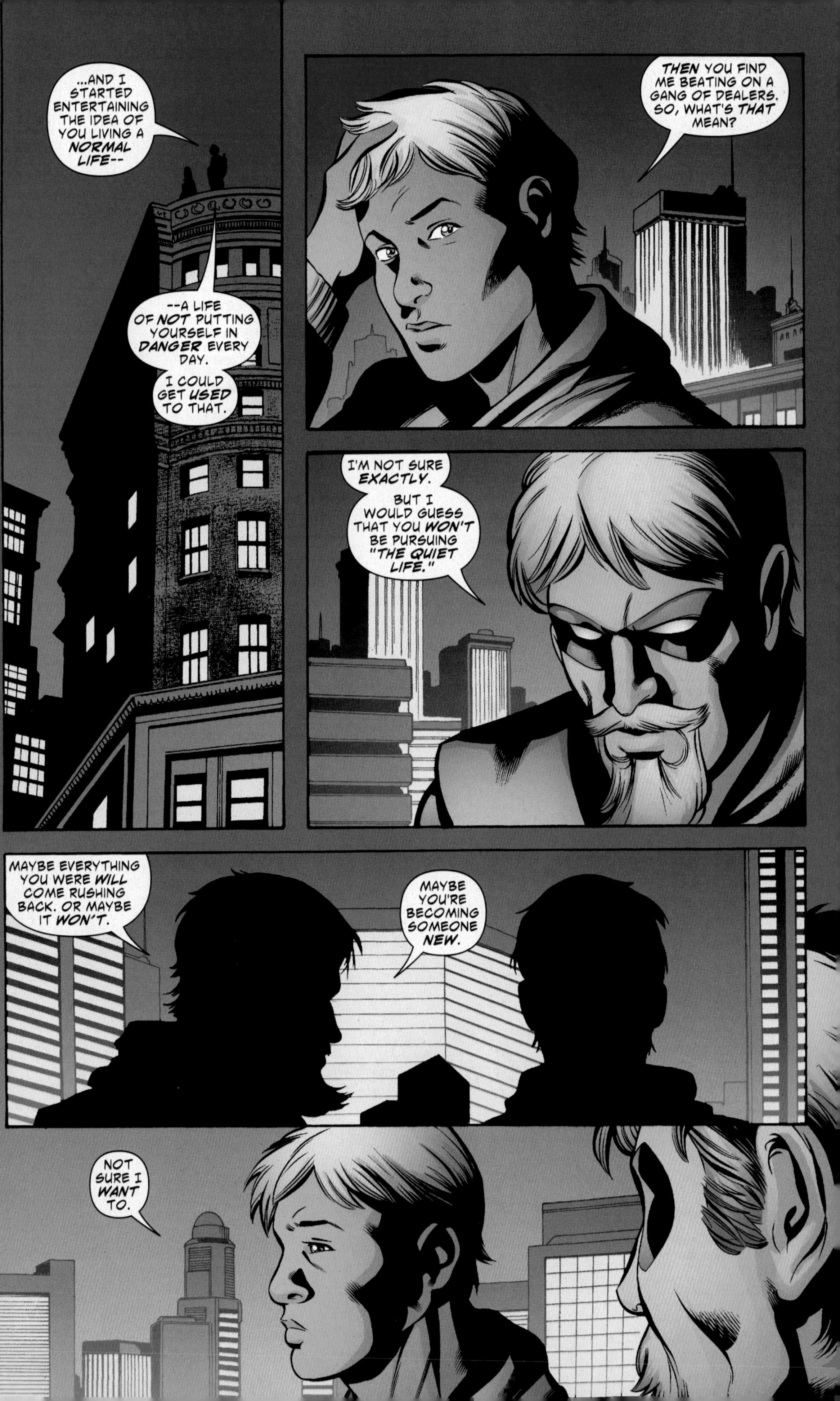
...AND I STARTED ENTERTAINING THE IDEA OF YOU LIVING A NORMAL LIFE--
--A LIFE OF NOT PUTTING YOURSELF IN DANGER EVERY DAY.
I COULD GET USED TO THAT.
THEN YOU FIND ME BEATING ON A GANG OF DEALERS. SO, WHAT'S THAT MEAN?
I'M NOT SURE EXACTLY.
BUT I WOULD GUESS THAT YOU WON'T BE PURSUING "THE QUIET LIFE."
MAYBE EVERYTHING YOU WERE WILL COME RUSHING BACK. OR MAYBE IT WON'T.
MAYBE YOU'RE BECOMING SOMEONE NEW.
NOT SURE I WANT TO.

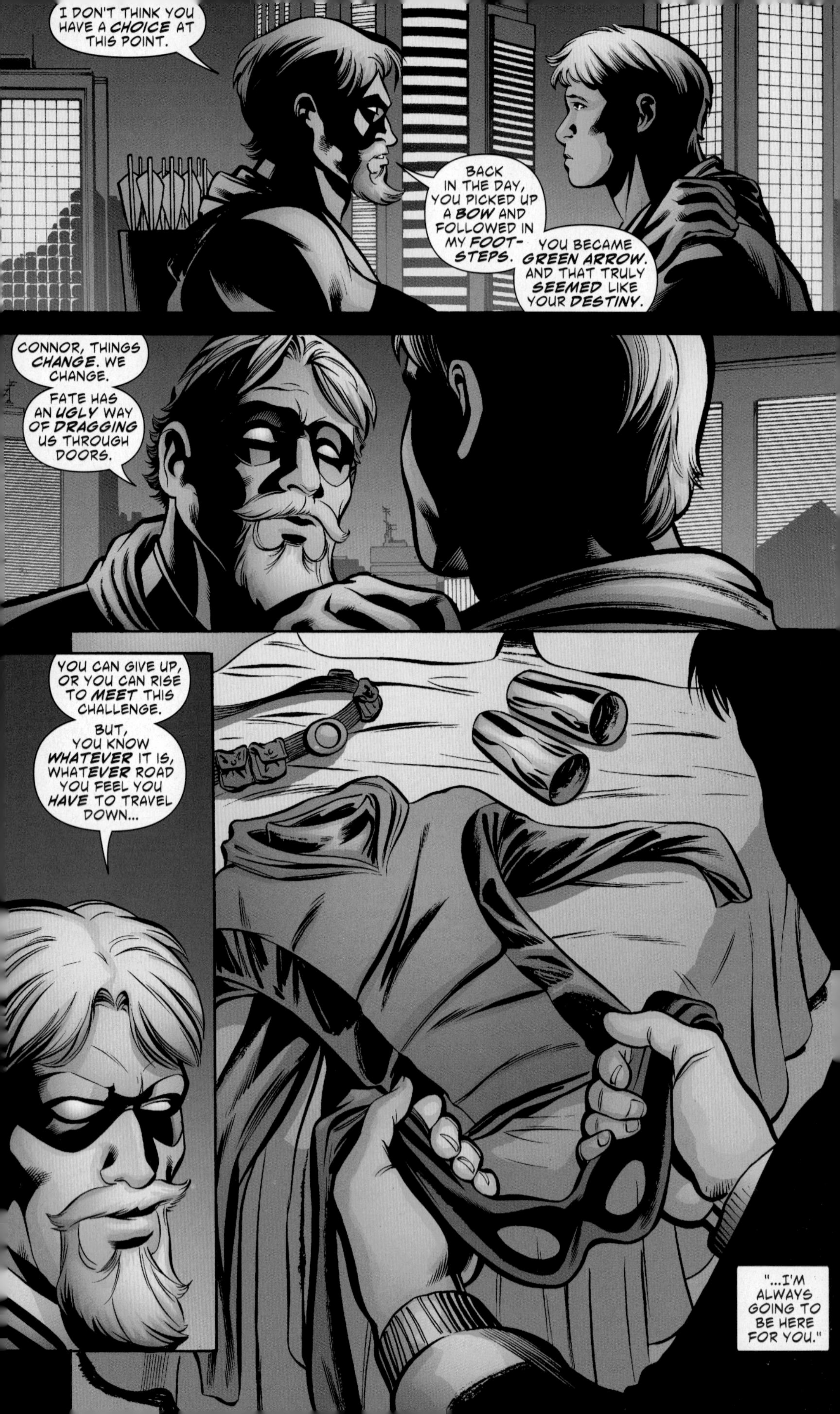

I DON'T THINK YOU HAVE A CHOICE AT THIS POINT.
BACK IN THE DAY, YOU PICKED UP A BOW AND FOLLOWED IN MY FOOT-STEPS.
YOU BECAME GREEN ARROW. AND THAT TRULY SEEMED LIKE YOUR DESTINY.
CONNOR, THINGS CHANGE. WE CHANGE.
FATE HAS AN UGLY WAY OF DRAGGING US THROUGH DOORS.
YOU CAN GIVE UP, OR YOU CAN RISE TO MEET THIS CHALLENGE.
BUT, YOU KNOW WHATEVER IT IS, WHATEVER ROAD YOU FEEL YOU HAVE TO TRAVEL DOWN...
"...I'M ALWAYS GOING TO BE HERE FOR YOU."

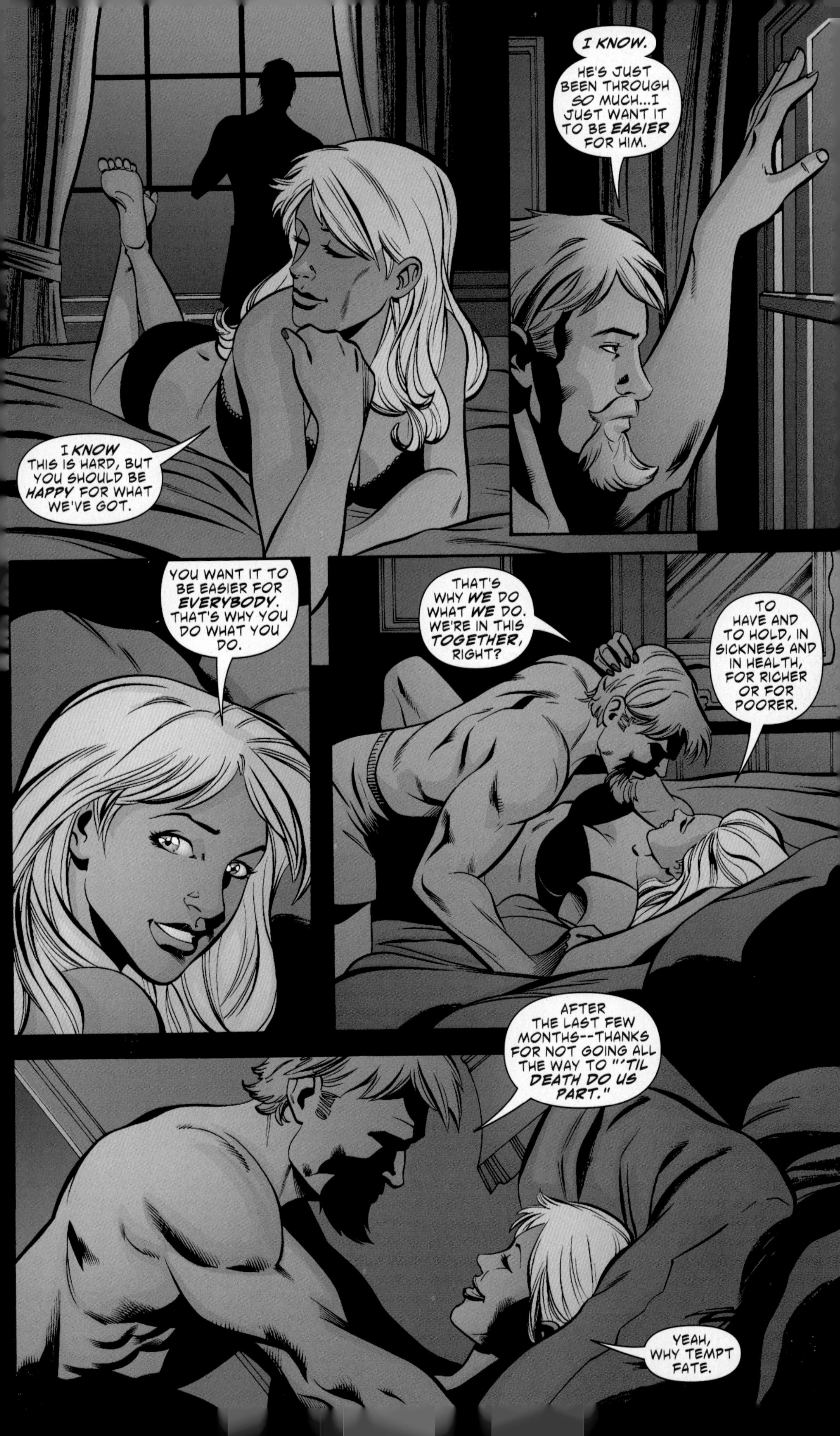
I KNOW THIS IS HARD, BUT YOU SHOULD BE HAPPY FOR WHAT WE'VE GOT.
I KNOW.
HE'S JUST BEEN THROUGH SO MUCH...I JUST WANT IT TO BE EASIER FOR HIM.
YOU WANT IT TO BE EASIER FOR EVERYBODY. THAT'S WHY YOU DO WHAT YOU DO.
THAT'S WHY WE DO WHAT WE DO. WE'RE IN THIS TOGETHER, RIGHT?
TO HAVE AND TO HOLD, IN SICKNESS AND IN HEALTH, FOR RICHER OR FOR POORER.
AFTER THE LAST FEW MONTHS--THANKS FOR NOT GOING ALL THE WAY TO "'TIL DEATH DO US PART."
YEAH, WHY TEMPT FATE.

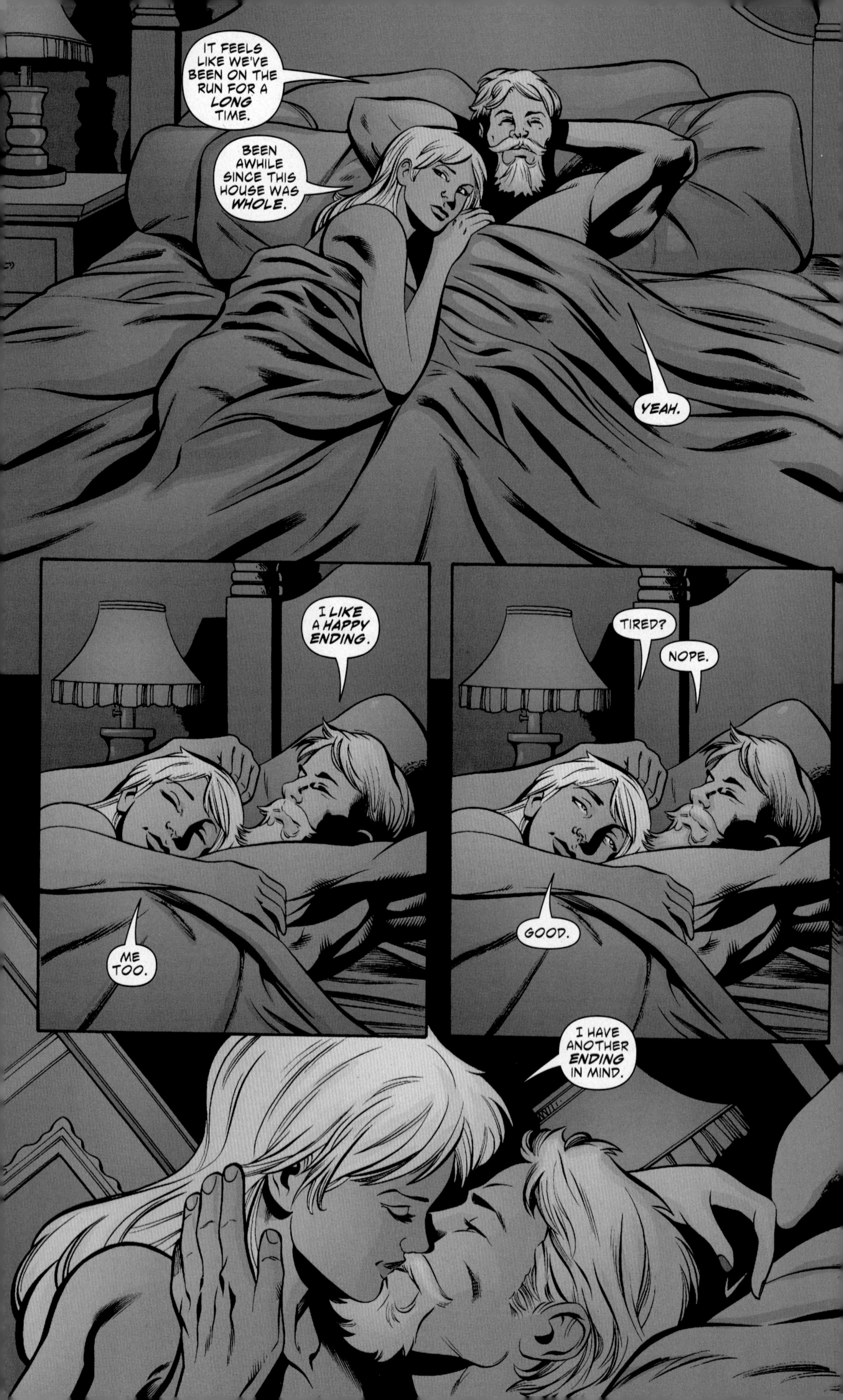
IT FEELS LIKE WE'VE BEEN ON THE RUN FOR A LONG TIME.
BEEN AWHILE SINCE THIS HOUSE WAS WHOLE.
YEAH.
I LIKE A HAPPY ENDING.
ME TOO.
TIRED?
NOPE.
GOOD.
I HAVE ANOTHER ENDING IN MIND.

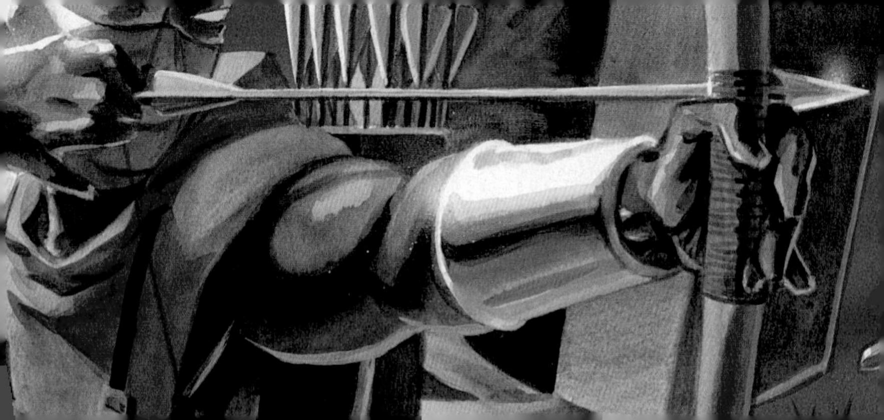

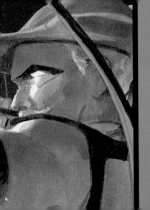

THE PARTING SHOT

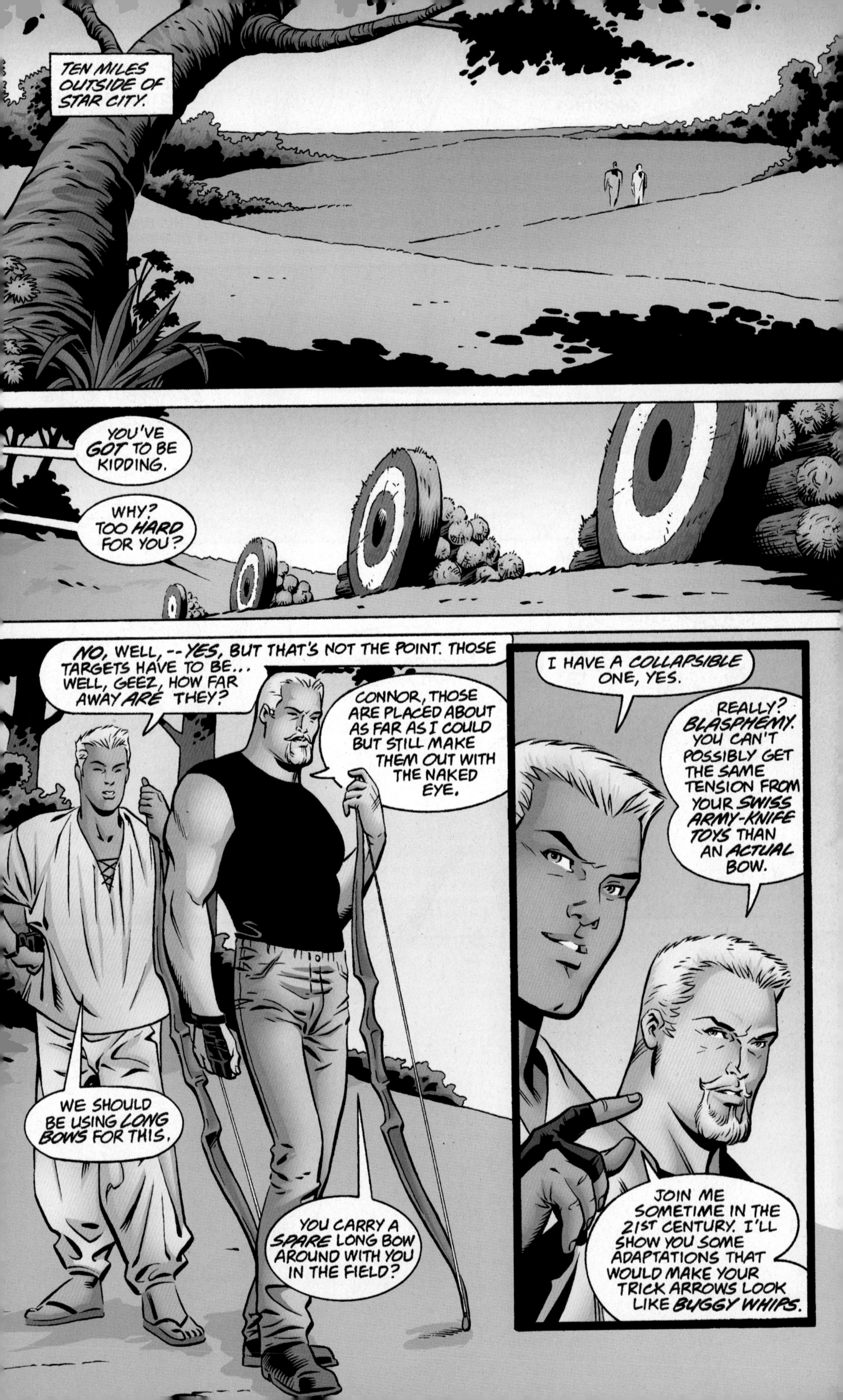
TEN MILES OUTSIDE OF STAR CITY.
YOU'VE GOT TO BE KIDDING.
WHY? TOO HARD FOR YOU?
NO, WELL, --YES, BUT THAT'S NOT THE POINT. THOSE TARGETS HAVE TO BE... WELL, GEEZ, HOW FAR AWAY ARE THEY?
CONNOR, THOSE ARE PLACED ABOUT AS FAR AS I COULD BUT STILL MAKE THEM OUT WITH THE NAKED EYE.
WE SHOULD BE USING LONG BOWS FOR THIS.
YOU CARRY A SPARE LONG BOW AROUND WITH YOU IN THE FIELD?
I HAVE A COLLAPSIBLE ONE, YES.
REALLY? BLASPHEMY. YOU CAN'T POSSIBLY GET THE SAME TENSION FROM YOUR SWISS ARMY-KNIFE TOYS THAN AN ACTUAL BOW.
JOIN ME SOMETIME IN THE 21ST CENTURY. I'LL SHOW YOU SOME ADAPTATIONS THAT WOULD MAKE YOUR TRICK ARROWS LOOK LIKE BUGGY WHIPS.

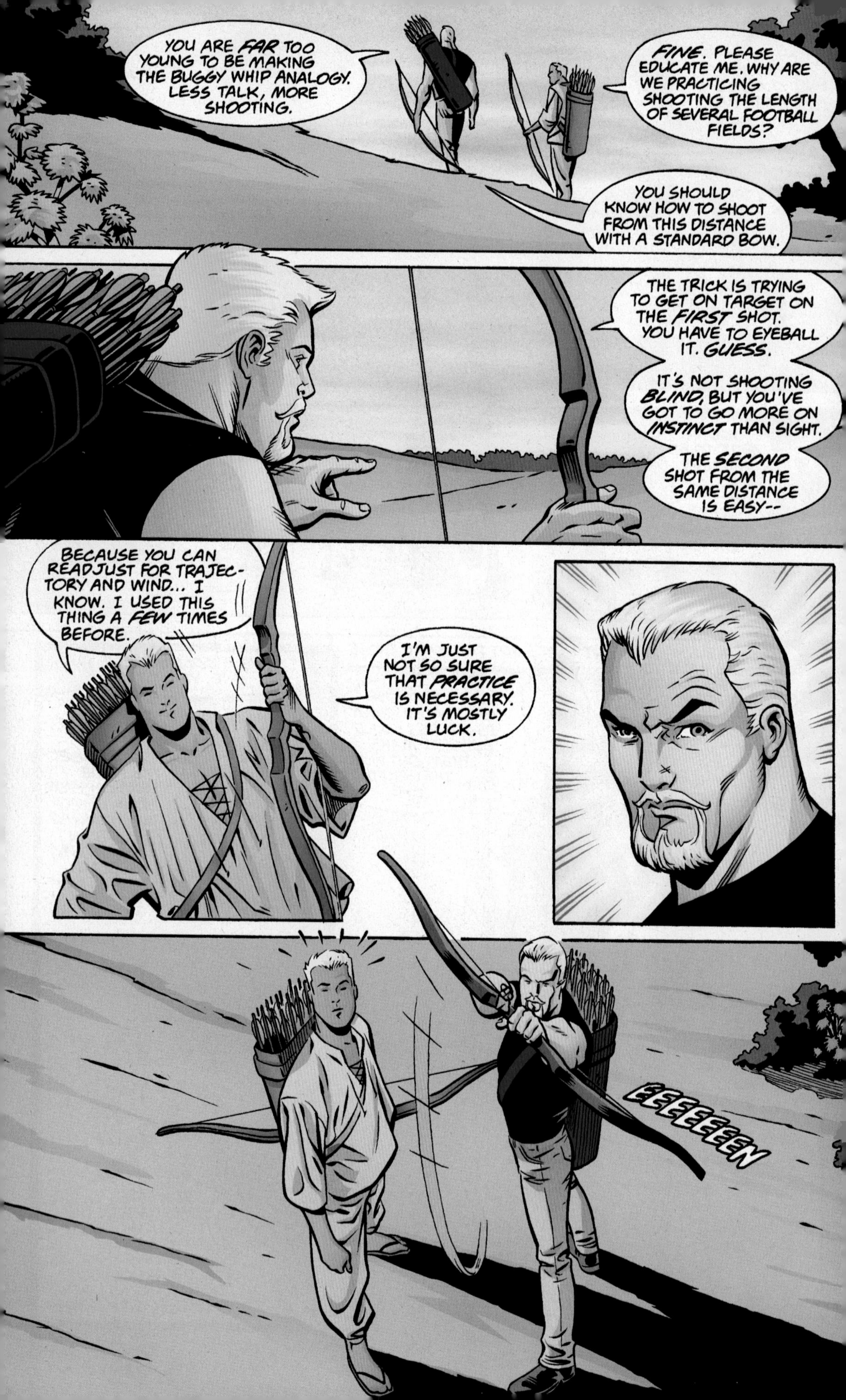
YOU ARE FAR TOO YOUNG TO BE MAKING THE BUGGY WHIP ANALOGY. LESS TALK, MORE SHOOTING.
FINE. PLEASE EDUCATE ME. WHY ARE WE PRACTICING SHOOTING THE LENGTH OF SEVERAL FOOTBALL FIELDS?
YOU SHOULD KNOW HOW TO SHOOT FROM THIS DISTANCE WITH A STANDARD BOW.
THE TRICK IS TRYING TO GET ON TARGET ON THE FIRST SHOT. YOU HAVE TO EYEBALL IT. GUESS.
IT'S NOT SHOOTING BLIND, BUT YOU'VE GOT TO GO MORE ON INSTINCT THAN SIGHT.
THE SECOND SHOT FROM THE SAME DISTANCE IS EASY--
BECAUSE YOU CAN READJUST FOR TRAJECTORY AND WIND... I KNOW. I USED THIS THING A FEW TIMES BEFORE.
I'M JUST NOT SO SURE THAT PRACTICE IS NECESSARY. IT'S MOSTLY LUCK.
EEEEEEEEN

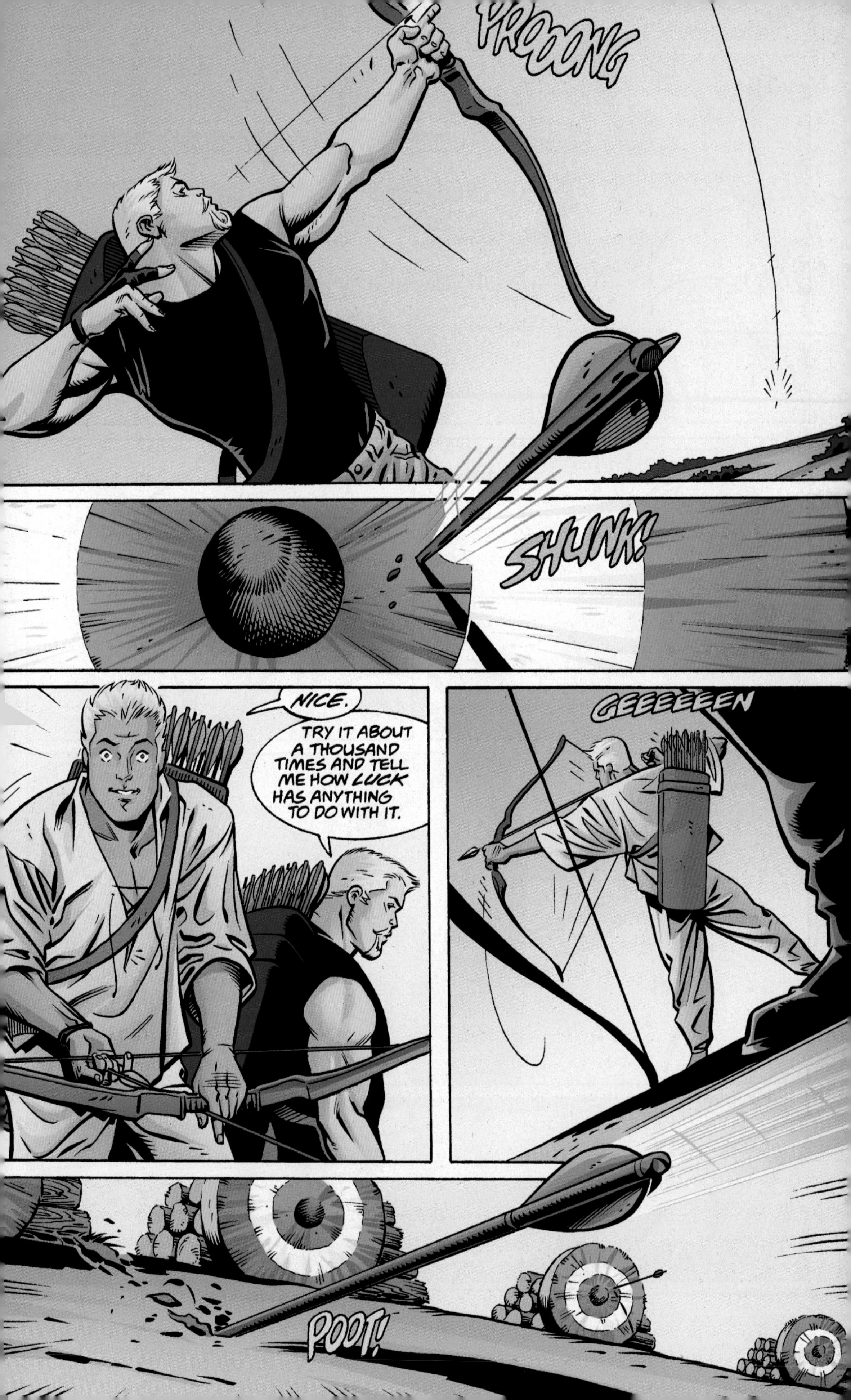
YROOOONG
SHUNK!
NICE.
TRY IT ABOUT A THOUSAND TIMES AND TELL ME HOW *LUCK* HAS ANYTHING TO DO WITH IT.
GEEEEEEN
POOT!

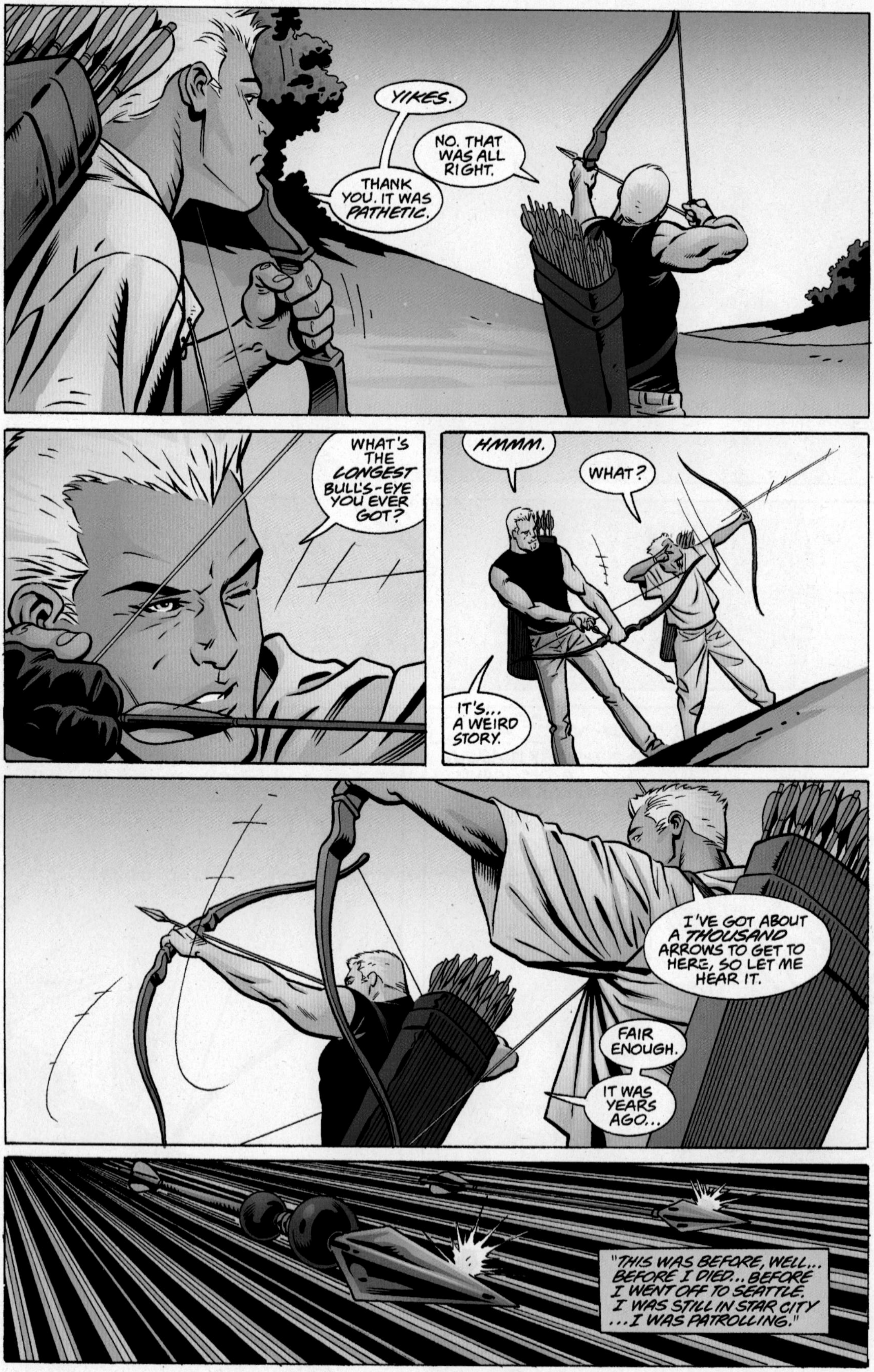
YIKES.
NO. THAT WAS ALL RIGHT.
THANK YOU. IT WAS PATHETIC.
WHAT'S THE LONGEST BULL'S-EYE YOU EVER GOT?
HMMM.
WHAT?
IT'S... A WEIRD STORY.
I'VE GOT ABOUT A THOUSAND ARROWS TO GET TO HERE, SO LET ME HEAR IT.
FAIR ENOUGH.
IT WAS YEARS AGO...
"THIS WAS BEFORE, WELL... BEFORE I DIED... BEFORE I WENT OFF TO SEATTLE. I WAS STILL IN STAR CITY ...I WAS PATROLLING."

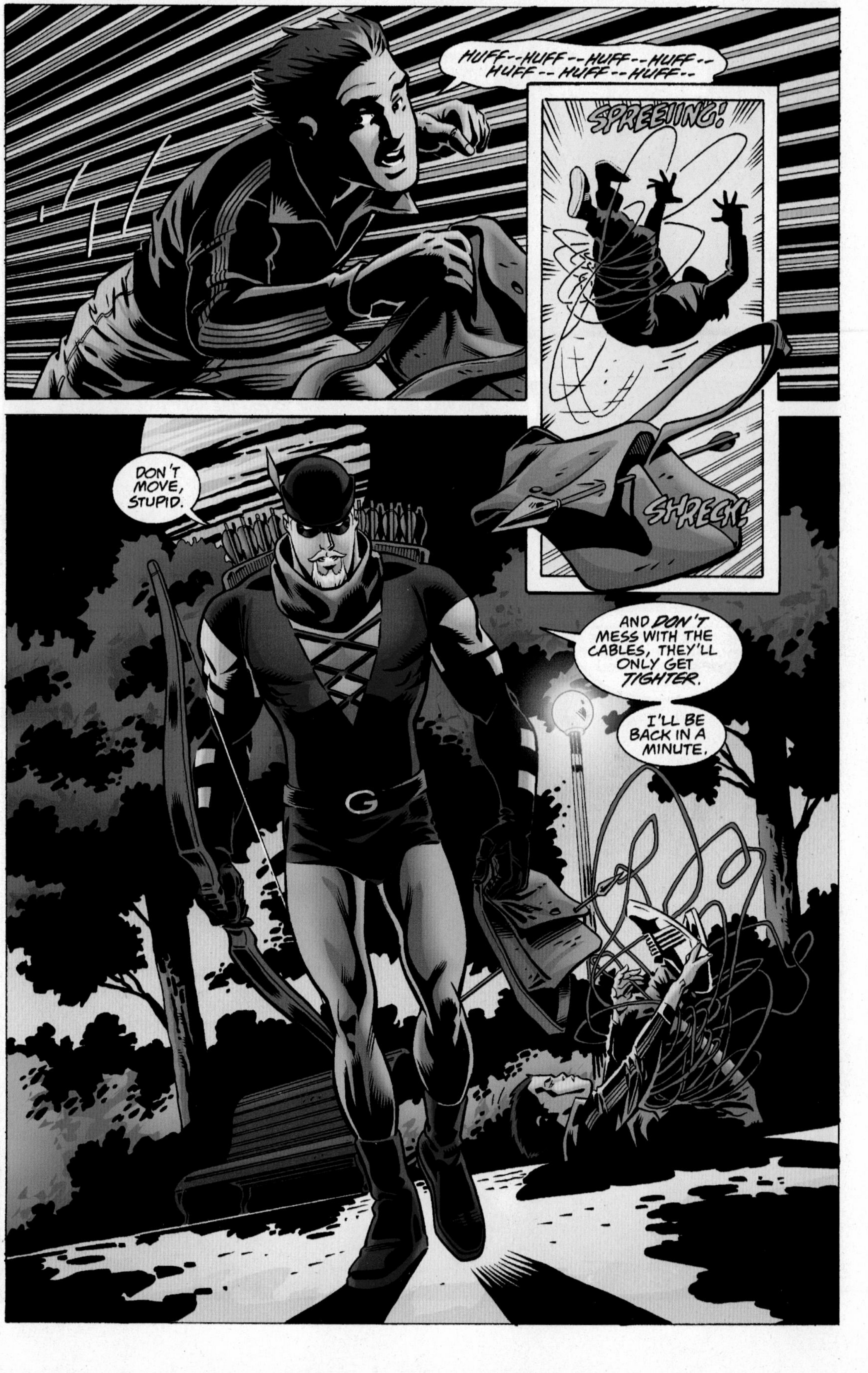
HUFF--HUFF--HUFF--HUFF--
HUFF--HUFF--HUFF--
SPREEIING!
DON'T MOVE, STUPID.
SHRECK!
AND DON'T MESS WITH THE CABLES, THEY'LL ONLY GET TIGHTER.
I'LL BE BACK IN A MINUTE.

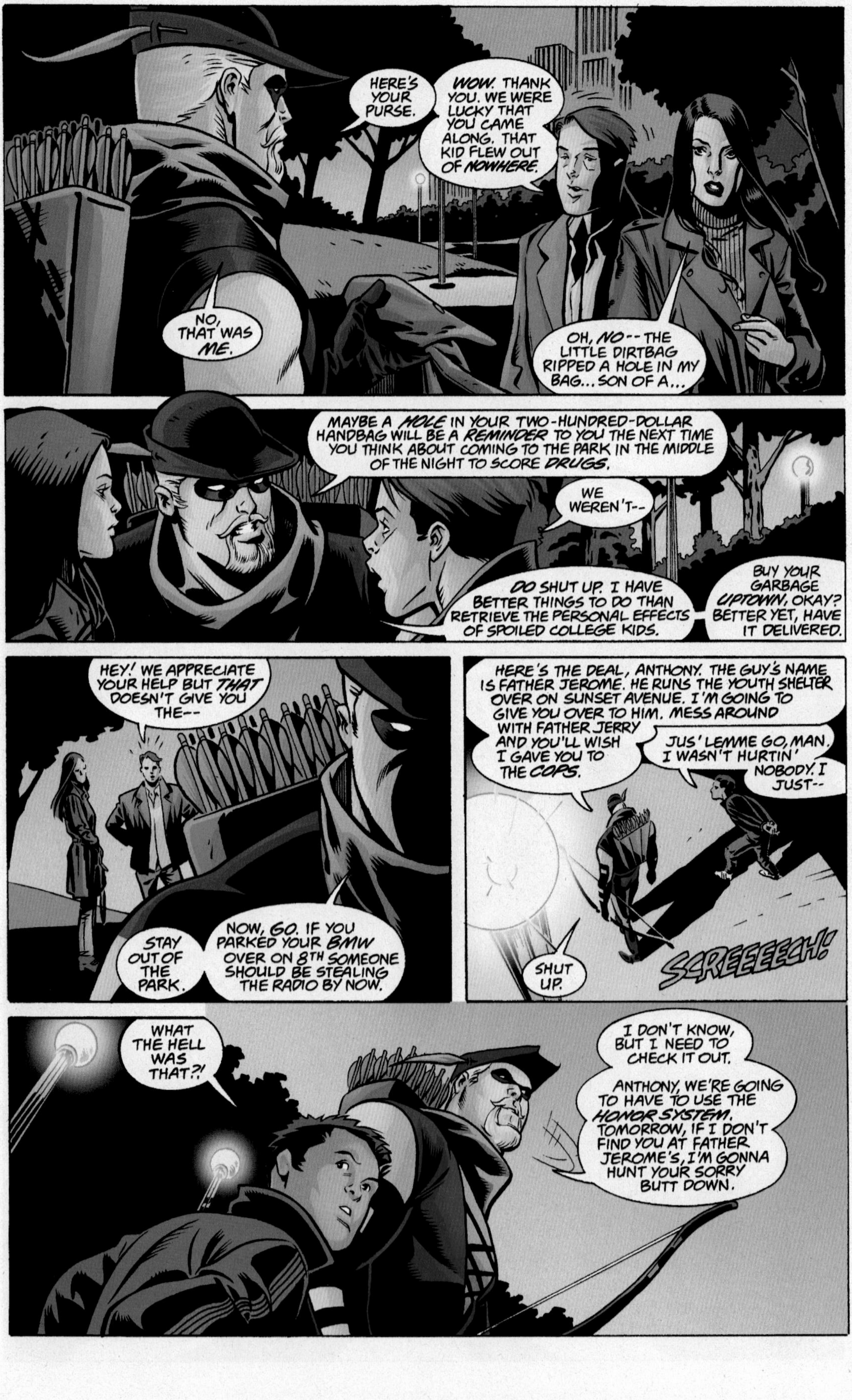

HERE'S YOUR PURSE.
WOW. THANK YOU. WE WERE LUCKY THAT YOU CAME ALONG. THAT KID FLEW OUT OF NOWHERE.
NO, THAT WAS ME.
OH, NO-- THE LITTLE DIRTBAG RIPPED A HOLE IN MY BAG... SON OF A...
MAYBE A HOLE IN YOUR TWO-HUNDRED-DOLLAR HANDBAG WILL BE A REMINDER TO YOU THE NEXT TIME YOU THINK ABOUT COMING TO THE PARK IN THE MIDDLE OF THE NIGHT TO SCORE DRUGS.
WE WEREN'T--
DO SHUT UP. I HAVE BETTER THINGS TO DO THAN RETRIEVE THE PERSONAL EFFECTS OF SPOILED COLLEGE KIDS.
BUY YOUR GARBAGE UPTOWN, OKAY? BETTER YET, HAVE IT DELIVERED.
HEY! WE APPRECIATE YOUR HELP BUT THAT DOESN'T GIVE YOU THE--
STAY OUT OF THE PARK.
NOW, GO. IF YOU PARKED YOUR BMW OVER ON 8TH SOMEONE SHOULD BE STEALING THE RADIO BY NOW.
HERE'S THE DEAL, ANTHONY. THE GUY'S NAME IS FATHER JEROME. HE RUNS THE YOUTH SHELTER OVER ON SUNSET AVENUE. I'M GOING TO GIVE YOU OVER TO HIM. MESS AROUND WITH FATHER JERRY AND YOU'LL WISH I GAVE YOU TO THE COPS.
JUS' LEMME GO, MAN. I WASN'T HURTIN' NOBODY. I JUST--
SHUT UP.
SCREEEEECH!
WHAT THE HELL WAS THAT?!
I DON'T KNOW, BUT I NEED TO CHECK IT OUT.
ANTHONY, WE'RE GOING TO HAVE TO USE THE HONOR SYSTEM. TOMORROW, IF I DON'T FIND YOU AT FATHER JEROME'S, I'M GONNA HUNT YOUR SORRY BUTT DOWN.

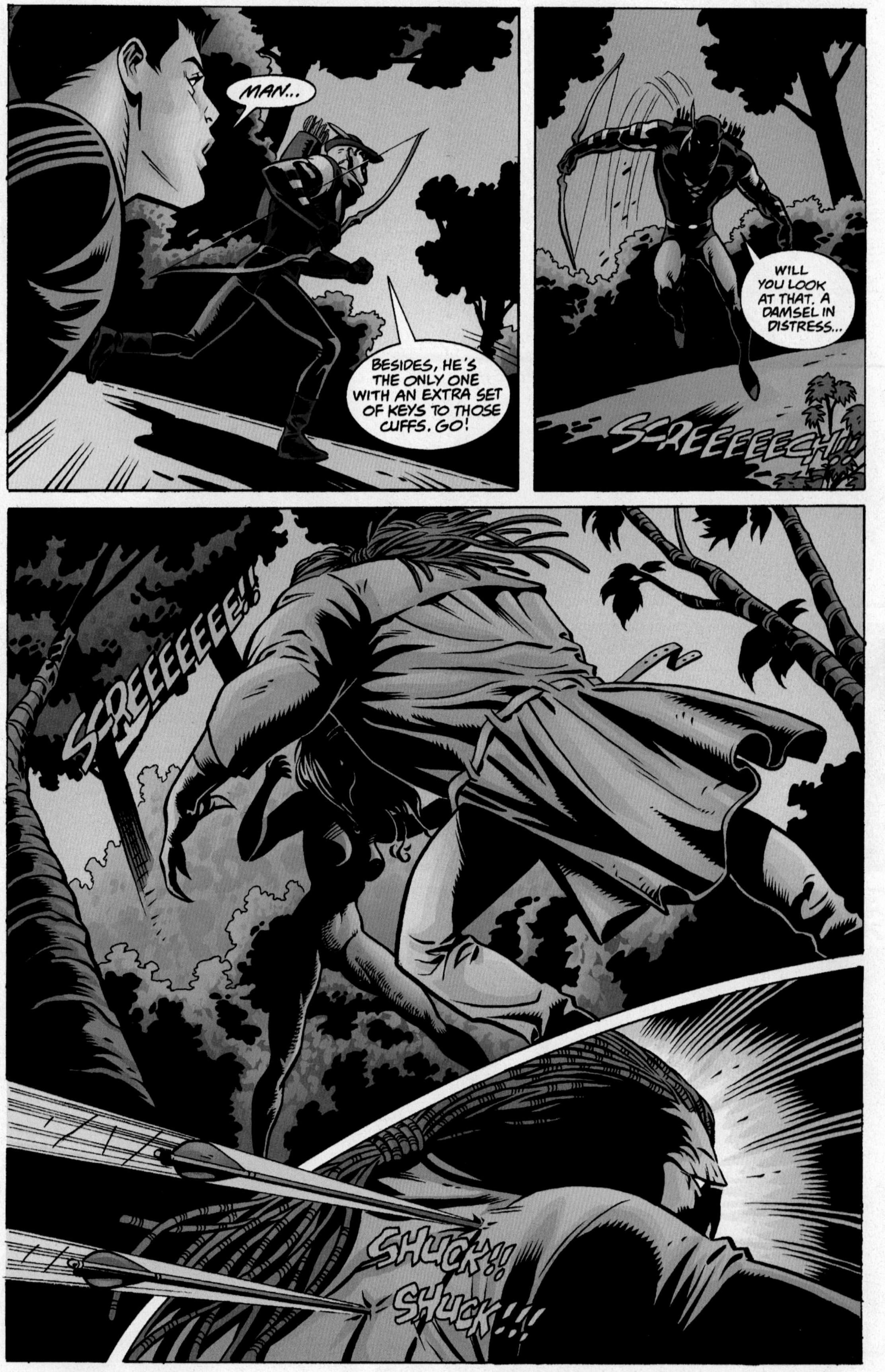
MAN...
BESIDES, HE'S THE ONLY ONE WITH AN EXTRA SET OF KEYS TO THOSE CUFFS. GO!
WILL YOU LOOK AT THAT. A DAMSEL IN DISTRESS...
SCREEEEEEECH!!
SCREEEEEEE!!
SHUCK!!
SHUCK!!!

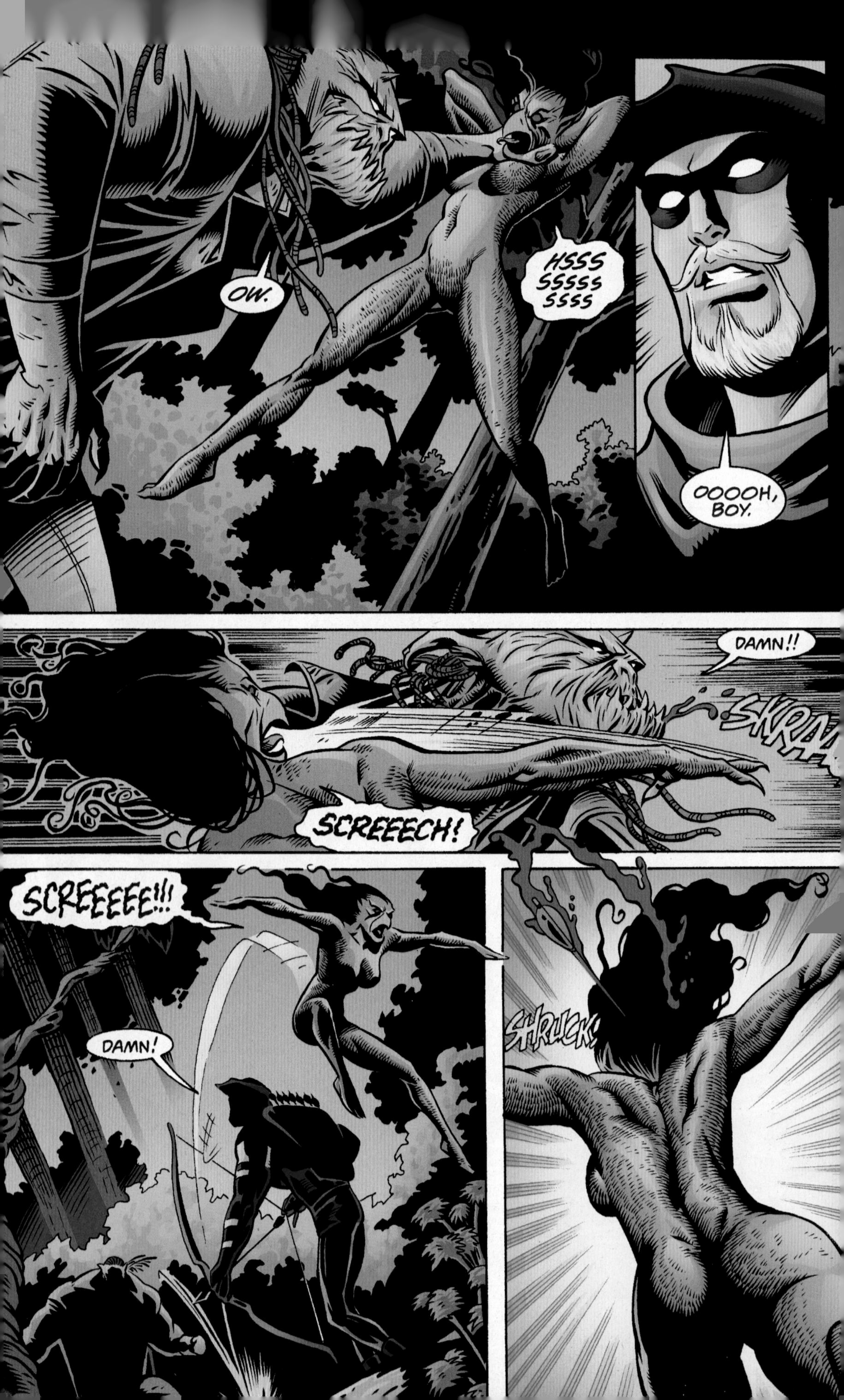
OW.
HSSS
SSSSS
SSSS
OOOOH, BOY.
DAMN!!
SKRA
SCREEECH!
SCREEEEE!!!
DAMN!
SHRUCK

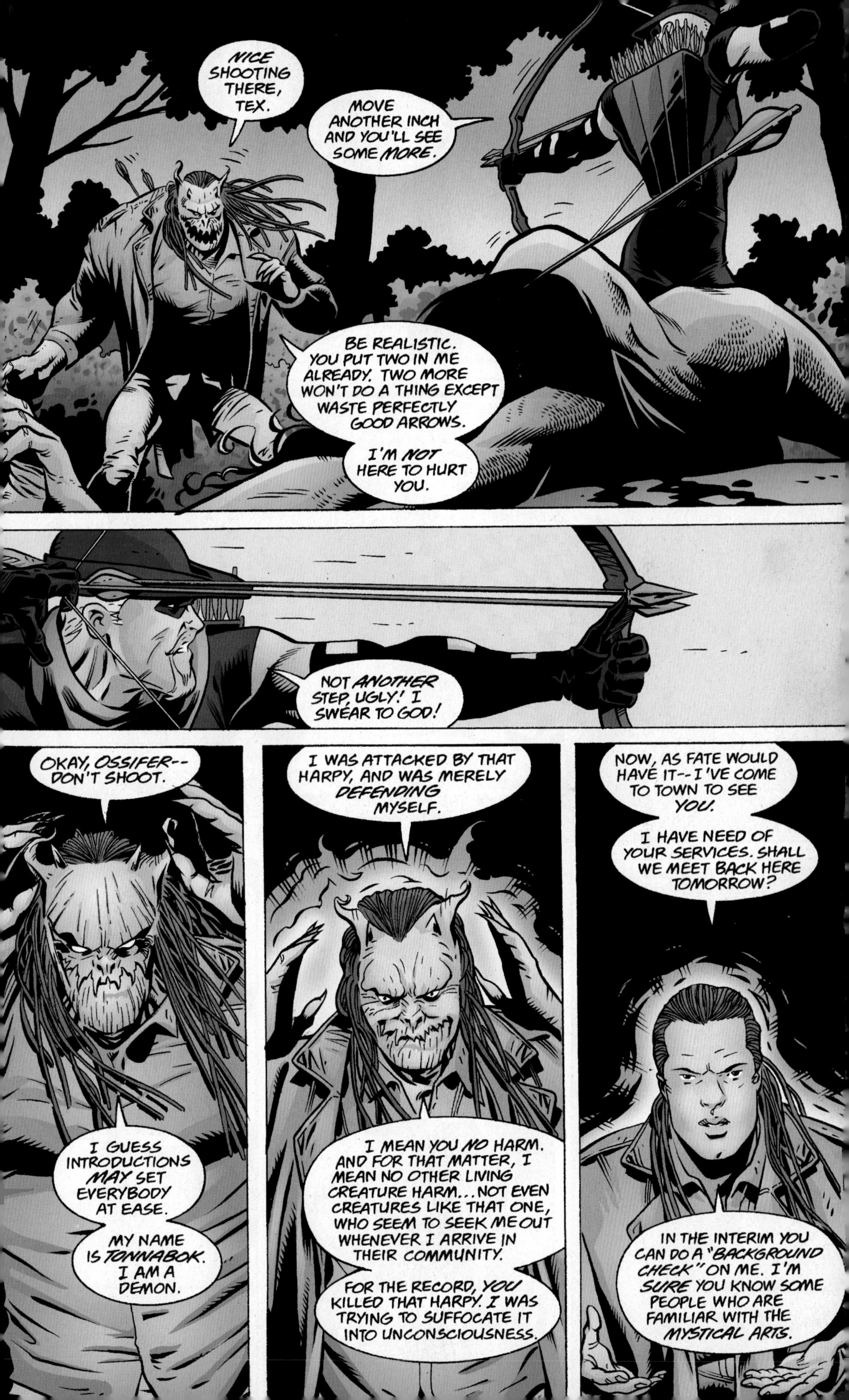
NICE SHOOTING THERE, TEX.
MOVE ANOTHER INCH AND YOU'LL SEE SOME MORE.
BE REALISTIC. YOU PUT TWO IN ME ALREADY. TWO MORE WON'T DO A THING EXCEPT WASTE PERFECTLY GOOD ARROWS.
I'M NOT HERE TO HURT YOU.
NOT ANOTHER STEP, UGLY! I SWEAR TO GOD!
OKAY, OSSIFER-- DON'T SHOOT.
I GUESS INTRODUCTIONS MAY SET EVERYBODY AT EASE.
MY NAME IS TONNABOK. I AM A DEMON.
I WAS ATTACKED BY THAT HARPY, AND WAS MERELY DEFENDING MYSELF.
I MEAN YOU NO HARM. AND FOR THAT MATTER, I MEAN NO OTHER LIVING CREATURE HARM...NOT EVEN CREATURES LIKE THAT ONE, WHO SEEM TO SEEK ME OUT WHENEVER I ARRIVE IN THEIR COMMUNITY.
FOR THE RECORD, YOU KILLED THAT HARPY. I WAS TRYING TO SUFFOCATE IT INTO UNCONSCIOUSNESS.
NOW, AS FATE WOULD HAVE IT-- I'VE COME TO TOWN TO SEE YOU.
I HAVE NEED OF YOUR SERVICES. SHALL WE MEET BACK HERE TOMORROW?
IN THE INTERIM YOU CAN DO A "BACKGROUND CHECK" ON ME. I'M SURE YOU KNOW SOME PEOPLE WHO ARE FAMILIAR WITH THE MYSTICAL ARTS.

ALL RIGHT.

SPLENDID.

DO YOU WANT THESE BACK?

THE HOME OF JASON BLOOD. THE HUMAN ALTER EGO OF THE DEMON ETRIGAN.

TONNABOK. OF COURSE I'VE HEARD OF HIM. HE'S A PERPETUAS DEMON, THE ONLY ONE OF THIS AGE...I NEVER THOUGHT I'D EVER COME ACROSS ONE. AMAZING CREATURES.

PERPETUAS DEMONS ARE IMMORTAL AND INDESTRUCTIBLE IN EVERY SENSE OF THE WORD. THEY JUST CAN'T DIE. THEY COULDN'T EVEN TAKE THEIR OWN LIVES.

OKAY, SO HE'S OLD.

NOT JUST OLD.

IN TERMS OF LIVING FLESH CREATURES-- HE IS ANCIENT. TONNABOK IS NEARLY ELEVEN HUNDRED YEARS OLD.

MORE IMPORTANT FOR YOU, HE CAN BE TRUSTED.

HE'S A GOOD DEMON, HUH?

IN TRUTH, YES. BUT THAT WASN'T ALWAYS THE CASE.

FOR THE FIRST THREE HUNDRED YEARS OF HIS EXISTENCE, THERE WAS NO GREATER SCOURGE ON EARTH.

HE STOLE, RAVAGED, TORTURED...MURDERED BY THE THOUSANDS. THERE ISN'T AN UN-SPEAKABLE ACT THAT HE DIDN'T PERPETRATE A HUNDRED TIMES OVER.

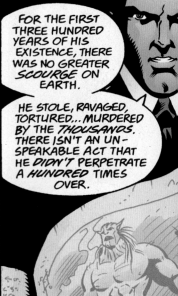

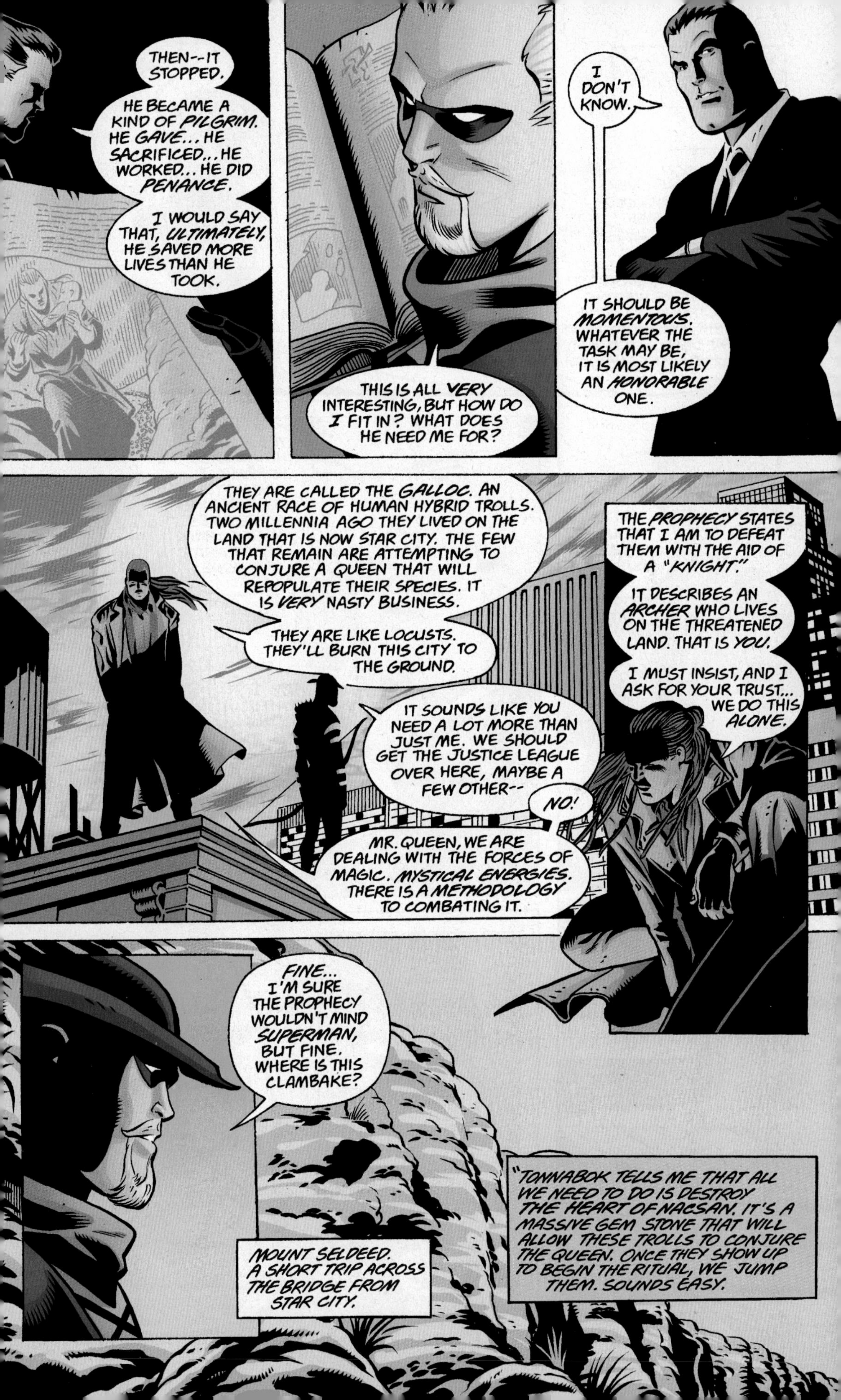

THEN--IT STOPPED.
HE BECAME A KIND OF PILGRIM. HE GAVE... HE SACRIFICED... HE WORKED... HE DID PENANCE.
I WOULD SAY THAT, ULTIMATELY, HE SAVED MORE LIVES THAN HE TOOK.
THIS IS ALL VERY INTERESTING, BUT HOW DO I FIT IN? WHAT DOES HE NEED ME FOR?
I DON'T KNOW.
IT SHOULD BE MOMENTOUS. WHATEVER THE TASK MAY BE, IT IS MOST LIKELY AN HONORABLE ONE.
THEY ARE CALLED THE GALLOC. AN ANCIENT RACE OF HUMAN HYBRID TROLLS. TWO MILLENNIA AGO THEY LIVED ON THE LAND THAT IS NOW STAR CITY. THE FEW THAT REMAIN ARE ATTEMPTING TO CONJURE A QUEEN THAT WILL REPOPULATE THEIR SPECIES. IT IS VERY NASTY BUSINESS.
THEY ARE LIKE LOCUSTS. THEY'LL BURN THIS CITY TO THE GROUND.
THE PROPHECY STATES THAT I AM TO DEFEAT THEM WITH THE AID OF A "KNIGHT."
IT DESCRIBES AN ARCHER WHO LIVES ON THE THREATENED LAND. THAT IS YOU.
I MUST INSIST, AND I ASK FOR YOUR TRUST... WE DO THIS ALONE.
IT SOUNDS LIKE YOU NEED A LOT MORE THAN JUST ME. WE SHOULD GET THE JUSTICE LEAGUE OVER HERE, MAYBE A FEW OTHER--
NO!
MR. QUEEN, WE ARE DEALING WITH THE FORCES OF MAGIC. MYSTICAL ENERGIES. THERE IS A METHODOLOGY TO COMBATING IT.
FINE... I'M SURE THE PROPHECY WOULDN'T MIND SUPERMAN, BUT FINE. WHERE IS THIS CLAMBAKE?
MOUNT SELDEED. A SHORT TRIP ACROSS THE BRIDGE FROM STAR CITY.
"TONNABOK TELLS ME THAT ALL WE NEED TO DO IS DESTROY THE HEART OF NACSAN. IT'S A MASSIVE GEM STONE THAT WILL ALLOW THESE TROLLS TO CONJURE THE QUEEN. ONCE THEY SHOW UP TO BEGIN THE RITUAL, WE JUMP THEM. SOUNDS EASY.

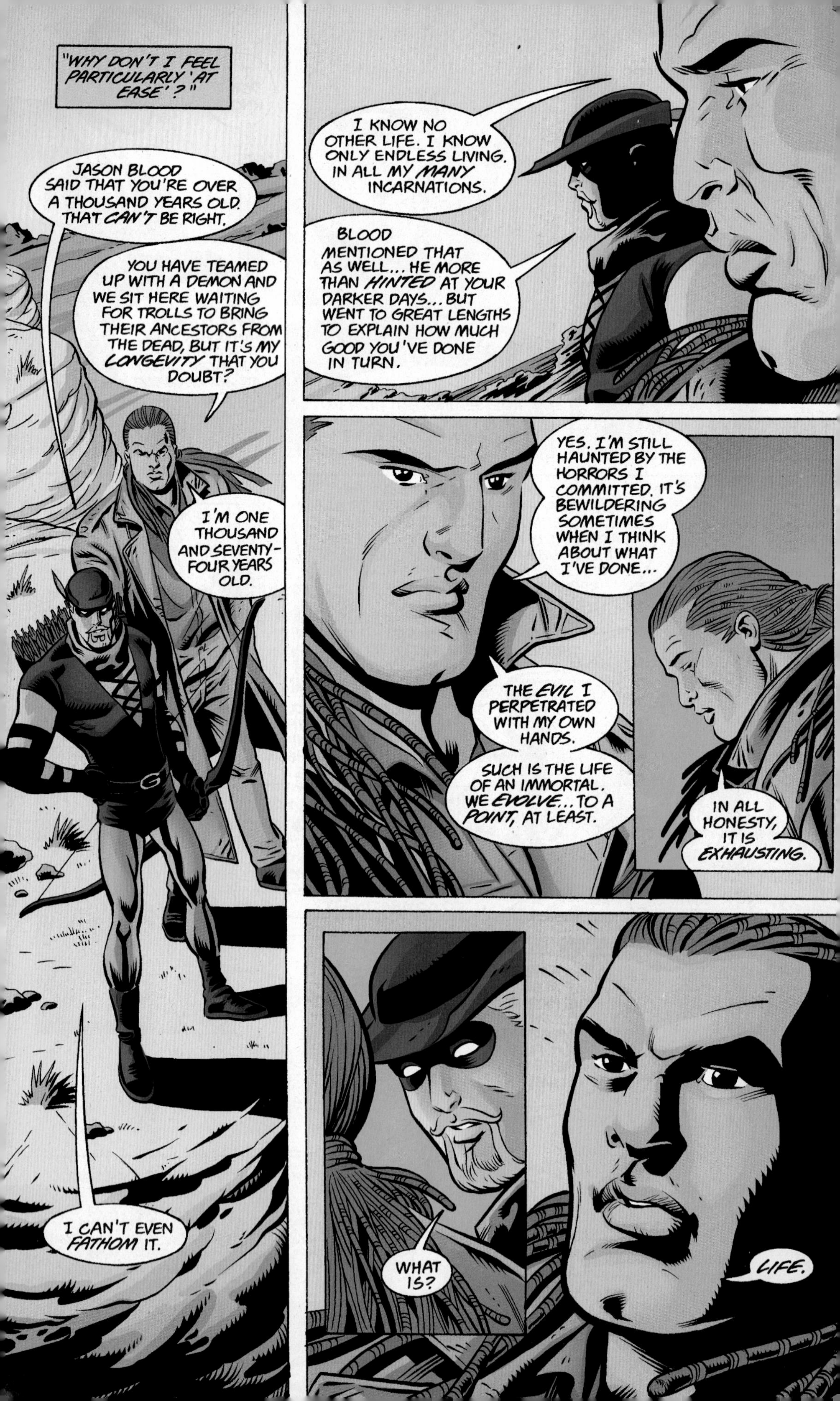
"WHY DON'T I FEEL PARTICULARLY 'AT EASE'?"
JASON BLOOD SAID THAT YOU'RE OVER A THOUSAND YEARS OLD. THAT CAN'T BE RIGHT.
YOU HAVE TEAMED UP WITH A DEMON AND WE SIT HERE WAITING FOR TROLLS TO BRING THEIR ANCESTORS FROM THE DEAD, BUT IT'S MY LONGEVITY THAT YOU DOUBT?
I'M ONE THOUSAND AND SEVENTY-FOUR YEARS OLD.
I CAN'T EVEN FATHOM IT.
I KNOW NO OTHER LIFE. I KNOW ONLY ENDLESS LIVING. IN ALL MY MANY INCARNATIONS.
BLOOD MENTIONED THAT AS WELL... HE MORE THAN HINTED AT YOUR DARKER DAYS... BUT WENT TO GREAT LENGTHS TO EXPLAIN HOW MUCH GOOD YOU'VE DONE IN TURN.
YES. I'M STILL HAUNTED BY THE HORRORS I COMMITTED. IT'S BEWILDERING SOMETIMES WHEN I THINK ABOUT WHAT I'VE DONE...
THE EVIL I PERPETRATED WITH MY OWN HANDS.
SUCH IS THE LIFE OF AN IMMORTAL. WE EVOLVE... TO A POINT, AT LEAST.
IN ALL HONESTY, IT IS EXHAUSTING.
WHAT IS?
LIFE.

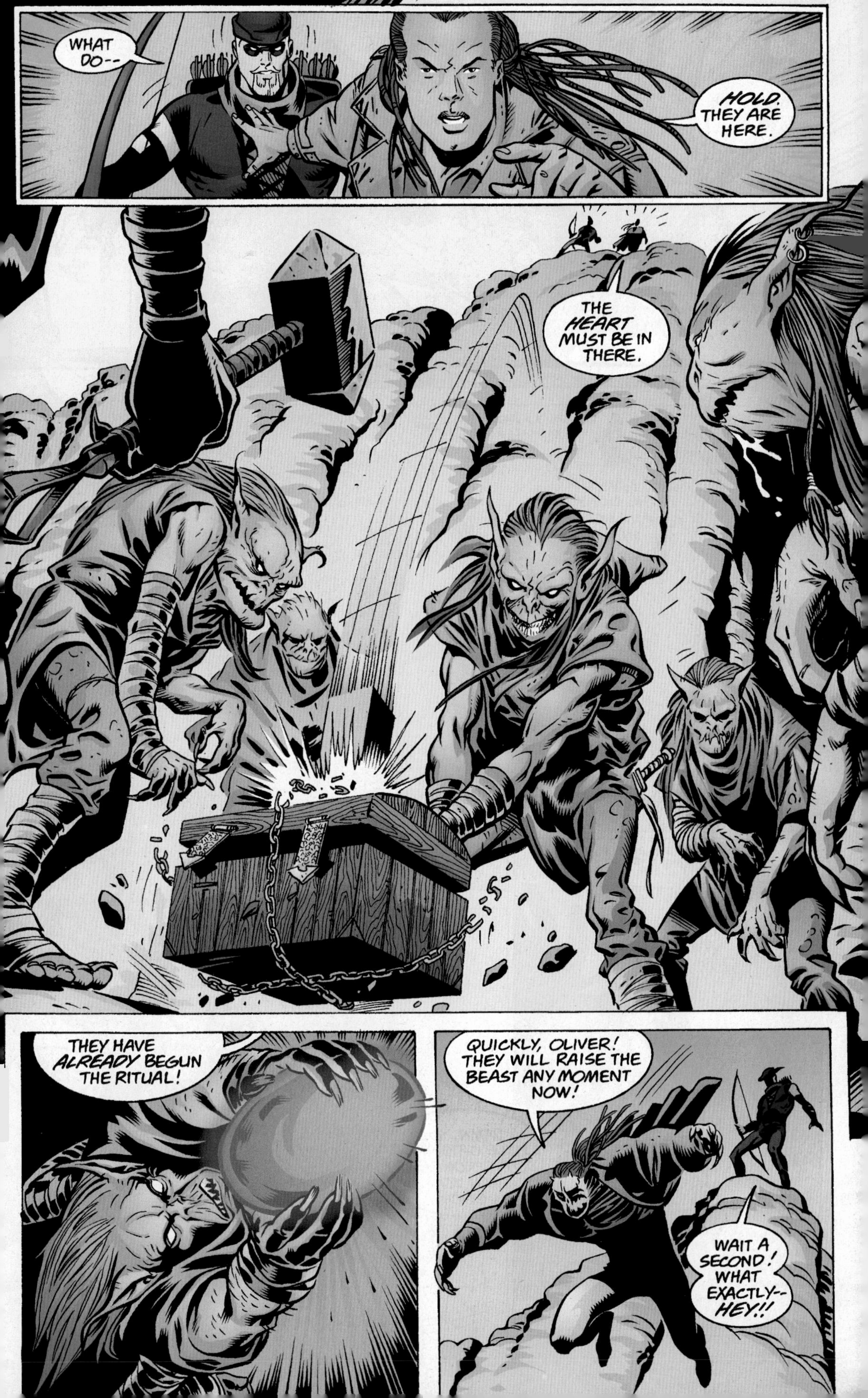
WHAT DO--
HOLD. THEY ARE HERE.
THE HEART MUST BE IN THERE.
THEY HAVE ALREADY BEGUN THE RITUAL!
QUICKLY, OLIVER! THEY WILL RAISE THE BEAST ANY MOMENT NOW!
WAIT A SECOND! WHAT EXACTLY-- HEY!!

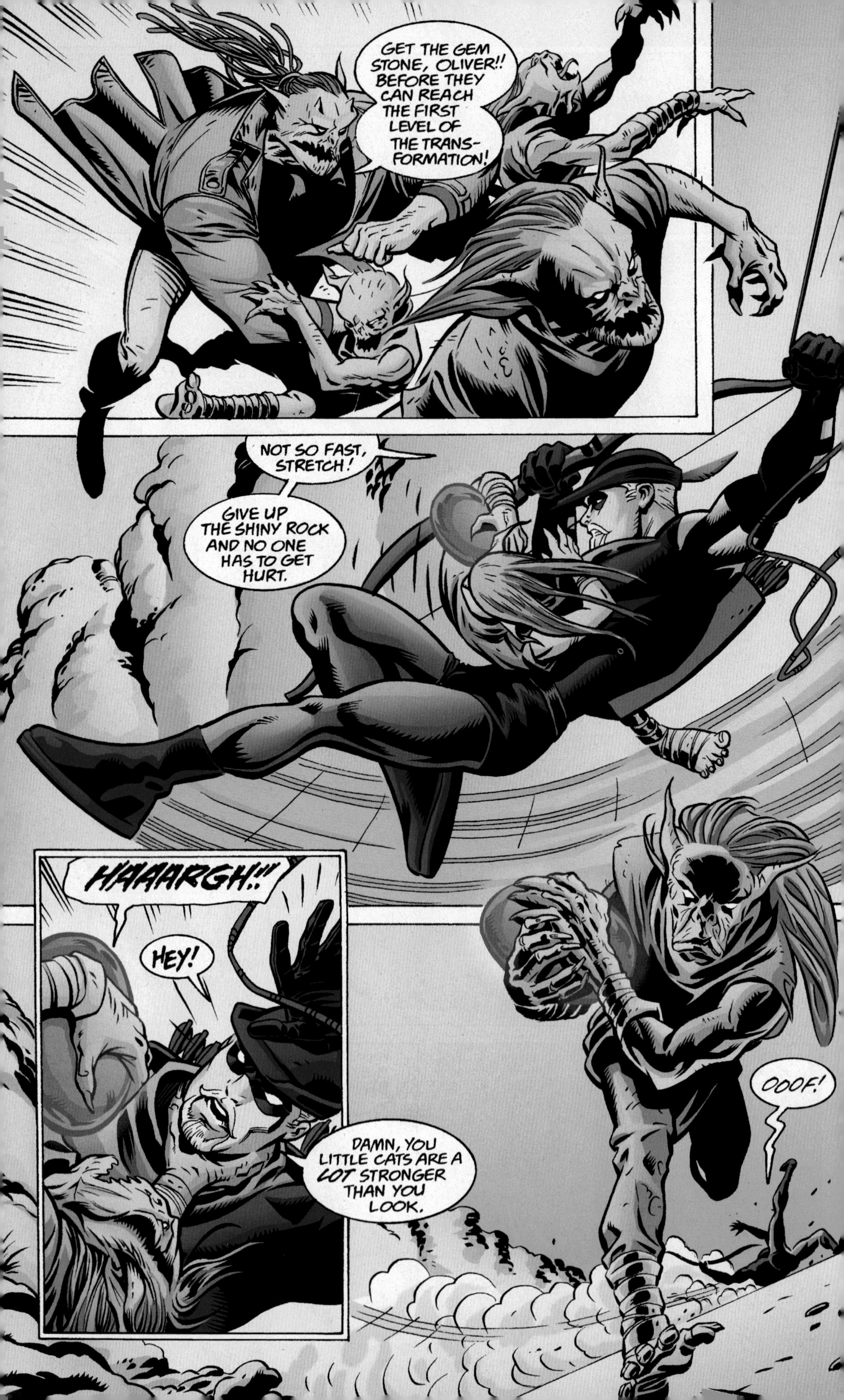
GET THE GEM STONE, OLIVER!! BEFORE THEY CAN REACH THE FIRST LEVEL OF THE TRANS-FORMATION!
NOT SO FAST, STRETCH!
GIVE UP THE SHINY ROCK AND NO ONE HAS TO GET HURT.
HAAAARGH!!
HEY!
DAMN, YOU LITTLE CATS ARE A LOT STRONGER THAN YOU LOOK.
OOOF!

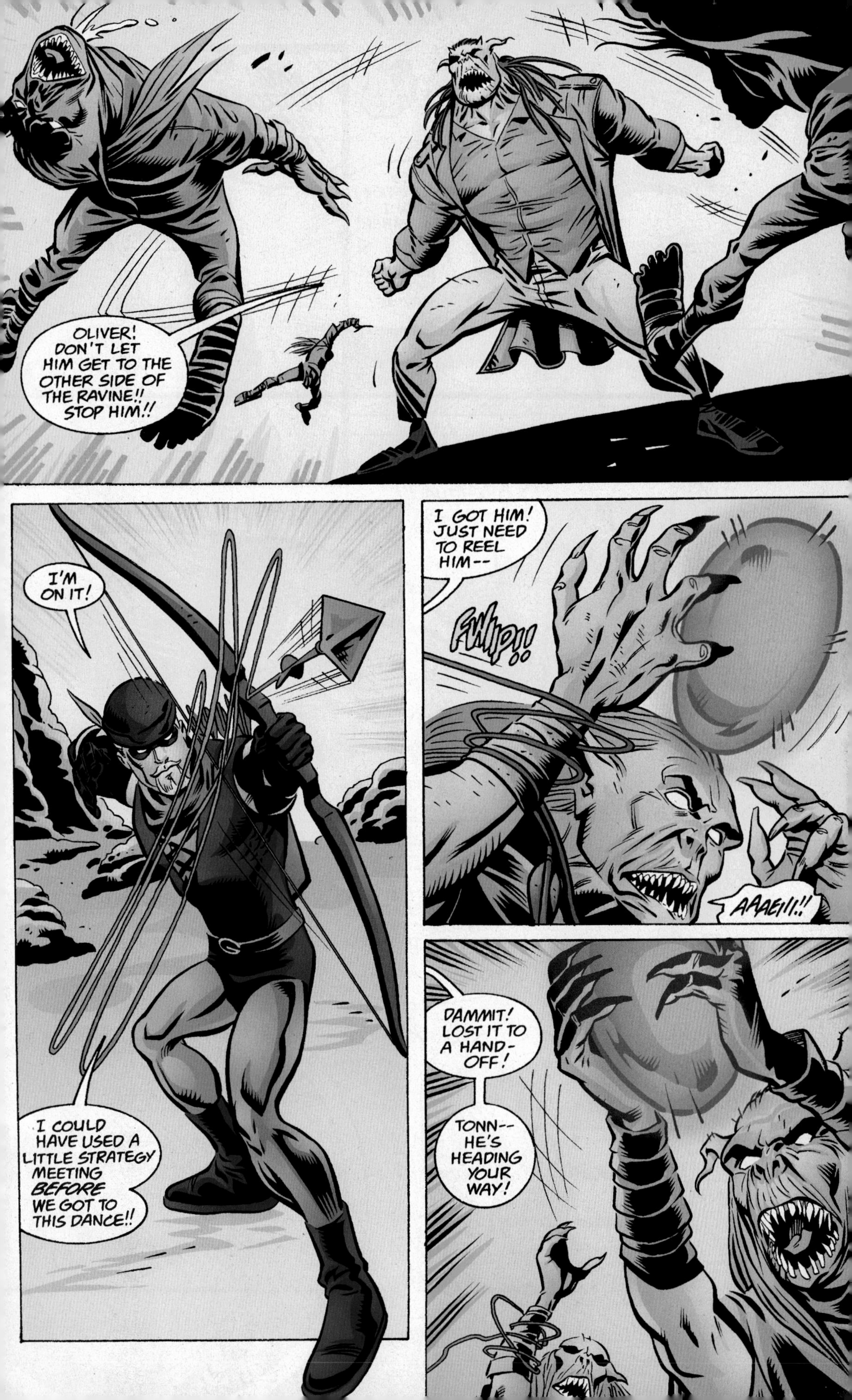
OLIVER! DON'T LET HIM GET TO THE OTHER SIDE OF THE RAVINE!! STOP HIM!!
I'M ON IT!
I COULD HAVE USED A LITTLE STRATEGY MEETING *BEFORE* WE GOT TO THIS DANCE!!
I GOT HIM! JUST NEED TO REEL HIM--
FWIP!!
AAAEIII!!
DAMMIT! LOST IT TO A HAND-OFF!
TONN-- HE'S HEADING YOUR WAY!

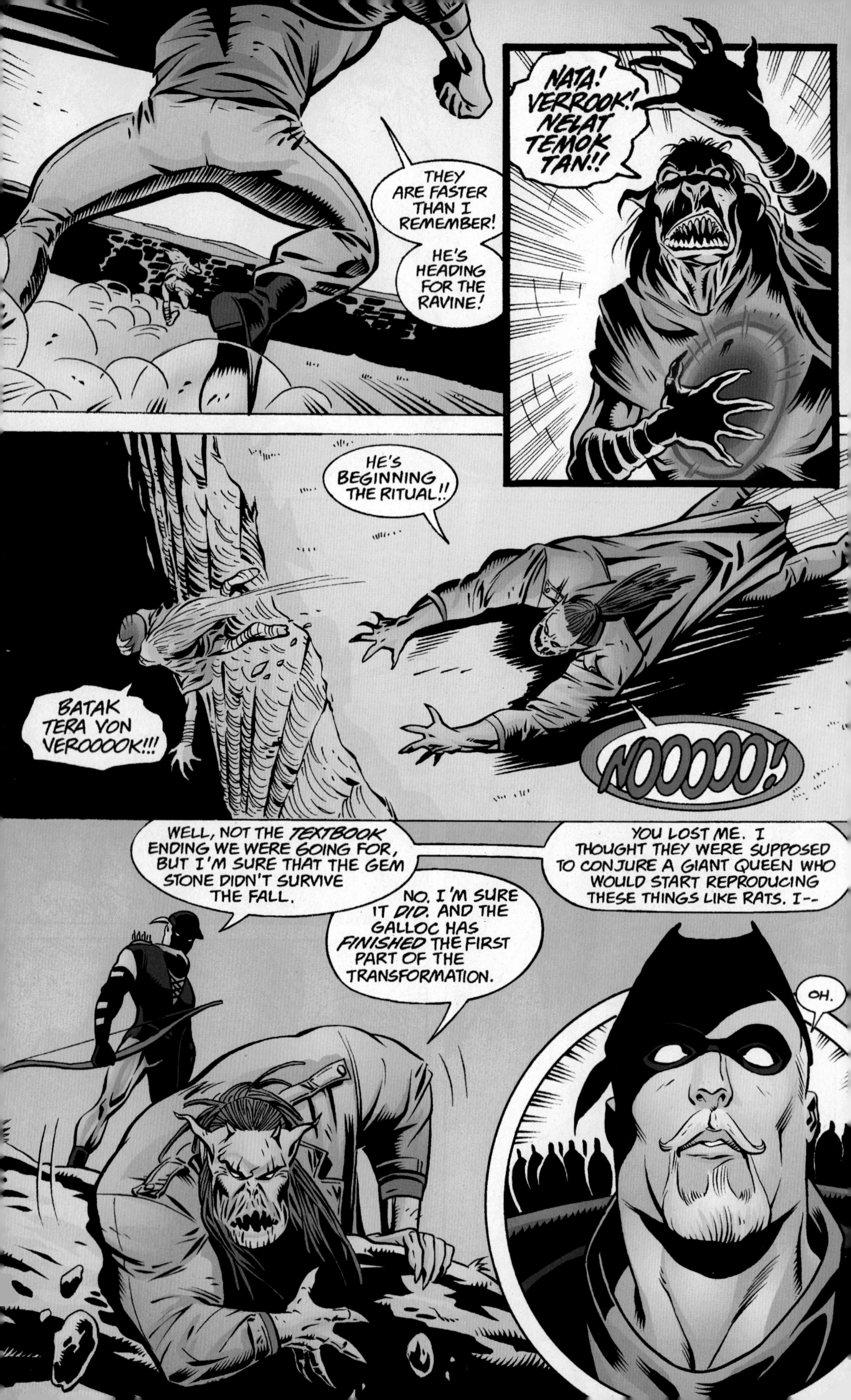

THEY ARE FASTER THAN I REMEMBER!
HE'S HEADING FOR THE RAVINE!
NATA! VERROOK! NELAT TEMOK TAN!!
HE'S BEGINNING THE RITUAL!!
BATAK TERA VON VEROOOOK!!!
NOOOOO!
WELL, NOT THE *TEXTBOOK* ENDING WE WERE GOING FOR, BUT I'M SURE THAT THE GEM STONE DIDN'T SURVIVE THE FALL.
NO. I'M SURE IT *DID*. AND THE GALLOC HAS *FINISHED* THE FIRST PART OF THE TRANSFORMATION.
YOU LOST ME. I THOUGHT THEY WERE SUPPOSED TO CONJURE A GIANT QUEEN WHO WOULD START REPRODUCING THESE THINGS LIKE RATS. I--
OH.

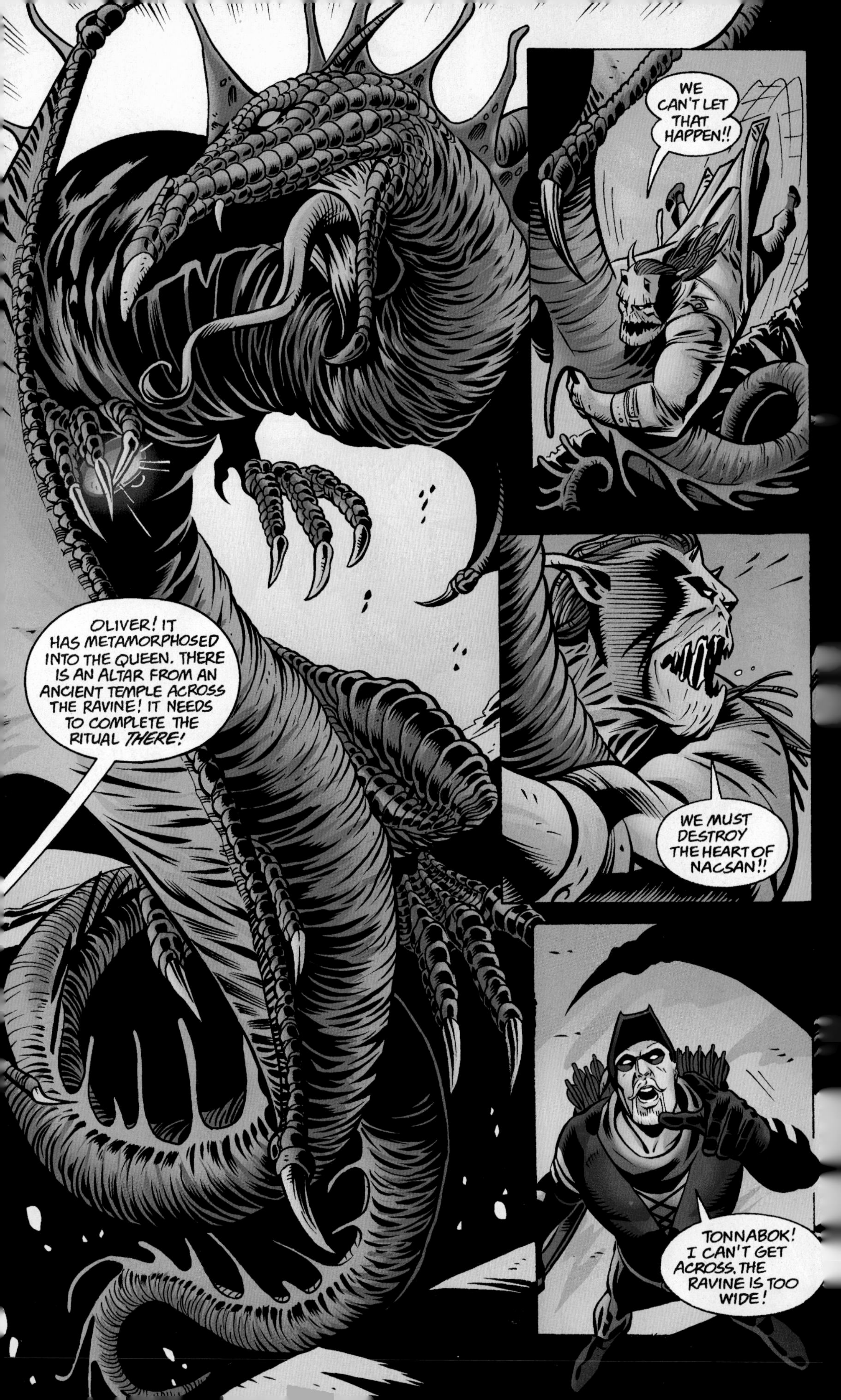
WE CAN'T LET THAT HAPPEN!!
OLIVER! IT HAS METAMORPHOSED INTO THE QUEEN. THERE IS AN ALTAR FROM AN ANCIENT TEMPLE ACROSS THE RAVINE! IT NEEDS TO COMPLETE THE RITUAL THERE!
WE MUST DESTROY THE HEART OF NACSAN!!
TONNABOK! I CAN'T GET ACROSS. THE RAVINE IS TOO WIDE!

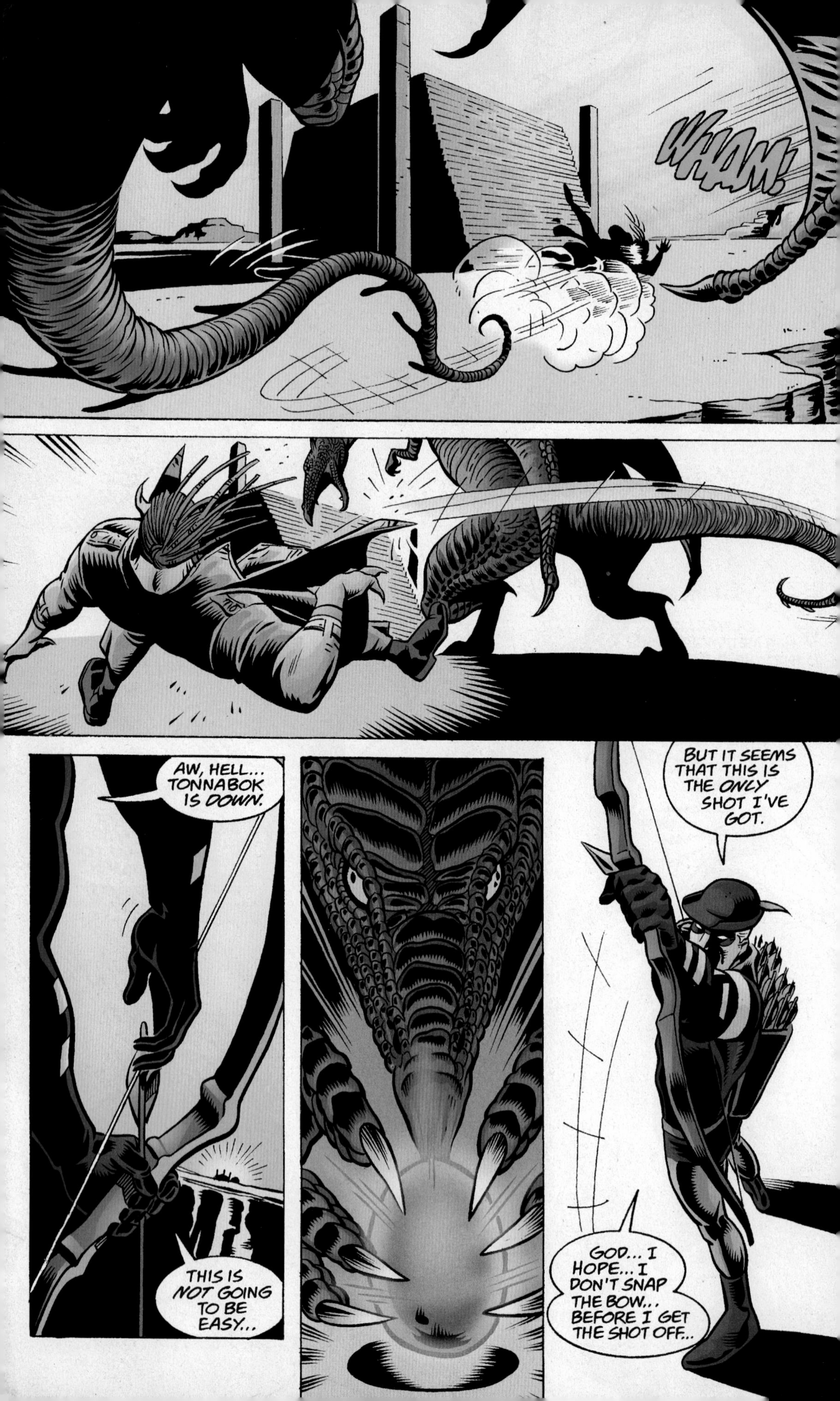
WHAM!
AW, HELL... TONNABOK IS *DOWN*.
THIS IS *NOT* GOING TO BE EASY...
BUT IT SEEMS THAT THIS IS THE *ONLY* SHOT I'VE GOT.
GOD... I HOPE... I DON'T SNAP THE BOW... BEFORE I GET THE SHOT OFF...

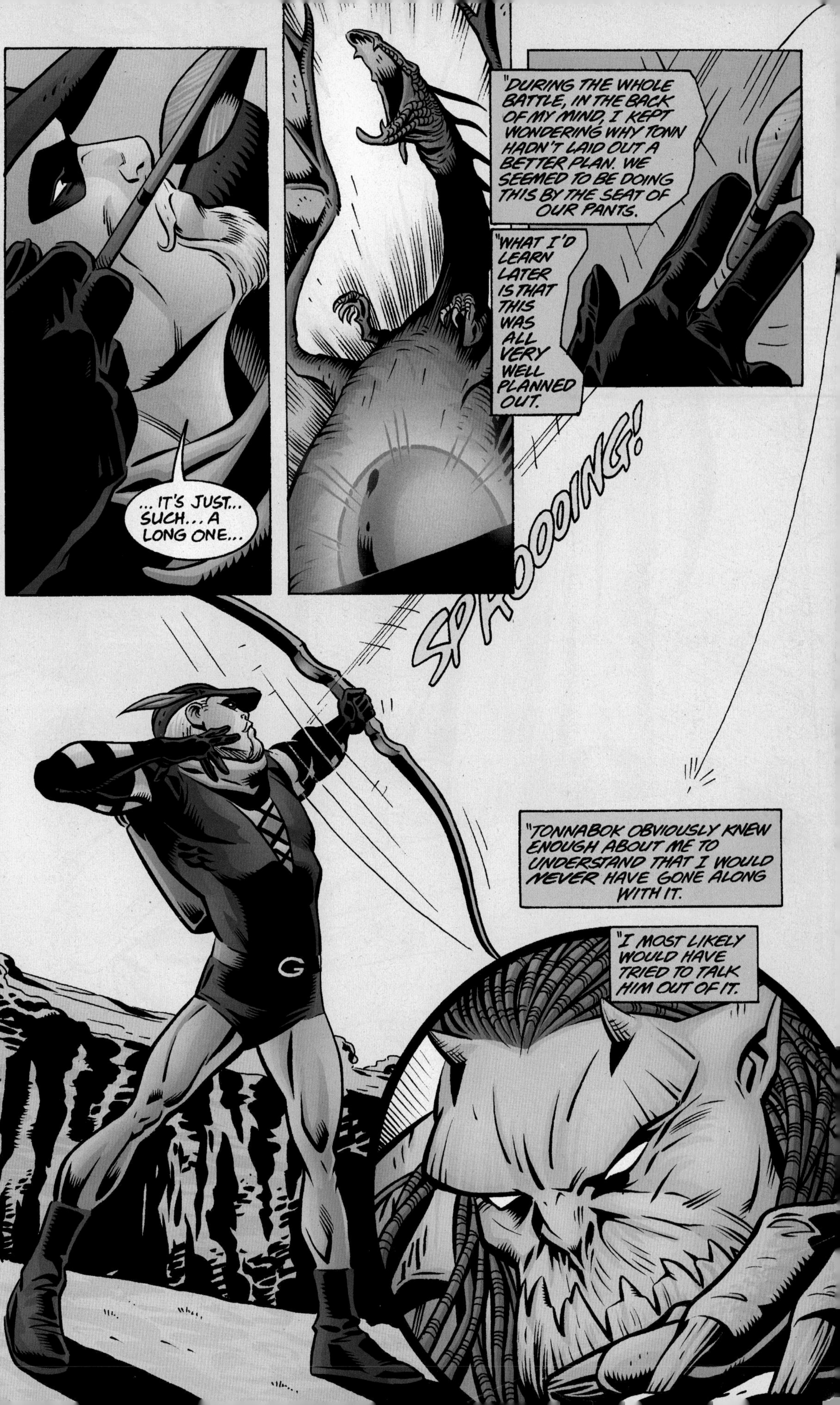

"DURING THE WHOLE BATTLE, IN THE BACK OF MY MIND, I KEPT WONDERING WHY TONN HADN'T LAID OUT A BETTER PLAN. WE SEEMED TO BE DOING THIS BY THE SEAT OF OUR PANTS.
"WHAT I'D LEARN LATER IS THAT THIS WAS ALL VERY WELL PLANNED OUT.
...IT'S JUST... SUCH... A LONG ONE...
SPROOOING!
"TONNABOK OBVIOUSLY KNEW ENOUGH ABOUT ME TO UNDERSTAND THAT I WOULD NEVER HAVE GONE ALONG WITH IT.
"I MOST LIKELY WOULD HAVE TRIED TO TALK HIM OUT OF IT.

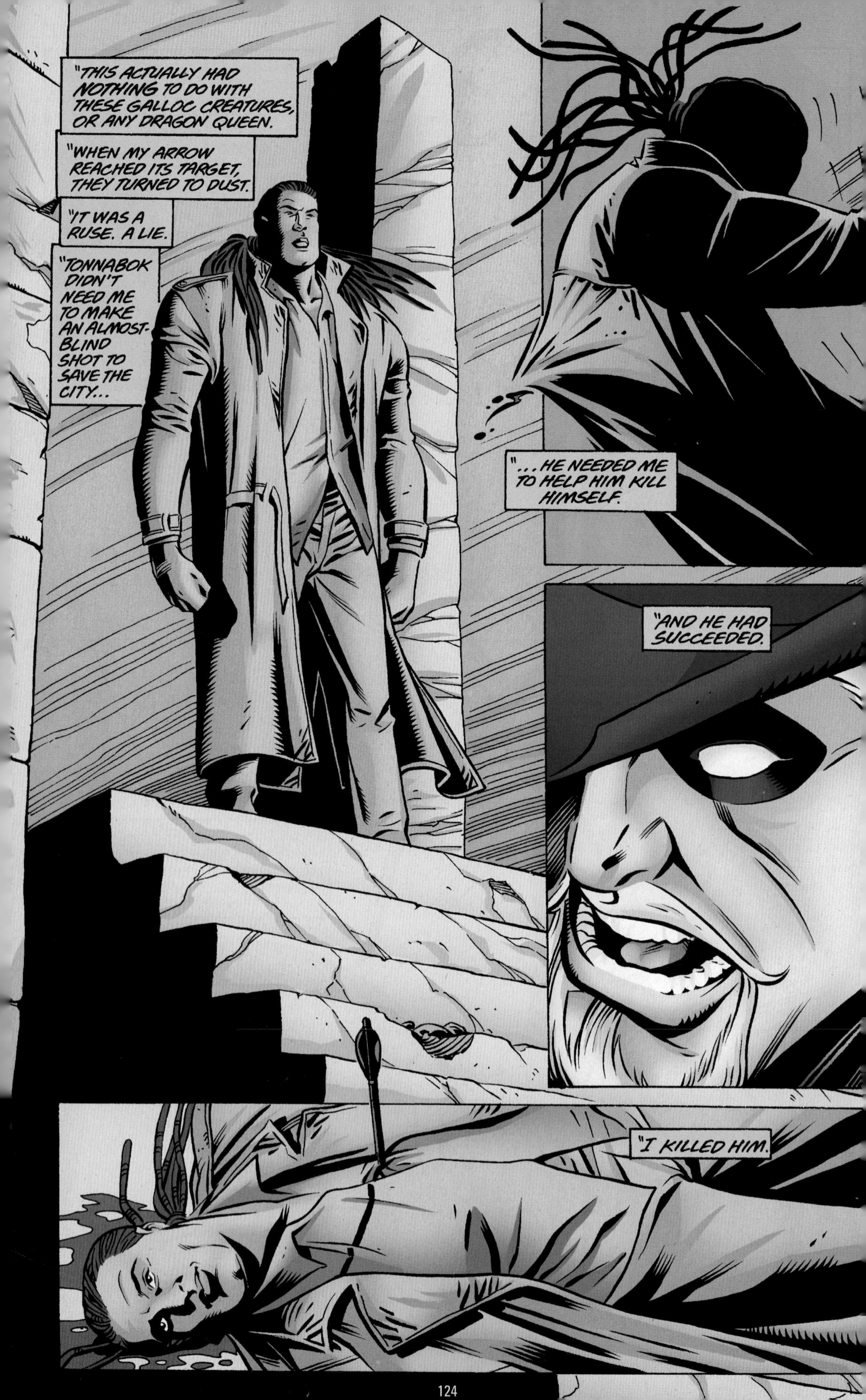
"THIS ACTUALLY HAD NOTHING TO DO WITH THESE GALLOC CREATURES, OR ANY DRAGON QUEEN.
"WHEN MY ARROW REACHED ITS TARGET, THEY TURNED TO DUST.
"IT WAS A RUSE. A LIE.
"TONNABOK DIDN'T NEED ME TO MAKE AN ALMOST-BLIND SHOT TO SAVE THE CITY...
"...HE NEEDED ME TO HELP HIM KILL HIMSELF.
"AND HE HAD SUCCEEDED.
"I KILLED HIM.

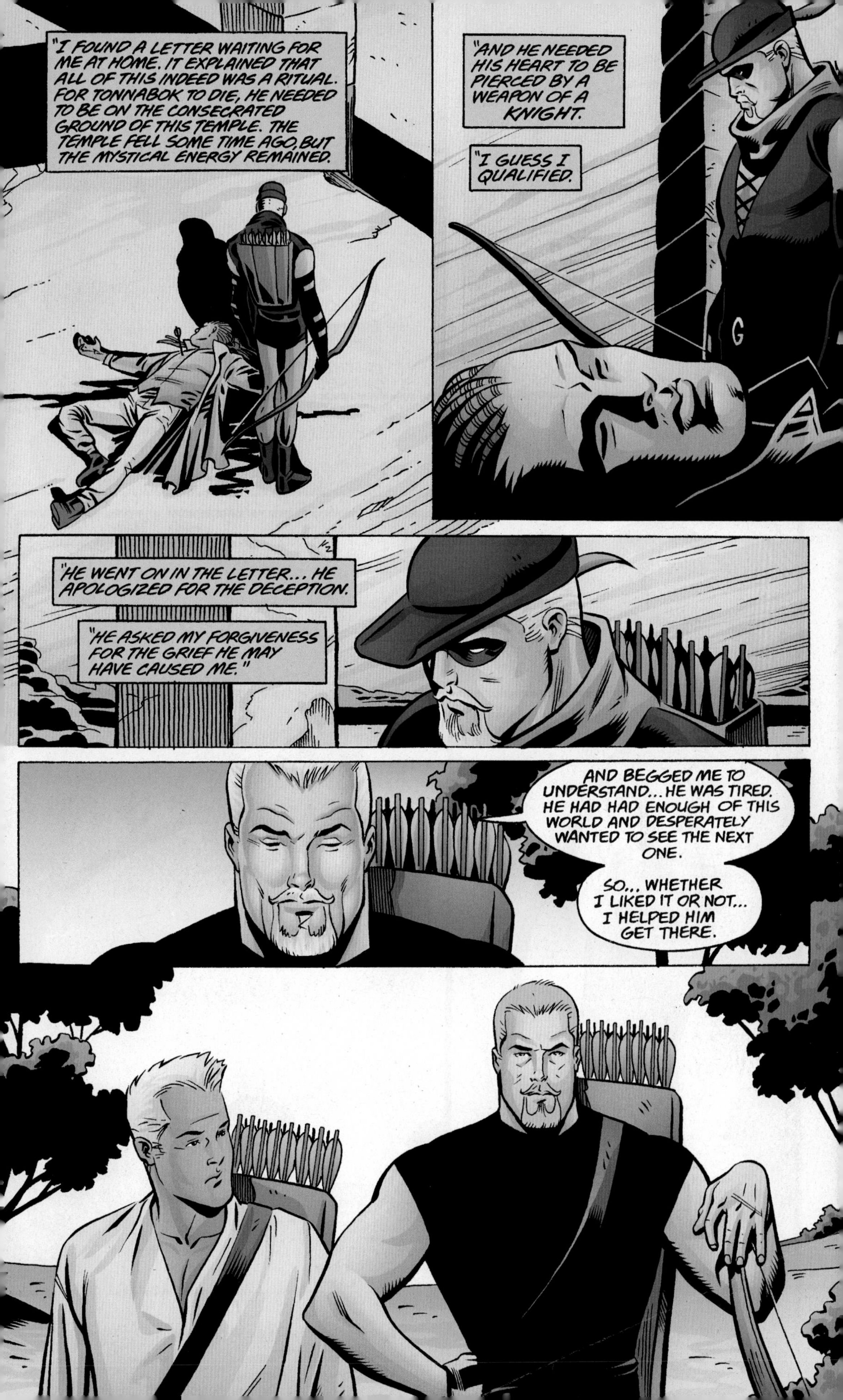
"I FOUND A LETTER WAITING FOR ME AT HOME. IT EXPLAINED THAT ALL OF THIS INDEED WAS A RITUAL. FOR TONNABOK TO DIE, HE NEEDED TO BE ON THE CONSECRATED GROUND OF THIS TEMPLE. THE TEMPLE FELL SOME TIME AGO, BUT THE MYSTICAL ENERGY REMAINED.
"AND HE NEEDED HIS HEART TO BE PIERCED BY A WEAPON OF A KNIGHT.
"I GUESS I QUALIFIED.
"HE WENT ON IN THE LETTER... HE APOLOGIZED FOR THE DECEPTION.
"HE ASKED MY FORGIVENESS FOR THE GRIEF HE MAY HAVE CAUSED ME."
AND BEGGED ME TO UNDERSTAND... HE WAS TIRED. HE HAD HAD ENOUGH OF THIS WORLD AND DESPERATELY WANTED TO SEE THE NEXT ONE.
SO... WHETHER I LIKED IT OR NOT... I HELPED HIM GET THERE.

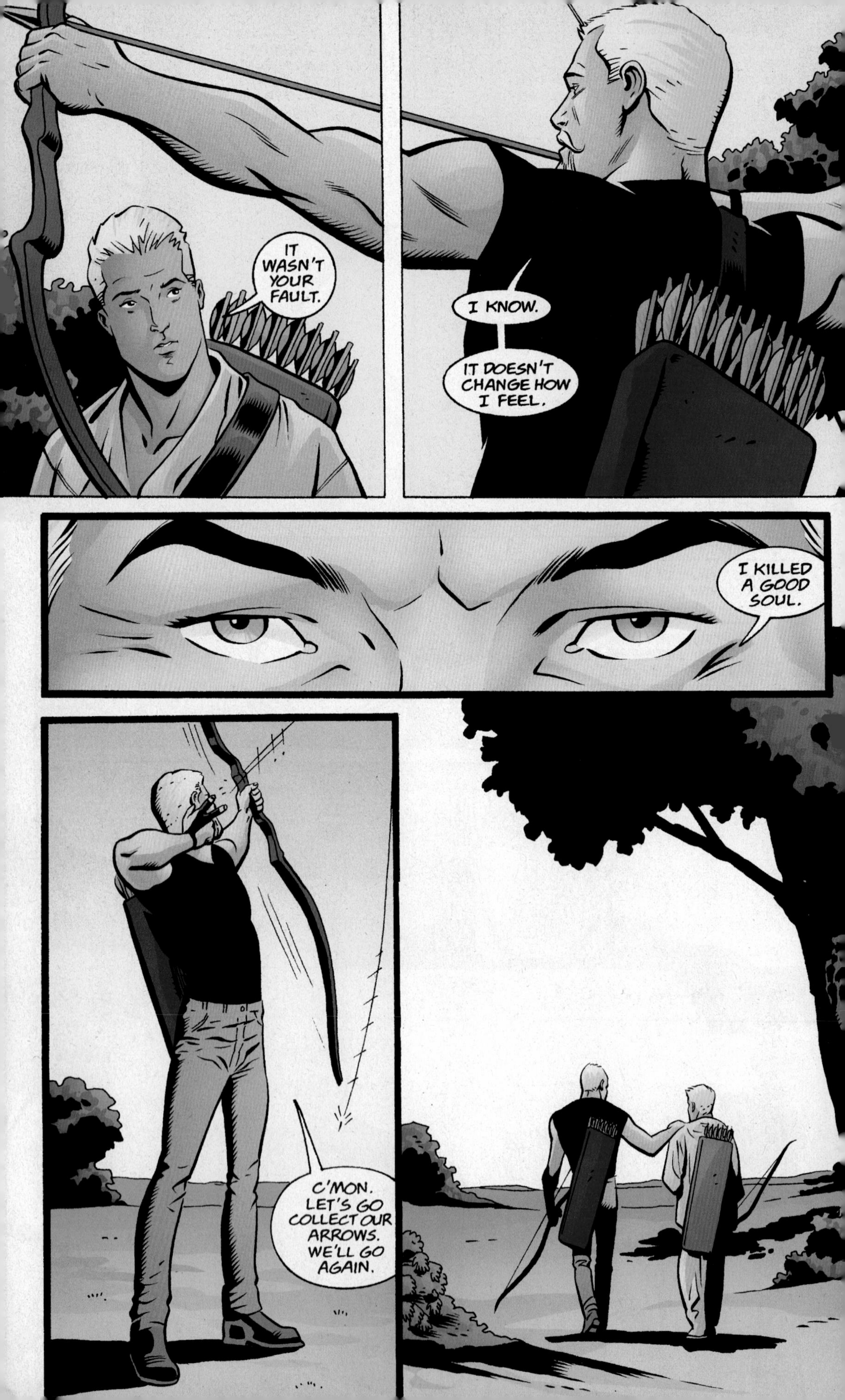
IT WASN'T YOUR FAULT.
I KNOW.
IT DOESN'T CHANGE HOW I FEEL.
I KILLED A GOOD SOUL.
C'MON. LET'S GO COLLECT OUR ARROWS. WE'LL GO AGAIN.

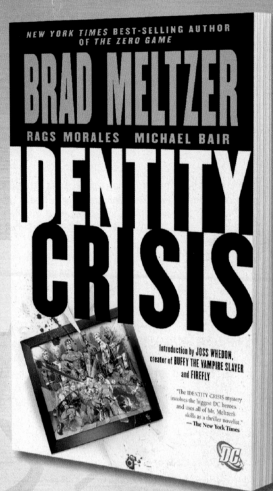

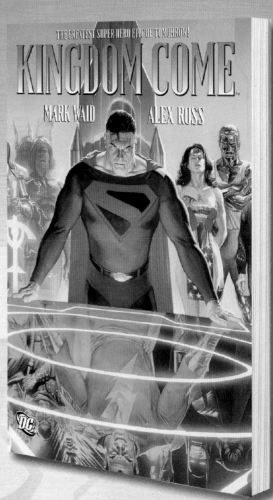
 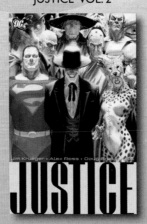